GLAD NEWS!

GOD LOVES YOU,
MY MUSLIM FRIEND

أخبار سارة   الله يحبك يا صديقي المسلم

GLAD NEWS!

GOD LOVES YOU,
MY MUSLIM FRIEND

by

أخبار سارة   الله يحبك يا صديقي المسلم

Samy Tanagho

God promised Abraham:

"And as for Ishmael, I have heard you: I will surely bless him; I will make him fruitful and will greatly increase his numbers." (Genesis 17:20)

I dedicate this book to my precious Muslim acquaintances, friends, neighbors, and all the sincere Muslims in the world who are earnestly seeking to have a complete relationship with the Living God (*Allah AL*-Hayy, in Arabic).

My dear reader, I believe God orchestrated many events to get this book in your hands to have you read it. He wants to say to you,

"I know you. You matter to Me. Because I love you, I want to give you the best life possible here on earth. I want you to live with Me forever and enjoy My kingdom, My presence, and My love. This is my purpose for creating you.

This is My joy; to love you and see you happy."

Glad News!
God loves you, my Muslim friend.

God loves you so much and He wants to embrace you as a father embraces his child. Yes, God wants you to become His child. He wants to have a close relationship with you based not on fear but on mutual love! God created you to enjoy joyful unbroken fellowship with Him forever.

God does not desire our relationship with Him to consist only of religious rituals and traditions. There is something deeper God desires for each one of us to have. God wants you to know Him through a living relationship and experience His love, forgiveness, and divine presence. God never intended this relationship to be the exclusive privilege of one special group of people.

God is inviting you to enjoy His salvation and discover the depth of His love toward you.

Understanding and applying God's truth is a common right for all humanity—a right to become spiritually enlightened and alive! God desires to fill your life with joy, love, peace, and hope.

God designed us in such a way that we will never be completely satisfied and happy without experiencing His perfect will in our lives. The way to enjoy the right relationship with God is presented to you in this book.

"You will seek me and find me when you seek me with all your heart."

Jeremiah 29:13

Biblica Publishing
We welcome your questions and comments.

USA   1820 Jet Stream Drive, Colorado Springs, CO 80921 www.authenticbooks.com
India   Logos Bhavan, Medchal Road, Jeedimetla Village, Secunderabad 500 055, A.P.

Glad News! God Loves You My Muslim Friend
ISBN-13: 978-1-884543-91-3

Glad News! is also available in Arabic and Chinese. Many other translations are in
progress.
Please contact Glad News for Muslims Ministry:
PO Box 28961
Santa Ana, CA 92799
(714) 514-2558
www.muslimministry.com
e-mail: Samy@muslimministry.com

Cover design: Paul Lewis

Printed in the United States of America

CONTENTS

INTRODUCTION

Everyone searches for love, but for many it proves elusive. The Beatles sang "All You Need Is Love" and then they disbanded! Many couples think they have found love, but then it slips away from them. They wonder if it was true love after all. I want to tell you about *real love*, an unconditional love that will revolutionize your life. In fact, it is the greatest love story in human history—God's love for *you!*

The most prevalent characteristic revealed about God in the Bible is that He is a loving God. Love is not just one of God's glorious attributes; love is the essence of God's being. God is the source of love.

I have personally experienced God's deep love. During the past 29 years of my life, I have met thousands of true followers of Christ who have had and still have the same experience. It is stated in the Bible, ". . . we know and rely on the love God has for us. God is love!" (1 John 4:16).

The God of the Bible does not merely love you, and me, and all people . . . "God is love." In other words, love is the very essence of His moral nature. This is the message I want to share with you. My desire is that multitudes of Muslims will know and experience God's deep and personal love for them. This longing has prompted me to write to you. I grew up with Muslim schoolmates, and neighbors, eating and playing with them. My wife was born and raised as a Muslim. I love Muslims. By the way, all true followers of Jesus Christ should deeply and genuinely love all Muslims.

In fact, Muhammad himself relied on Christians when Muslims were being persecuted. Islamic historians and books record that Muhammad trusted his Christian friends in Abyssinia and sent his followers there to be protected by followers of Jesus Christ.

The Qur'an states, "Strongest among men in enmity to the Believers wilt thou find the Jews and Pagans; and nearest among them in love to the Believers wilt thou find those who say, "We are Christians . . ." (Surah 5:82).

It is interesting that the Qur'an mentions the name Jesus more than it does Muhammad. Throughout this book, I'd like to present to you a few important facts about Jesus Christ (*Isa AL-Masih* in the Qur'an) found in both the Qur'an and the Bible.

These undeniable facts will help you to develop an informed opinion about who Jesus really is. My prayer is that you will have an open mind and sincerity in your search for the truth. I also pray that you will ask God to guide you before, during, and after reading this book. The most important thing I encourage you to do is to prayerfully read the verses of Holy Scripture referenced in this book.

THE HEART OF GOD

My dear Muslim friend, God is speaking to me and to you:

"I know the plans I have for you declares the Lord, plans to prosper you and not to harm you, plans to give you hope and a future" (Jeremiah 29:11)

Please consider the heart of God toward you. The following passage gives a glimpse of God's love for you and all those who are not secure in the arms of God.

Jesus taught this parable:

What do you think? If a man owns a hundred sheep, and one of them wanders away, will he not leave the ninety-nine [secure sheep] on the hills and go to look for the one that wandered off? And if he finds it, I tell you the truth, he is happier about that one [lost] sheep than about the ninety-nine that did not wander off. In the same way your Father in heaven is not willing that any of these little ones should be lost. (Matthew 18:12–14)

Jesus wants us to know that God relentlessly pursues us at any time when we are lost.

As a further illustration of God's heart of love toward you, I would like to share a true story of a wealthy couple. They sat down with a marriage counselor in his office to solve their marital problems. Angrily, the husband said, "I don't understand my wife's problem. I gave her a diamond ring for our wedding anniversary, I bought a house in her name, and I gave her money to spend on herself every month." After he listed everything he gave her, the wife replied, "Yes it is true, Ameer, you have given me everything." With tears running from her eyes, she continued, "Everything except yourself!"

It is my hope and prayer that through reading this book you will see how God has actually given you the ultimate gift of love—Himself! "This is how we know what love is: Jesus Christ laid down His life for us . . ." (1 John 3:16).

My precious reader, it is not by accident you are reading this book right now. It is a divine appointment designed by the relational God to draw you to know Him because God is passionate in His love towards you.

You owe it to yourself and to God to investigate and see if what the Bible says is true.

Your servant

Samy Tanagho

SECTION ONE

THE QUR'AN'S TESTIMONY REGARDING THE AUTHENTICITY OF THE BIBLE

1

THE CREDIBILITY OF THE BIBLE

In this book, Islamic beliefs and verses from the Qur'an are addressed to help Muslims and Christians see the common ground and the differences between Islam and Christianity.

While I do not depend on the Qur'an to prove the credibility of the Bible, I find it significant and interesting that throughout its pages, the Qur'an testifies to the authenticity of the Bible. The Jews and the Christians are described in the Qur'an as "the people of the Book." The Jewish Scripture is the Torah; and the Christian Scripture is the Injeel. The Qur'an speaks with reverence and respect of the Torah (Old Testament), Zabur (the Psalms), and the Injeel (Gospel or New Testament). These Holy Scriptures have the status of the authentic Word of God, because they were God's revelation before the Qur'an.

The Torah can mean the "law" or the instruction God gave through Moses. Also, it can be any word God gave through the prophets. The word Torah (or Taurat) and Injeel are found many times in the Bible but are not translated to English as titles. For example, Injeel is translated "good news."

If someone says you should not read the Bible because it was annulled by the arrival of the Qur'an, my dear Muslim friend, there is no evidence to support that claim. Not one single verse in the Qur'an attests that the Bible has been invalidated by the arrival of the Qur'an. Furthermore, the Qur'an itself commands Muslims to profess belief in the Bible. We read in Surah 2:136: "Say ye: 'We believe in Allah, and the revelation given to us, and to Abraham . . . and that given to Moses and Jesus, and that given to (all) Prophets from their Lord: We make no difference between one and another of them . . ."

MISCONCEPTIONS ABOUT THE BIBLE

Many Muslims mistakenly think and teach that the Qur'an came to replace the Holy Scriptures of the Jews and the Christians (the Bible). There are misconceptions that it became corrupted, altered, outdated, or lost. I will briefly address such allegations and provide you with strong evidence to show the contrary.

The Qur'an confirms the previous Holy Scripture

Many years before the time of Muhammad (by AD 350), there was a uniform canon of the Bible. The Qur'an does not accuse Christians of changing the written words of their Holy Books. On the contrary, the Qur'an declares that it (the Qur'an) was given to confirm the previous revelations and not to replace them. Surah 5:48 says: "To thee [Muhammad] We sent the Scripture [Qur'an] in truth confirming the Scripture that came before it; and guarding it in safety . . ." This confirmation is repeated in many Qur'anic verses (Surah 2:89; 2:91, 97; 2:101; 6:92; and 46:12).

The Qur'an testifies that the Torah, the Zabur, and the Injeel are the Word of God. The testimony of the Qur'an is not ambiguous. Surah 3:3–4 states: ". . . And He [God] sent down the Law (of Moses) and the Gospel (of Jesus) before this as a guide to mankind."

The Qur'an's references to the Torah

Regarding the Torah, we read in Surah 5:44: "It was We who revealed the Law (to Moses) therein was guidance and light. By its standard have been judged the Jews, by the prophets who bowed (as in Islam) to Allah's will." In this passage, "guidance" refers to conduct, and "light" refers to spiritual insight provided by God. Other verses in the Qur'an that discuss the Torah are as follows:

"... We gave Moses the Book, completing (Our favor) to those who would do right, and explaining all things in detail—and a guide and a mercy . . ." (Surah 6:154)

"We [God] gave Moses the Book and followed him up with a succession of Messengers [Jewish prophets] . . ." (Surah 2:87)

Please refer also to Surah 4:54; Surah 28:43; Surah 32:23; Surah 40:53–54; and Surah 45:16.

The Qur'an's references to the Zabur and Injeel

Regarding the Zabur, the Qur'an states in Surah 21:105, "Before this We [God] wrote in the Psalms . . ."

Regarding the Injeel, the Qur'an declares in Surah 5:46 that Christ confirmed the Torah as true and that Christ's Gospel contains guidance, light, and admonition. It reads, "And in their footsteps We sent Jesus the son of Mary, confirming the law that had come before him: We sent him the Gospel: therein was guidance and light and confirmation of the law that had come before him: a guidance and an admonition to those who fear Allah." Please also read Surah 57:27.

The importance of reading the Gospel

Many Muslims think that it is unnecessary to read the Bible. Their opinion contradicts even the Qur'an itself. The Qur'an states clearly that all Muslims must follow and obey the teachings of the previous Holy Scripture (The Bible). The following Surahs are clear on this subject:

Surah 2:136 states: "Say ye: 'We believe in Allah and the revelation given to us and to Abraham . . . and that given to Moses and Jesus and that given to (all) Prophets from their Lord we make no difference between one and another of them: and we bow to Allah (in Islam)."

Surah 2:285 states: "The Messenger believeth in what hath been revealed to him from his Lord, as do the men of faith. Each one (of them) believeth in Allah, His angels, His books, and His Messengers . . . 'We make no distinction (they say) between one and another of His Messengers.' And they say: 'We hear and we obey . . .'"

Surah 4:136 reads: "O ye who believe! Believe in Allah and His Messenger and the scripture which He hath sent to His Messenger and the scripture which He sent to those before (him). Any who denieth Allah, His angels, His Books, His Messengers, and the Day of Judgment hath gone far, far astray."

My dear Muslim reader, to enjoy a right and complete relationship with God, you must read the Gospel (the New Testament). It will increase your understanding of Jesus Christ (Al-Masih, Isa). It will also help you to understand the Salvation God wants you to experience through faith in Him.

The Qur'an mentions the Glad News of Jesus in Surah 3:45 "Behold! The angel said: 'O Mary! Allah giveth thee Glad Tidings of a Word from him: His name will be Christ Jesus . . .'"

According to the Qur'an, all Holy Books are Equal

In Surah 2:285 and Surah 4:136 cited above, notice that "His Books" is plural. This means all the Holy Books. In Surah 2:136, please discern the important phrase, "We make no difference between one and another of them." This is a clear command that Muslims should regard all Holy Books as equal revelation.

As we read in Surah 4:136, if any Muslim ignores or rejects any part of God's revelation in the Torah or in the Gospel, he has "gone far, far astray." Also, God would condemn him as an infidel, as noted in Surah 40:70–72: "Those who reject the Book and the (revelations) with which We sent Our messengers: But soon shall they know—when the yokes (shall be) round their necks, and the chains; They shall be dragged along—In the boiling fetid fluid; Then in the Fire shall They be burned."

Clearly, the Qur'an commands all people to read and obey God's revelations in the Bible; this is an essential part of being a Muslim. It is very clear that Muhammad himself considered the Holy Scriptures of the Jews and the Christians to be books that lead people to become fully submitted to God.

The Qur'an also indicates that the Jews and Christians, who lived in Muhammad's time, rejected the Qur'an. You can read about this in Surah 2:91: "When it is said to them: 'Believe in what Allah hath sent down,' they say, 'We believe in what was sent down to us.' Yet they reject all besides, even if it be truth confirming what is with them . . ."

It is a fact that Muhammad wanted Arab Christians and Jews to accept him as a prophet in the line of Biblical prophets. The Qur'an also recorded that Jews and Christians rejected Muhammad (Surah 2:120).

The Qur'an considers the Bible Preeminent

Surah 10:94 is a command given to Muhammad (and all Muslims) to treat the Bible as the primary source of enlightenment: "If thou [Muhammad] wert in doubt as to what We have revealed unto thee then ask those who have been reading the Book from before thee . . ." This verse clearly instructs all the Muslim believers to refer to the Bible when questions arise regarding the Qur'an's meaning. It is clear from this verse that in the event of any doubt about certain revelations in the Qur'an, Muhammad is commanded by God to consult with the Jews and Christians who have been reading their Holy Scriptures. So Surah 10:94 is a command to Muhammad to test the truthfulness of his own message by the contents of the Holy Scriptures of the Jews and the Christians. This verse clearly shows that the Qur'an does not supersede the Gospel.

If Muhammad had doubt and was commanded to ask, then you, as a Muslim, have the permission–and the obligation–to examine all things. Think about all the information you receive so you can, by God's guidance, determine the whole truth.

My dear friend, the Qur'an does not claim that God sent it to prevent corruption or to replace the Holy Word of God, which is the entire Bible (Torah and the Injeel). On the contrary, the Qur'an confirms Biblical authenticity.

Jesus declared that He did not come to abrogate previous revelations. Jesus said, "Do not think that I have come to abolish the law or the prophets; I have not come to abolish them but to fulfill them" (Matthew 5:17). He also said, "Heaven and earth will pass away, but My words never pass away" (Matthew 24:35).

The Qur'an recognizes that the Jews possess the Word of God

There are many passages in the Qur'an that assure us that the Torah was available in an unadulterated form during the time of Muhammad. For example, a dispute had arisen among the Jews in Medina, and it had come to the attention of Muhammad. The Qur'an addresses Muhammad, "But why do they come to thee for decision, when they have (their own) law before them? Therein is the (plain) command of Allah . . ." (Surah 5:43). Notice the expression "before them" in this verse.

It is also clear from Surah 5:43 that it was not necessary for the Jews to go to Muhammad for judgment because they had the Torah, which is the Word of God that contained all the needed guidance and light.

Consider also Surah 2:101 which states, "And when there came to them a Messenger from Allah, confirming what was with them." Notice the expression "with them." These verses clearly teach that the Jews of Medina had the true Torah (Old Testament) in their possession at the time of Muhammad, and it was reliable to settle their own disputes.

Throughout their history, the Jews have known only the Holy Scripture in the Books of the Old Testament. The Qur'an never states that the Torah is a book different from that which the Jews themselves accepted as the Torah.

The Qur'an recognizes that the Christians possess the Word of God

The Qur'an also confirms Biblical authenticity with regard to the New Testament. Surah 5:47 states, "Let the people of the Gospel judge by what Allah hath revealed therein. If any do fail to judge by (the light of) what Allah hath revealed, they are (no better than) those who rebel." How could the Christians be expected to judge by the Injeel unless they had it in their possession? The Christian world has known only one Injeel, which existed centuries before Muhammad's time and continues to exist today. The Qur'an never states that the Gospel is a book different from the one Christians used at the time of Muhammad. And the Qur'an never accuses the Jews and Christians of changing the actual text of the Biblical manuscripts.

Have you noticed my precious Muslim reader what this verse said? "Let the people of the Gospel judge by what Allah hath revealed therein . . ." So the Christians, who are the people of the Gospel, should rely on the Gospel. They do not need the Qur'an.

It is clear then–the Qur'an does not supersede the Gospel!

The Qur'an in Surah 5:47 uses the word *Injeel*, which is the same title that the followers of Jesus use. Please refer to Mark 1:1: "The beginning of the gospel about Jesus Christ . . ."

In fact, Christian Arabs still use the Arabic word *Injeel*, for the Gospel.

Additional references to the Torah and the Gospel

It is important to note that the Qur'an does not claim to give all the teachings of Jesus, nor the whole story of His life. You need to read the New Testament to discover all that Jesus taught.

The Qur'an confirms its support of the Torah and the Gospel and urges the Jews and the Christians to recognize the authority of their Holy Book. It says in Surah 5:68, "Say: 'O People of the Book! Ye have no ground to stand upon unless ye stand fast by the Law, the Gospel, and all the revelation that has come to you from your Lord . . .'"

This verse is another clear example showing that the Jews and Christians had the Word of God in their possession prior to the writing of the Qur'an. Since Jews and Christians are commanded to observe the precepts contained in their Scripture, it would have been impossible for them to know the commandments they must obey if their Book had perished. Or if the Bible had been previously corrupted, they would have gone astray if they obeyed it.

There is no indication in the Qur'an whatsoever that the Holy Scriptures the Jews and Christians had in their possession were anything other than the original Holy Books God had revealed to them.

Surah 5:68, which we just read, is another clear example that Islam, as recorded in the Qur'an, did not and should not abrogate the Christian faith which preceded it. On the contrary, the Qur'an commands all Jewish and Christian believers to follow their Holy Scriptures.

Because the Qur'an testifies that the Holy Scriptures of the Jews and Christians is the word of God, the Muslim should submit to the authority of the Qur'an on this point. The Muslim should look no further. If the words of Muslim teachers or even Traditions (Hadith)[1] contradict what the Qur'an states, the true Muslim should follow the Qur'an because the Qur'an is much higher in authority according to Islamic law and beliefs.

Early Muslim scholars uphold Bible integrity

For hundreds of years after the death of Muhammad, many of the well-known Muslim scholars upheld the integrity of the Bible. At Tabari was a former Christian whose life was marked by his defense of Islam in front of the Jews and the Christians while he was at Baghdad (capital of the Muslim world in his time). He wrote under the direction of the reigning Abbasid Caliph Mutawakkil (AD 847–861). At no time did he charge the Jews or the Christians with corrupting their Scriptures. He acknowledged that the authentic Torah and Gospel remained in the hands of the Jews and the Christians. In his famous book, *The Book of Religion and Empire*, he wrote, "As to the Gospel which is in the hands of the Christians, the greater part of it is the history of the Christ, His birth and His life."

Another scholar, Al-Ghazzali (AD 1058–1111), is considered one of the greatest Muslim theologians in the history of Islam. In his writings he never challenged the Bible's integrity. He even wrote treatises on the Trinity in which he quoted many passages from the Bible, without questioning the trustworthiness of the text.[2]

At Tabari, one of the earliest authoritative commentators on the Qur'an, comments on Surah 5:68. He noted that Ibn Abbas, one of Muhammad's companions, said that some Jews wanted to know if Muhammad believed the Torah. And so they asked Muhammad,

"Oh Muhammad, do you not claim that you walk in the steps of Abraham's Community and religion, and do you not believe in The Torah which we have and confess that it is God's truth?"

The messenger [Muhammad] said, "Of course I do but you have read into the Scripture things that are not there and you have rejected God's Covenant with you. You have concealed what you had been commanded to make known to the people. Therefore, I disown your innovations."

They replied, "We abide by what is in our hands {The Torah}; we follow the truth and the guidance and we do not believe in you nor do we follow you."[3]

Here we see that Muhammad admits that the Torah is God's truth, but accuses the Jews of concealing its teaching.

Many traditions (Ahadith) record that when Muhammad was asked to judge on some disputes, he asked for the Torah to be read aloud to him. These traditions are further evidence that Muhammad considered the Torah to be holy and uncorrupted.

For example, I read in the most acknowledged biography on Muhammad's life, by Ibn Hisham, a story about a man and a woman who were caught in adultery. In that story, the people asked Muhammad to be the judge. Muhammad asked a rabbi to read the passage about adultery.

As the rabbi read from the Torah, Abdullah B. Salam struck the rabbis hand saying, "This, oh prophet of God, is the verse of stoning which he refuses to read to you." Muhammad then said, "Woe to you Jews! What has induced you to abandon the judgment of God which you hold in your hands?"[4]

2

WAS THE BIBLE ALTERED, AS SOME MUSLIMS CLAIM?

My dear Muslim reader, it is only fair that you examine the evidence with objectivity. Any accusation that the Bible was altered raises serious questions which demand answers from those people who have made this claim. When could this alleged alteration of the Holy Scriptures have occurred?

A. Before Muhammad's time?

All the verses pointed out in the previous chapter clearly demonstrate that Muhammad did not believe the Bible to be corrupt in his time.

B. After the death of Muhammad?

It is not possible for the Bible to have been altered after the death of Muhammad because by AD 600 Christianity had spread as far as Asia, Africa, and Europe.

If the Jews and Christians tampered or changed the teachings of the Torah and the Gospel (changed the original manuscript of the Holy Books), then the testimony of the Qur'an supporting their authenticity is false. Muslim teachers claiming that the Bible was corrupted after Muhammad died are, in effect, saying that the Allah of the Qur'an could not foresee that the Bible would be altered. In both cases, if the Bible became corrupted, then such a claim would make the Qur'an untrustworthy.

Comparisons of Bible translations reveal textual accuracy

Those who had embraced Christianity in Asia, Africa, and Europe had no common language. The Bible was circulating in many different languages around the world. This would make any attempt to falsify the Holy Scriptures impossible, and comparisons of these Bible translations in the various languages reveal complete accuracy of the Bible text.

An impossible conspiracy

It is not rational to suppose that Christians and Jews throughout the world could meet and agree on the alterations of their Holy Scripture. History shows that Jews and Christians have had major doctrinal differences between them, and they have been in disagreement regarding many religious issues. (See Surah 2:113.)

We also read in many verses in the Qur'an (such as in Surah 3:19 and Surah 98:4) that Christians were divided into sects. So if the Scriptures had been changed to alter doctrine, at least one of the many sects that existed within Judaism or Christianity at that time would have protested. Yet there is no historical mention of any such accusation or dissension.

By the time Muhammad lived, Judaism and Christianity had spread throughout the world. Therefore, it would have been impossible for anyone or any group to collect all the Holy Books, manuscripts, and writings containing Scriptural references from all the churches, synagogues, schools, libraries, and homes to make the changes. Then the replacements would have had to be returned without detection. How could everyone who had a Bible be convinced to exchange it for a revised (corrupted) version, and yet leave no evidence of such a monumental feat?

More evidence for textual purity of the Bible

Many sincere Christian scholars during the time of Muhammad, such as the Abyssinians who loved Muslims and befriended them, would have exposed any attempted changes in the Scriptures.

Surah 5:82 describes these Christians. It reads: "Strongest among men in enmity to the believers wilt thou find the Jews and pagans; and nearest among them in love to the believers wilt thou find those who say: 'We are Christians' because amongst these are men devoted to learning and men who have renounced the world, and they are not arrogant."

Note that this verse describes these Christians as "devoted to learning." Since these dedicated Christians knew very well the revelations given to them from God, they would have discovered any attempted tampering. The verse also describes these Christians: "They have renounced the world, and they are not arrogant," which means these Christians were living a godly life. Hence they would not have committed such a terrible sin of changing or corrupting their Holy Scriptures.

Lack of evidence for textual corruption

Surah 5:66 which states ". . . there is from among them a party on the right course . . ." shows that there were a significant number of Jews and Christians who did not compromise, but were faithful and stood fast by the Law and the Gospel. Such a steadfast group would have exposed any attempt to corrupt their Holy Scriptures.

In addition, from Muhammad's time forward, many Jews and Christians in lands conquered by the Muslim army embraced Islam. Since Muslims revered the Holy Books of the Jews and the Christians, the Jews and Christians who became Muslims would have retained their original Scriptures. Yet no texts have been discovered that differ from today's Bible.

If the Jews and Christians had collaborated to corrupt the Bible, surely some of these Muslim converts would have been able to produce unaltered copies of the Holy Books. In fact, hundreds of manuscripts exist today from the fourth and fifth centuries (Islam started in the sixth century). These manuscripts agree with today's translations of the Scripture (Injeel). Any variances are minor and do not affect any essential doctrine. So the New Testament of Muhammad's day is the same as the New Testament today. This is a well-established fact that is widely agreed upon.

Challenging the basis for the accusations

These circumstances render it impossible for Jews and Christians to have come together after the death of Muhammad to alter their Holy Scriptures. Those Muslims who claim that today's Bible is altered or corrupt, need to answer the following questions:

- When and where did this corruption take place?

- Who were the perpetrators?

- How did they reach a consensus?

- If there were an original Bible different from the one that exists today, where is it so that we can make a comparison? What specific textual changes were made to the original manuscripts?

- What evidence proves any alterations of doctrines?

ACCORDING TO GOD, THE BIBLE CANNOT CHANGE

The Word of God is unchangeable as God originally presented it in the Holy Scriptures of the Jews and the Christians. The Qur'an itself asserts repeatedly that no one can alter the Word of God. Surah 6:34 states, ". . . There is none that can alter the Words (and Decrees) of Allah . . ." Surah 10:64 states,

". . . No change can there be in the Words of Allah." Both Surah 6:115 and Surah 18:27 state, "None can change His Words."

In addition, the Bible emphasizes that the Word of God does not change. In the Old Testament, Isaiah 40:8 reads, "The grass withers, the flowers fall, but the Word of our God stands forever."

Jesus said, "Heaven and earth will pass away, but my words will never pass away" (Matthew 24:35).

Therefore, whoever claims that the Bible is corrupted or changed calls God a liar and actually accuses God of being unable to protect and preserve His Word.

Abdullah Ibn Abbas has judged on this subject of corruption or *Tahrif* (as recorded by Imam Al-Bukhari). He declared, "The word 'Tahrif' (corruption) signifies to change a thing from its original nature; and there is no man who could corrupt a single word of what proceeds from God, so that the Jews and Christians could corrupt only by misrepresenting the meanings of the words of God."[1] (To read more about Abdullah Ibn Abbas, please refer to the appendix in this book.)

When any of my Muslim acquaintances or friends tell me, "The Bible is corrupted," I reply, "God forbid," or in Arabic, "Astaghfar Allah."

The earliest revelation is the foundation

We know counterfeit currency can be made after the authorized one is first given. What is the standard that we use to examine currency to see if it is authentic or counterfeit? Do we use the original authorized currency or a recent one? Obviously the same principle applies when we ask if a book is God's Word or not. Of course the standard should be the earlier holy books not the most recent book.

Therefore, it is not possible, as some Muslims claim, that God first sent the Torah, the Zabour (Psalms), and the Injeel (the Gospel), and then allowed them to be corrupted.

Even the Qur'an indicates harmony with this principle. For in Surah 10:94 a command is given to Muhammad and all Muslims to treat the Bible as the primary source of enlightenment. The verse reads, "If thou wert in doubt as to what We have revealed unto thee then ask those who have been reading the Book from before thee."

HOW COULD IT POSSIBLY BENEFIT THE JEWS OR THE CHRISTIANS TO CORRUPT HOLY SCRIPTURES?

What purpose or benefit would it have been to the Christians and the Jews to corrupt their own Holy Scriptures? Why then would they continue to believe their Scripture? If they had done this, how could they bring themselves to pass it on to their children? Such allegation is irrational.

Some Muslims claim the Bible may have contained prophecies related to Muhammad and that they were deleted. Where is the evidence? If such prophecies were originally found in the Bible, Christians and Jews would have acknowledged Muhammad. They would have followed him and benefited by sharing in the spoils given to Muslims at the conquests of Persia, Syria, Palestine, Egypt, and many other lands.

In the Torah, God warned the Jews, "Do not add to what I command you and do not subtract from it, but keep the commands of the Lord your God that I give you" (Deuteronomy 4:2). (See also Deuteronomy 12:32.) If such prophecies about Muhammad did exist, why would Jews and Christians bring upon themselves and their beloved children sufferings here on earth and forever by eliminating those prophecies and thus altering the Word of God? In fact, the temptation would be greater to try to find prophecies of Muhammad rather than to eliminate any. For example, by becoming Muslims they could have avoided a disadvantaged status as a minority at the time when Muhammad died and Islam was spreading rapidly through conquest.

Also, when you read the Bible, you will find many statements and paragraphs that show the bad actions and sins of Jewish religious leaders.

It does not make any sense that Jews had corrupted the Bible without deleting all the negative words that still exist all over the Bible against them.

3

THE GOSPEL IS GOD'S GLAD NEWS

While I was talking with one of my dear Muslim friends, he told me the Qur'an mentions only one Gospel, but the Bible has four Gospels. I answered, "The word *Gospel* does not refer to one book, but to the Glad News of God's love toward everyone, which came to us through Jesus Christ. Gospel means 'good news.' The Qur'an calls it 'glad tidings' (Surah 3:45)."

The Glad News provided in the Gospel for the human race was written by clear revelation from God. It shows us how we can be saved from hell and enjoy eternal life with God.

The living revelation of God

We know from reading the Bible that Jesus Christ, a living person, is the perfect revelation of God to the human race. We read in the Gospel that "Jesus went throughout Galilee . . . preaching the good news [Gospel] of the kingdom, and healing every disease and sickness among the people" (Matthew 4:23). Thereafter, Jesus commanded His disciples to proclaim the Gospel (the good news which He revealed to them) to all the people of the world. (See Acts 1:8 and Matthew 28:18–20).

The Gospel tells us that the Messiah, the Savior who was foretold by the prophets, has come. (See John 1:45). Four different disciples of the Messiah recorded (in the Injeel) His coming and His life on earth.

Divine inspiration comes from the Holy Spirit

There is only one Gospel and only one Messiah, Jesus. God inspired Jesus' apostles through the guidance of the Holy

Spirit to tell us about the person, life, and teachings of Jesus. The Bible states: "All Scripture is God-breathed and is useful for teaching, rebuking, correcting and training in righteousness, so that the man of God may be thoroughly equipped for every good work" (2 Timothy 3:16–17). This verse means God "breathed" His words and thoughts through His selected messengers. God is the ultimate Author of the message and doctrines of the Gospel.

We read in the Bible, "Knowing this first, that no prophecy of Scripture is of any private interpretation. For prophecy never came by the will of man, but holy men of God spoke as they were moved by the Holy Spirit" (2 Peter 1:20–21 NKJV). It is clear that the Holy Spirit moved men to write each word as revealed by God.

Biblical scholar David W. Shenk explains *divine inspiration*. He wrote:

> Divine inspiration does not mean Divine dictation. Christians do not believe that the prophets who spoke or wrote the Word of God were [mindless] tubes through which God's words flowed. In all of the Biblical scriptures, the personality of the different writers is evident . . . God's inspiring activity does not cancel human involvement in the process. The imprint of human personality is part of the content of Biblical revelation. The Bible is the marvelous revelation in human language and thought forms. The Bible is the marvelous drama of God revealing Himself to persons, and the inspired prophets of God expressing that revelation in human language and thought forms.[1]

Over 2000 times in the Old Testament alone, there are clauses such as, "God spoke to Moses" and "God said, 'The Word of the Lord came unto Jonah,'" and many more.

Four presentations of the one Gospel of God

If we had only one account of the life of Jesus, many people would be suspicious and wonder if the one account were true. God gave us four accounts written by four separate and distinct individuals. Matthew and John were eyewitnesses and two of Jesus' twelve disciples. Luke, a historian (Luke 1:1–4) received his information from eyewitnesses (Luke 1:2). Mark spent extensive time with Peter, one of Jesus' closest friends who witnessed all the major events in His life.

Four followers of Christ, Matthew, Mark, Luke, and John, wrote testimonies of Jesus' life and recorded His teachings. None of their writings contradict. All their writings proclaim the glad news of God's love shown through Jesus. Each writer simply tells the story in a different way.

Jesus assured the gospel writers that the Holy Spirit would guide each one's writings and remind them of what He had spoken, "The Helper, the Holy Spirit, whom the Father will send in My name, He will teach you all things, and bring to your remembrance all things that I said to you" (John 14:26 NKJV).

My dear reader, when you study the Gospel as recorded by John, you are studying the Glad News of the kingdom of God as taught by Jesus. John, who was inspired by the Holy Spirit and a close companion of Jesus, could easily keep notes of His teachings.

Each of the four writers presents a different aspect of the character of Jesus. Matthew was one of Jesus' disciples and shows the Jews that Jesus is the long expected Messiah.

Mark was one of Jesus' followers and introduces Jesus as the Servant and powerful Savior.

Luke, who knew Jesus' disciples, describes Jesus as the Perfect Man and personal Savior who had been rejected by Israel. God also used Luke to write the book of Acts, which records what Jesus continued to do and teach (by the Holy Spirit) through His Apostles (Acts 1:1).

John was an eyewitness to the death, resurrection, and ascension of Jesus, as were Matthew and nine other disciples.

The Apostle John assures us that the disciples actually walked and talked with Jesus:

"That which was from the beginning [Jesus], which we have heard, which we have seen with our eyes, which we have looked at and our hands have touched—this we proclaim concerning the Word of life. The life appeared; we have seen it and testify to it" (1 John 1:1–3).

God guided His writers to accurately record what happened (Luke 1:1–4). Their writings precisely connect with actual historical events. The entire New Testament contains the greatest love story ever told. God's love for you and me and for all the people He created is revealed in the Bible.

All of the disciples wrote one message, which is the Gospel of Jesus Christ. Jesus even prophesied seventeen times about the spreading of the Gospel (e.g., Matthew 24:14).

Other New Testament writings

In addition to the four presentations of the Gospel, the New Testament also contains inspired teachings and letters written by apostles and disciples of Jesus to different groups of Christians and ultimately to all believers. The apostle Paul said, "For I received from the Lord what I also passed on to you" (1 Corinthians 11:23). (See also 1 Thessalonians 2:13.) The Qur'an also acknowledges that God inspired many messengers (e.g., Surah 21:7).

All the words written in the New Testament are significant echoes of Jesus' teachings. They help us to grow morally and spiritually. The four presentations of the Gospel and the other writings of the New Testament are interdependent.

The Apostles were the channel of God's truth in the New Testament just as the prophets were in the Old Testament (Hebrew 2:3).

For example, Peter makes known to us that the Apostles were actual eyewitnesses to the life of Jesus. Peter declared, "For we did not follow cleverly invented stories when we told you about the power and coming of our Lord Jesus Christ, but we were eyewitnesses of his majesty" (2 Peter 1:16).

The Apostles repeatedly challenged people living at that time to question any of the hundreds of eyewitnesses for verification of the life, death, resurrection, and teachings of Jesus. (See Acts 2:22–24; 5:30–32; 26:25–26; Luke 1:2.) The whole New Testament was written soon after Jesus' death (AD 40–96).

In about AD 42, Jesus' disciples were called Christians (Acts 11:26). Some Muslims wonder where the name "Christian" came from. The letters "ian" in those days meant "belonging to." So the followers of Jesus were called Christians because everybody knew that they belonged to Christ.

Different translations of the Bible

A notable fact is that Muslims scholars consider only the Arabic Qur'an to be the actual Word of God. Any translation of the Arabic Qur'an to a different language is not considered to be the actual Word of God.

Some Muslim scholars point to the different translations of the Bible to prove that it could not be the Word of God.

The Old Testament was written in Hebrew with a few chapters in Aramaic. And the New Testament was written in Greek. Converting those languages into English or any other language is referred to as a translation. Followers of Christ recognize the credibility of a translation of the Bible as long as it retains the teaching and the meaning found in the original language.

With the passage of time, words change in meaning. Words continue to slowly fall in and out of use. New translations of the Bible have helped a variety of people to understand more clearly the Bible in their contemporary languages.

None of these new translations conflict with any doctrinal teaching. The differences between these translations are relatively insignificant. It should also be pointed out that there is a division of philosophy among the different translators.

1. The literal equivalent translations seek to render (give, express and present) the source language into English as precisely as possible. In this translation the choice of words is meant to reflect the actual words of the source language. These translations include, "King James Version (KJV)," "New King James Version (NKJV)."

2. The dynamic equivalent translations seek to translate the idea rather than the very words of the source language. While these translations are handy, for occasionally illuminating the text, they often overstep the role of a translation and in reality become an interpretation of the Bible rather than a translation. These translations include, "The New Living Translation," and "The Message."

The New International Version (NIV) falls between these two camps.

The original manuscripts of the Bible, known as autographs were given by revelation of God. Obviously a translation or a copy is authoritative only to the extent that it accurately reproduces the autographs.

A typo mistake in a copy of the Bible or an inaccurate translation of a word or a passage cannot be used as proof that the

Bible is corrupted. In the same way a scratch in a Mercedes car does not mean the car is no longer a genuine Mercedes.

There are several different English translations of the Arabic Qur'an. For example, Surah 19:88, as translated by Yusuf Ali, says:

"They say: (Allah) Most Gracious has begotten a son!"

But Pickthal and Daryebadi in their translations use the word "taken" instead of begotten.

My Muslim friend, the most important proof that the Gospel is the divine Word of God comes when it is prayerfully read. God's Word will enlighten your mind and God will knock softly on the door of your heart. He will truly speak to you and change your life!

The words of Jesus and His disciples in the New Testament contain the highest moral standards ever said and written, which is strong evidence that the words came from God.

THE CERTAINTY OF THE BIBLE

The word "Bible" is taken from the Greek word "biblia," which means "book." The Bible is divided into two parts: the Old Testament books and the New Testament books. The word "testament" means "covenant," which refers to the relationship between God and His people. The Old Testament contains the Torah, the Psalms, and the books of the Prophets.

There are hundreds of books presenting conclusive evidence that demonstrate the authenticity and reliability of the Bible. One popular book is *The New Evidence that Demands a Verdict*, by Josh McDowell.[2]

You may be asking, "How do I know with *certainty* that any writing is from God?" Test it. The Bible warns its readers to "test everything and hold onto the truth" (1 Thessalonians 5:21).

Regardless of the opinions of friends or family, our own individual destiny lies in the balance. Our choice of a Holy Book should be carefully and prayerfully considered. God has given us minds to test such things. To ignore that gift because of pressures from others would be fearing created beings more than the *Creator*! So what kind of test is there to see if something is supernaturally inspired by God? There are two key tests:

1. Is it *Prophetic* with Accuracy?

This question is the most important test. In the Bible, God revealed that the test for true prophecy is that it must be fulfilled with 100 percent accuracy. Prophets who were not 100 percent accurate were deemed false and were to be stoned to death (Deuteronomy 18:20). Why is such a test in the Bible and not in any other religious books? And why does the Bible contain a great number of specific *historical* prophecies—which have been fulfilled accurately—while other religious books contain almost none?

2. Is it *Reliable*?

The evidence for reliability of the Biblical manuscripts far exceeds the evidence for all other ancient writings. Researchers Geisler and Nix conclude, "In contrast to the total number of over 5,000 New Testament manuscripts known today, other religious and historical books of the ancient world pale in significance." Two classical books: *From God to Us: How We Got Our Bible,* by Norman Geisler and William Nix[3], and *The New Testament Documents: Are They Reliable?* by F.F. Bruce[4] provide evidence for the trustworthiness of the Bible.

The entire Bible is harmonious even though forty authors who came from a variety of educational and cultural backgrounds wrote its sixty-six books. They lived on three different continents (Africa, Asia, and Europe) and wrote in three different languages. The Bible also covers many controversial topics and was written over a period of more than 1,500 years. Accordingly, one would expect such a book to contain contradictions or inconsistencies in its message, symbolism, and content. Who could get forty authors in a room today to agree 100% on even one controversial topic? Yet the Bible is consistent point by point throughout its text. It has one doctrinal system and one plan of salvation. This unity, itself, is a miracle.

PROPHETIC PROOF

In the Bible, God declares that He is outside of time. ". . . I am God, and there is no other; I am God, and there is none like me. I make known the end from the beginning, from ancient times, what is still to come." (Isaiah 46:9–10).

To test any supposed holy work, the first consideration should be to find proof. Are words proofs? Of course not, for any word can be alleged to be true. Is belief proof? People can be indoctrinated to believe anything.

However, if someone could always foretell the future with total accuracy, that is the specific predictions are always fulfilled and historically verifiable, it would establish that the information came from God. Only *God* possesses the ability to know fully what is to come.

In analyzing any work claimed to be "from God," one should find evidence that supports the divine inspiration. For example, hundreds of Bible prophecies have been fulfilled and are historically accurate. These prophecies were written far in advance of their fulfillment. Only God can write history in advance!

THE BIBLE'S PROPHECIES

Historical prophecies

Archeology affirms the accuracy of the Bible. In 1974, Time Magazine published an article, which stated, "After more than two centuries of facing the heaviest scientific guns that could be brought to bear, the Bible has survived, and is perhaps better for the siege. Even on the critic's own terms, historical fact, the scriptures seem more acceptable now than when the rationalists began the attack." Even during the mid-1700's through the mid-1900's, archeology has systematically proved the historical veracity of the Bible.

Archeological findings by both Christians and non-Christians have confirmed the reliability and the accuracy of the Biblical writers regarding numerous customs, names, places, and events. (See Halley's Bible handbook for artifacts.)

Only the Bible amazingly predicts precise historical events centuries in advance of their fulfillment. These prophecies are supported by archaeological evidence.

In about AD 32, Jesus predicted the destruction of the city of Jerusalem. (See Luke 19:43–44.) Just as Jesus had predicted, in AD 70 the Roman General Titus destroyed Jerusalem.

Messianic prophecies

There are 332 specific prophecies in the Old Testament concerning Jesus' birth, life, ministry, trial, crucifixion, death, and resurrection. Every single one was fulfilled with 100 percent accuracy in the life of Jesus Christ. For example, the exact location of the birth of the Messiah was prophesied to be in the city of Bethlehem (Micah 5:2). Consider the staggering probability of any one person fulfilling only 8 of these 332 predictions. "We find that the chance that any man might have lived down to the present time and fulfilled all eight prophecies is 1 in 10^{17} (10 to the 17th power)."[5] Five times in the New

Testament, Jesus affirmed Himself to be the theme or reoccurring message throughout the Old Testament (Matthew 5:17; Luke 24:27, 44; John 5:39; Hebrews 10:7).

Roy Gustafson, an internationally known authority on prophecy, correctly said, "The Old Testament is explained in the New Testament, the New Testament authenticates the Old Testament. The Old Testament foreshadows the New Testament. The New Testament fulfills the Old Testament. The Old Testament predicts a person. The New Testament presents that person. This person is the Lord Jesus Christ—who fully validated the Old Testament."[6]

Many of the Messianic prophecies are explained in chapter eleven.

Scientific prophecies

Another form of prophecy is the scientific information found in the Bible. This wisdom was given to Biblical authors 2,000 years or more before modern science discovered it. One example from astronomy is that the Bible recorded approximately 3,000 years ago that the sun follows a circular path through the universe. "It [the sun] rises at one end of the heavens and makes its circuit to the other; nothing is hidden from its heat" (Psalm 19:6). Certainly we know today that this is a fact.

The Bible records that the earth is round (Isaiah 40:22). And the earth *hangs* on nothing in space ". . . He suspends the earth over nothing" (Job 26:7).

In his book, *Science and the Bible*, Dr. Henry Morris identifies many of the scientific prophecies found in the Bible. This fascinating book gives detailed information on prophesied scientific facts.[7]

Many religious leaders have claimed that their writings were holy, but *none* have stood the test of complete and accurate prophecy. Only the Bible passes this test. Its detailed, fulfilled, historical prophecies provide evidence for its authenticity without a doubt. You will read throughout this book more about fulfilled prophecies. Another excellent reference is *Every Prophecy of the Bible,* by John F. Walvoord.[8]

RELIABILITY

The testimony of the ancient manuscripts

Today Christians have in their possession many ancient manuscripts of the Bible that date back many generations before Muhammad started the Islamic religion and before the Qur'an was written. Today's modern Bible does not differ from these ancient biblical manuscripts.

1. Codex Vaticanus (dated AD 325–350)

The Codex Vaticanus manuscript includes all of the books of the Bible up to the New Testament book of Hebrews (9:14).[9] The remaining portion of the New Testament is included by a later writer.[10] Codex Vaticanus is currently located in the Vatican library.

2. Codex Alexandrinus (dated AD 400)

The Codex Alexandrinus manuscript contains almost the entire Bible. This preserved manuscript is kept in the British Museum.[11]

3. Codex Sinaiticus (dated AD 350)

The Codex Sinaiticus manuscript contains the entire New Testament and a portion of the Old Testament. It is also found in the British Museum.[12]

The fact that these manuscripts existed at least two hundred years before Muhammad founded Islam means that the only Holy Book in the hands of the Christians at Muhammad's time consisted of the same Old and New Testaments we have today.

THE OLD TESTAMENT (TORAH)

The Dead Sea Scrolls

Manuscripts of the entire Old Testament, except the book of Esther, were found in 1947 in a series of caves along the northwestern portion of the Dead Sea. The documents had been placed in these caves about AD 70 by a sect of Jews known as the Essenes. They placed parchments in clay jars and hid them in the caves near the present-day ruins of Khirbet Qumran.

After scientific scrutiny, many scrolls appeared to have been written at least 200 years prior to their placement in the caves in AD 70. The documents remained hidden and protected for nearly 2,000 years. When discovered in 1947, the scrolls were compared letter by letter to today's Hebrew Holy Scriptures (Torah). Virtually no difference could be found![13] The Old Testament was passed down accurately, proving that the prophecies about Jesus Christ were made long before He arrived.[14]

The Septuagint

The Septuagint is the Greek translation of the Hebrew Torah.[15] This version was transcribed around 270 BC and is well documented in both Jewish and secular history. The content shows consistent accuracy with today's Old Testament and verifies all the prophecies of the coming Messiah that were translated from Hebrew into Greek almost three hundred years before Christ was born!

THE NEW TESTAMENT

Numerous copies of the manuscripts

Today there are nearly 24,000 early manuscripts of portions of the New Testament. These Greek New Testament manuscripts have been preserved since the first century after Christ. They form the contents of the New Testament available today.

Contrary to popular belief among many Muslims, there is no evidence suggesting that the life and teachings of Jesus Christ were different from that which is recorded in the Bible. Not even a shred of evidence exists.

In addition to the numerous existing first century manuscripts, the integrity of the New Testament text is established by applying the three basic tests of historiography: the bibliographical test, the internal test, and the external test. A full description is given in the book *The New Evidence that Demands a Verdict* (cited previously).

4

DID MUHAMMAD COME TO ESTABLISH A NEW RELIGION?

Many Muslim teachers claim that Muhammad's mission was to establish a new religion. However, according to the Qur'an itself, Muhammad's mission was not to establish a new religion but to preserve the religion of Abraham in the Torah (Old Testament). Some such Qur'anic passages are:

> "So we have taught thee [Muhammad] the inspired (message), "Follow the ways of Abraham the True in Faith . . ." (Surah16:123)

> "Say: "Verily, my Lord hath guided me to a way that is straight—a religion of right—the path (trod) by Abraham the True in Faith . . ." (Surah 6:161)

> "Say: "Allah speaketh the Truth: follow the religion of Abraham . . ." (Surah 3:95)

> "Who can be better in religion than one who submits his whole self to Allah, does good, and follows the way of Abraham the true in faith? For Allah did take Abraham for a friend." (Surah 4:125)

As proved earlier, the Qur'an never states that its words replaced the words of the previous Holy Scriptures of the Jews and Christians. The Qur'an does state that some of its verses abrogate other verses in the Qur'an. (See Surah 2:106 and 16:101.)

THE QUR'AN ITSELF SAYS MUHAMMAD DID NOT COME TO TEACH NEW DOCTRINES

As I showed you in chapter one, the Qur'an frequently affirms that Muhammad was given revelations to confirm what was already revealed in the Holy Books of the Jews and Christians. It does not claim to correct, replace, add to, or annul the Bible. Let me mention some Qur'anic passages as a confirmation:

"Nothing is said to thee [Muhammad] that was not said to the Messengers before thee . . ." (Surah 41:43)

"The same religion has He [God] established for you as that which He enjoined on Noah . . . and that which we enjoined on Abraham, Moses, and Jesus: namely, that ye should remain steadfast in Religion, and make no divisions therein . . ." (Surah 42:13)

"Say [Muhammad]: 'I am no bringer of new-fangled doctrine among the messengers, nor do I know what will be done with me or with you.'" (Surah 46:9)

MUHAMMAD'S STATUS ACCORDING TO THE QUR'AN

The Qur'an clearly states Muhammad's purpose. For example:

"Muhammad is no more than a Messenger: many were the Messengers that passed away before him . . ." (Surah 3:144)

"Say: [Muhammad] 'It is not in my power to cause you harm, or to bring you to right conduct'" (Surah 72:21)

"Say: 'I am but a man like yourselves . . .'" (Surah 18:110)

Who was the Qur'an intended for?

Some verses in the Qur'an indicate that the Qur'an was given for the people of Mecca. For example, "Thus have We sent by inspiration to thee an Arabic Qur'an: That thou mayest warn the Mother of Cities and all around her . . ." (Surah 42:7).

We read in the Qur'an that it is for Arabic speaking people. For example:

"We have sent it down as an Arabic Qur'an, in order that ye may learn wisdom" (Surah 12:2).

"A Book, whereof the verses are explained in detail- A Qur'an in Arabic, for people who understand" (Surah 41:3).

"We have made it a Qur'an in Arabic, that ye may be able to understand" (Surah 43:3).

"Verily, We have made This (Qur'an) easy, in thy tongue, in order that they may give heed" (Surah 44:58).

"And before this, was the Book of Moses as a guide and a mercy: And this Book confirms (it) in the Arabic tongue . . ." (Surah 46:12).

SUBMISSION TO GOD WITHOUT FOLLOWING MUHAMMAD

It is significant that even according to the Qur'an believers in God submitted their lives to Him without following Muhammad or the teachings of the Qur'an.

According to the Qur'an, the followers of Jesus are superior and people should follow Jesus until the last day. The Qur'an states: "Behold! Allah said: O Jesus! . . . I will make those who follow thee superior to those who reject faith, to the Day of Resurrection . . ." (Surah 3:55).

The Qur'an declares that followers of Jesus worship the One and only true living God (Surah 2:139).

The Qur'an states that Abraham and Jacob submitted their lives to God (Surah 2:131–133).

It is well known that the Qur'an classified Jesus (Isa) and all the prophets as ones who submit their lives to God (Surah 2:136). The Qur'an also describes the followers of Jesus as ones who submit their lives to God (Surah 3:52). (See also Surah 5:111.)

According to the Qur'an, a Muslim is one who submits his whole self to God and is a doer of good (Surah 2:131). It is significant that a person can submit his life to God without following Muhammad or the Qur'an.

My dear Muslim reader, when you read the Bible, you will discover that the true believers in God and followers of Jesus Christ are called to surrender their lives completely and submit their whole being to the One and only living God, the Creator of heaven and earth. This is the clear teaching of Jesus and His disciples. The Bible urges believers to submit themselves to God (James 4:7).

The believers who truly submit their lives to God are brave enough to live by what God has revealed in the Holy Scriptures. They do not follow the opinions of men or Tradition (Hadith) that contradict the clear revelation of God.

Also, genuine believers do not follow their own preference or their own interpretation. Those who submit their lives completely to God do not revere the traditions of men more than the Word of God. They keep all the words of God in their hearts and minds and ask God continually to guide them. They establish their beliefs based on balanced assimilation of the Word of God.

An Invitation

My dear reader, are you burdened, worried, or lonely? Do you feel spiritually or emotionally thirsty? The God of the Bible does not desire for you to live life this way. Jesus offers a comforting invitation: "'If anyone is thirsty, let him come to me and drink. Whoever believes in me, as the Scripture has said, streams of living water will flow from within him'" (John 7:37–38).

As physical water satisfies your body, Jesus promised that He will satisfy your heart.

SECTION TWO

ADAM IN THE QUR'AN
AND IN THE BIBLE

5

ADAM IN ISLAM

My dear reader, this section is exciting because it reveals the desire of God's heart, which is to fellowship with people and to relate to us personally!

Adam created perfectly by God

The Qur'an states that God created Adam in a perfect condition. We read in Surah 95:4, "We have indeed created man in the best of molds." Surah 2:30 states that Adam was God's representative ("Khalifah"). In addition, we read in Surah 15:29, "When I have fashioned him [Adam] and breathed into him of My Spirit."

Adam and Eve's perfect circumstances

According to the Qur'an, God gave Adam and Eve perfect circumstances. He created them in the Heavenly Garden. God gave them everything they needed to enjoy and live a righteous life. Surah 2:35 states: "We said: 'O Adam! Dwell thou and thy wife in the Garden [Jannatu], and eat of the bountiful things therein as (where and when) ye will . . .'"

God desires to interact with people

We read in Surah 2:31: "And He [God] taught Adam the names of all things." This verse indicates that God talked to Adam many times and Adam had a personal, direct, and wonderful relationship with God. According to the Qur'an, Adam and Eve were able to enjoy perfect fellowship with Him. As you will clearly see, it was the original intention of the almighty, transcendent God to personally relate to the people He created because He is gracious and humble.

Satan tempted Adam and Eve, and they fell

We read in the Qur'an a clear warning to Adam: "We said: 'O Adam! Dwell thou and thy wife in the Garden; and eat of the bountiful things therein . . . but approach not this tree, or ye run into harm and transgression'" (Surah 2:35).

The Qur'an states that Satan tempted and deceived Adam and Eve and that they failed to represent God. They disobeyed God and sinned. ". . . They both ate of the tree, Thus did Adam disobey his Lord, and allowed himself to be seduced" (Surah 20:121).

The Qur'an described what happened in Surah 2:36: "Then did Satan make them slip from the (Garden) and get them out of the state (of felicity) in which they had been. We said: 'Get ye down, all (ye people), with enmity between yourselves. On earth will be your dwelling place . . .'"

The Arabic Qur'an named the place where Adam and Eve lived before they disobeyed God as "Jannatu." (The English translation is "garden"), which is the same name that the Qur'an gives to heaven. (see Surah 9:72)

There is a strong indication in the Qur'an that Adam and Eve were created in heaven itself and enjoyed peace and felicity until they disobeyed God and were cast out of heaven.

God's penalty extended to all mankind

Note that in Surah 2:36, the form used in Arabic is the imperative *ahbituu,* "get ye down," which means "get down, descend, crash down."[2] The widely acclaimed Muslim scholar and commentator of the Qur'an, Pickthall, says, "Here the command is in the plural, as addressed to Adam's race."[3]

Abdullah Yusuf Ali explained the phrase "Get ye down, all (ye people)" (Surah 2:36), in his popular translation and commentary of the Qur'an: "Allah's decree is the result of man's action. Note the transition in Arabic from the singular number in Surah 2:33 to the dual in Surah 2:35 and the plural here, which I have indicated in English by 'All ye people.' Evidently Adam is the type of all mankind . . ."[4]

The Qur'an teaches the fall of Adam and implicates the whole human race in this fall. In Surah 2:38, we read that the same command given to Adam and Eve was given to their offspring: "Get ye down all [jamean] from here."

Note the Arabic word *jamean* is taken to mean a "host, congregation, all, together, altogether."[5] Therefore, God's command to depart from the Garden was intended for not only Adam and Eve, but to all their descendants. This verse points to the fact that humankind as a whole was affected by the disobedience of Adam and Eve. The Hadith confirms this truth.[6]

Adam was the first human created. He is the father of all human kind. We all originate from him. His disobedience affected all the members of his family. It is from this point of origin that mankind has had to face its ultimate problem—the result of Adam's fall into sin.

6

THE RESULTS OF THE FALL

According to the Gospel, when God created man, His purpose was that man might enjoy constant and beautiful fellowship with Him. God placed man in the Garden of Eden and communed with him there.

Adam's sin separated him from God

God's intention for man was being fulfilled while Adam walked in fellowship with Him. But Adam disobeyed God. Adam's relationship with God was broken as a result of sin.[1] The prophet Isaiah declared, "Surely the arm of the LORD is not too short to save, nor His ear too dull to hear. But your iniquities have separated you from your God . . ." (59:1–2). Adam's sin and our sin caused the separation between mankind and the Holy God.

Adam was created morally pure because he reflected the image of God. Since God created Adam completely pure it was reasonable for Him to demand total purity. When he disobeyed God he lost the ability to be completely moral, which is known as the Fall.

Adam chose to rebel

God gave mankind the freedom of choice, and man chose to rebel against God in the person of Adam.

God placed a certain tree in the middle of the garden as a symbol of His authority over man. Adam was granted the freedom to choose. The moment Adam and Eve chose to eat the fruit from the forbidden tree, they intentionally challenged and violated the authority of God. Their sin was an act of defiance against the authority of Almighty God. Because Adam and Eve ate of the forbidden fruit, God banished them from the Garden.

No one can make light of Adam's sin by saying he just forgot God's command. Adam could not have possibly forgotten the only command God gave him, especially since Satan had just reminded him of God's prohibition (Surah 7:20).

Sin infected all humanity

The original sin of Adam and Eve had a devastating effect on the whole human race. The effect of their sin became universal and all humanity now plunges into a world where sin and death reign. My dear friend, sin became an integral part of human nature as an immediate result of Adam's sin (disobedience).

God created man in His own image and gave him the freedom of choice. Man chose to rebel against God. Consequently, Adam's sin distorted God's image in mankind. The human nature fell captive to the power of sin, thereby becoming intrinsically corrupt. Man cannot purify his soul to the state it was in before the Fall. Even Muhammad said, "Satan runs in the body of Adam's son (i.e., man) as his blood circulates in it."[2]

I was discussing the topic of Adam with a Muslim acquaintance and he responded, "This is not fair and does not make any sense that we suffer because of Adam and Eve's wrong choice and their disobedience to God." I explained to him that this principle is logical and observable even today. For example, when a leader wages war, people are killed; a whole country can suffer from its leader's wrong decision. Another example is when parents live an immoral lifestyle and their children suffer because of their parents' wrong choices.

These types of instances have been repeated among mankind since the beginning.

Adam's sin tainted human nature

Sin permanently tainted human nature. Fallen humanity experiences sin's effect daily through self-centeredness, jealousy, envy, hate, etc. None of Adam's descendants are able to live the pure and sinless life for which God created them to live.

According to the following verses in the Qur'an, all humans are captive to the power of sin:

Surah 12:53, ". . . The (human) soul is certainly prone to evil . . ."

Surah 16:61, "If Allah were to punish men for their wrongdoing, He would not leave, on the (earth), a single living creature . . ."

Muhammad said: "Every son of Adam is a sinner."[3] Surely all of us can testify that we are prone to indulge ourselves. At times we violate our conscience and yield to our selfish nature which is sin. Even within the best of all human hearts remains an evil nature.

The devastating consequences of sin

God created Adam as a perfect human being who would live forever. Man was not originally created to die. He was not originally programmed for death. God warned Adam of the devastating consequences of sin, ". . . for when you eat of it, you will surely die" (Genesis 2:17).

Sin sentenced us to a slow death. We were like flowers planted in God's garden. Sin cut us off from God's presence like a flower plucked from its source of life. It is just a matter of time before that flower dies completely and no human effort can restore life to it.

We need a miracle. And the practice of religious duties and rituals cannot bring us life. We need Someone who can give us life (raise us from the dead) because our sin caused our soul to die.

Sin affects us in that our body dies a physical death and our spirit (detached from God, the source of spiritual life) dies a spiritual death. Our body, spirit, and soul are eternally separated from God. And no amount of works or efforts on our part can bridge the distance between God and us.

The Bible states, ". . . Sin entered the world through one man, and death through sin, and in this way death came to all men, because all sinned" (Romans 5:12). All men continue to sin because sin is now an integral part of human nature.

It is apparent that the circumstances of life did not bring sin to man, but rather it is man who brought sin to the world. It is clear that the descendants of Adam inherited all the characteristics of his fallen nature. As a consequence, we all became subject to the condemnation of God because of the sins we committed against Him. He is Holy and Righteous and cannot tolerate sin. God's law and justice are stated in the Bible: "The wages [consequences] of sin is death . . ." (Romans 6:23).

After years of studying Islamic religion, I discovered the majority of Muslim scholars teach that mankind only needs to follow appropriate teaching and guidance. I believe they are mistaken in their optimistic diagnosis of the human nature. The reality is that we need a radical solution and transformation of our nature. Our works or efforts cannot accomplish this.

As you shall see in the coming pages of this book, God provided the remedy for us. And it is glorious, Glad News!

7

RECONCILIATION IS POSSIBLE

Part of the Good News that God wants you to know is that "God is love" (1 John 4:16). His nature is love. He desires a loving personal relationship with you! You will surely discover this marvelous fact by the time you finish reading this book.

God's plan to save mankind

God's eternal love for mankind did not change because of man's disobedience. God planned a way to save mankind, that is, to restore our relationship with Him. God's holiness demanded justice and punishment toward sinners, while His immeasurable love pleaded for mercy and forgiveness for them. The God of the Bible has not stood still waiting for us to find Him. He came to us in the person of Jesus Christ! (2 Corinthians 5:18–19) Therefore, Jesus Christ (the Living Word of God) became flesh and, on the cross, suffered the consequences of our sin. God's total judgment against sin fell upon Jesus.

In Jesus, we see an accurate picture of the balance between God's righteous anger and God's love.

On our behalf, Christ voluntarily paid the price we should have paid for all the sins we have committed, and ever will commit, against God. Christ loves each one of us. The Apostle Paul said about Jesus, ". . . [Jesus] loved me and gave himself for me" (Galatians 2:20).

Jesus, the only sinless, perfect man

The Gospel, in Luke 4, teaches that Satan tempted Jesus to act independently from God's will and offered the kingdoms of the world if He worshiped him. Unlike Adam and Eve, who lost their relationship with God through their disobedience, Jesus had complete victory over Satan's temptations to sin. In the Gospel, Jesus is recognized as the perfect man who submitted every moment of His life to the will of God.

All other people throughout human history have yielded to Satan's temptations and have sinned regularly. Jesus was the only exception. According to the teaching of both the Qur'an and the Gospel, Jesus was the only man to live a life without committing one single sin.

Because Jesus alone lived His life in perfect obedience to God, He is the only One able to restore us to a right relationship with God.

God's gift of grace came to us through Jesus

Grace is undeserved favor. We cannot do enough to earn God's favor or acceptance. It is a gift. "For it is by grace you have been saved, through faith—and this not from yourselves, it is the gift of God—not by works, so that no one can boast" (Ephesians 2:8–9).

Do you want to obtain this gift from God? Read on to discover how to receive God's gift of grace that was purchased by Jesus with His invaluable sacrifice.

The Bible contrasts the sin of Adam and its deadly consequences for mankind with the gift of Jesus and its redeeming benefits to mankind.

> . . . For if the many died by the trespass of the one man, how much more did God's grace and the gift that came by the grace of the one man, Jesus Christ, over-flow to the many! . . . The judgment followed one sin and brought condemnation, but the gift followed many trespasses and brought justification. For if, by the trespass of the one man, death reigned through that

one man, how much more will those who receive God's abundant provision of grace and of the gift of righteousness reign in life through the one man, Jesus Christ. Consequently, just as the result of one trespass was condemnation for all men, so also the result of one act of righteousness was justification that brings life for all men. For just as through the disobedience of the one man the many were made sinners, so also through the obedience of the one man the many will be made righteous. (Romans 5:15–19)

How to become spiritually alive

The Bible explains creation, degeneration, and regeneration. *Creation* is the original generation of life. *Degeneration* is the Fall of man, which made us spiritually dead. *Regeneration* is when people become spiritually alive. When Jesus taught about regeneration, He declared, "I tell you the truth, no one can see the kingdom of God unless he is born again" (John 3:3). Because of our sinful nature and our individual sins, we are spiritually dead and separated from God.

Jesus has the power to give spiritual and eternal life to all those who believe in Him and follow Him. The Gospel declares, "For since death came through a man, the resurrection of the dead comes also through a man. For as in Adam all die, so in Christ all will be made alive" (1 Corinthians 15:21–22).

As an electric light bulb becomes full of light and useful when it is connected with electrical power, you will become full of life when you put your faith in Jesus Christ as your Savior. You will start fulfilling the purpose for which you were created.

What does it mean to be "born again"?

To become "born again" means you are newly created in your heart and transformed in the very depths of your being.

The Holy Spirit comes to dwell within you and gives you many spiritual blessings. He gives you a new heart (with new affections and desires), new power, and a new destination. You develop a new view of people around you, a new nature, and a new purpose! The Bible declares, "If anyone is in Christ, he is a new creation . . ." (2 Corinthians 5:17). Adam was the head of the old creation, whereas Christ is the head of the new creation. Certainly, you will enjoy an unimaginable inner peace, which fills your inner most being when you are "born again."

God looks at the heart

The Bible teaches that God is concerned about our hearts not our rituals. Jesus quoted Isaiah's prophecy: "These people [religious Jews] honor me with their lips, but their hearts are far from Me. They worship me in vain; their teachings are but rules taught by men" (Matthew 15:8–9). Jesus said of those who cancel the Word of God for the sake of tradition, "You hypocrites!" (vs. 7).

Consider an example of two men attempting to get close to God. One man performs all the rituals he learned from his religious teachers. He memorizes and utters all the prescribed prayers, bows down with proper body movements, and washes his body for cleansing. However, he is keeping a sin in his heart. The other man was never taught the prescribed rituals and prayers, but he recognizes his sins and humbly asks God with all his heart to forgive him and guide him. According to the Bible, God would surely hear and answer the prayer of the second man.

According to the Bible, repentance (*toba* in Arabic) is making a decision and commitment to forsake all sins and to submit to God's will. Repentance involves humbling self, confessing unworthiness, and receiving God's mercy and grace that came to us through Jesus.

The wonderful truth is that if you believe in what Jesus Christ (AL-Masih Isa) did for you on the cross, and you confess your sins and repent (*toba* in Arabic), you will be born again! God will grant you acceptance. Upon your new birth, you will begin to enjoy a peaceful, personal, and living relationship with your Creator!

My dear reader, will you decide to take a step of faith? Will you demonstrate your faith through a simple and yet most vital decision? Will you decide in your heart and declare with your mouth to God that you believe and rely on Jesus' death on the cross to pay the penalty for your sins?

The decision is as simple as trusting a chair to hold your weight when you sit upon it. When you put your faith in Jesus for the forgiveness of your sin—not in yourself or your works or anything else—you will experience God's forgiveness and enjoy amazing rest.

The Holy Spirit dwells within the true followers of Christ

True believers and followers of Christ are people who have experienced a new birth. Note that there are many people who claim to be *Christians*. Perhaps they have Christian parents, or received a Christian education, or were born in a supposedly Christian nation, or accept Christianity as a good religion. They might even be attending a church, or trying to do good works, or agreeing with Christian beliefs intellectually. However, none of those things can make someone a true follower of Christ. Only those people who experience the new birth become true followers of Christ. The evidence of the new birth is the presence of the Holy Spirit within, confirming a person to be God's child.

The Holy Spirit in you will help you to realize that God knows you personally and you are so special to Him.

God's mercy to us through Jesus

What a loving God! He showed us mercy through Jesus Christ. Because of Jesus, we can actually trade judgment for forgiveness! We can trade our sin for the righteousness of Jesus. The Bible declares,

> As for you, you were dead in your transgressions and sins, in which you used to live when you followed the ways of this world . . . All of us also lived among them at one time, gratifying the cravings of our sinful nature and following its desires and thoughts. Like the rest, we were by nature objects of wrath. But because of his great love for us, God, who is rich in mercy, made us alive with Christ even when we were dead in transgressions . . . (Ephesians 2:1–5)

Even the Qur'an states that Jesus is a mercy from God. "And (we wish) to appoint him . . . a Mercy from us" (Surah 19:21).

Jesus reconciles us to God forever!

The Bible reveals that God wants mankind to spend eternity enjoying joyful fellowship with Him (1 Timothy 2:3–4).

Jesus Christ offers us the opportunity to be born into His spiritual family. Jesus is alive now. And through our union to Him, He alone grants us eternal life. Remember, eternal life was God's original intent for Adam and his descendants. Through Adam we all forfeited eternal life. Therefore God sent Jesus, who willingly came to bring us back into an eternal relationship with God. Jesus died in our place in order to take away our sins. What awesome glad news! Jesus reconciles us to God forever!

The Bible states, "All this is from God, who *reconciled* us to himself through Christ . . . God was reconciling the world to

himself in Christ, not counting men's sins against them . . ."
(2 Corinthians 5:18–19).

Some Muslims respond to this truth saying, "It is not fair that Jesus paid for our sins. Each one who has committed sin must account for it. Where do you find in a court of law someone else being hanged for another?"

I usually answer, "This incredible sacrifice is not something we requested or forced someone else to give for us. It is what God Himself has done for us—as a gift. And God is simply asking you to accept His gift of reconciliation."

I also remind my Muslim friends that Jesus freely chose to rescue us, Jesus said: ". . . I lay down my life. . . . no one takes it from me, but I lay it down of my own accord" (John 10:17-18).

A few times, I have seen fathers and mothers sacrificing their lives in order to save their children's lives.

I would like to share with you a story. Once there was a rich king who was also the lawgiver and supreme judge of his kingdom. One day his beloved son committed serious violations of the law. The penalty of these violations amounted to paying a fine of a large amount of money, which his son did not have. His father, the king, because he was a just judge, ordered his son to pay this fine because he did not want to violate his own laws. The son was terrified because if he did not pay this fine he would have to go to prison for a long time.

The son realized his mistakes and repented from all his heart for breaking the laws. The king decided to offer to pay the fine from his personal finances. The son humbly and joyfully accepted his father's gift. Out of his gratitude and love for his father, the son decided to dedicate the rest of his life to serve his father and his kingdom.

There are similarities between this story and our relationship with God. It is a small picture of what the God of the Bible has done for us. He personally paid the price we owed.

My Muslim friend, please ponder in your heart the necessity of putting your faith in Jesus. If you ever become terminally ill, the best medicine in the world will not help you unless you take it.

Imagine there is a door that opens heaven for you and even gives you access to the presence of God. And God provides the key for you. That door remains locked until you use the key. Jesus said, "I am the gate; whoever enters through me will be saved" (John 10:9) The Bible tells us that Jesus is the key to heaven.

SOME BIBLICAL FACTS ABOUT JESUS

1. God the Father sent Jesus Christ. (John 8:29,42)

2. Jesus always did the Father's will. (John 5:30)

3. Jesus could do nothing independently of the Father. (John 5:19)

4. Jesus lived to please the Father. (John 8:29)

5. Jesus Christ received all His authority from the Father. (John 5:27)

6. Jesus received His message from the Father. (John 14:10)

   Jesus said, "For I did not speak of my own accord but the Father who sent me commanded me what to say and how to say it. I know that his command leads to eternal life. So whatever I say is just what the Father has told me to say." (John 12:49–50)

7. The Father gave to Jesus Christ the works to accomplish. (John 5:36 and 17:4)

8. Jesus was submitted to the Father. (Matthew 26:39,42)

9. Jesus Christ's kingdom was appointed to Him by the Father. (Luke 22:29)

10. Jesus Christ will ultimately deliver up the kingdom unto the Father. (1 Corinthians 15:24)

11. Jesus Christ Himself will be subjected unto the Father. (1 Corinthians 15:27–28)

12. God the Father is the God of Jesus Christ. (John 20:17) Jesus Christ bore the relation of man to God the Father.

13. Jesus Christ functioned under the Father's headship. (1 Corinthians 11:3)

    Jesus said, ". . . the Father is greater than I." (John 14:28)

14. Jesus Christ served as a man. (Philippians 2:5–8)

15. Jesus Christ, as a human, was subject to hunger, thirst, agony, and death. (Matthew 21:18; John 19:28,33–37)

16. The goal of Jesus was not to receive glory for Himself. (John 8:50)

    Jesus came, lived, suffered and died to glorify God the Father.

17. Jesus' mission was to make it possible for us to have fellowship with God, the Bible tells us:

    "For Christ died for sins once and for all . . . to bring you to God."(1 Peter 3:18)

SECTION THREE

ABRAHAM IN THE QUR'AN AND IN THE BIBLE

8

THE LIFE OF ABRAHAM

Abraham is given the title "friend of God" in both the Qur'an and the Bible. Surah 4:125 teaches: ". . . For Allah did take Abraham for a friend."

Abraham, the friend of God

In the Bible (James 2:23), Abraham is described as the friend of God. The title suggests a very close relationship with God. It implies that God shared with Abraham many of His secret plans for the future that He would not otherwise have revealed to someone who was only His servant.

Abraham, a model of faith for Muslims and Christians

The Bible also calls Abraham the "father of all who believe" (Romans 4:11). In Galatians 3:7, it is written, "Understand, then, that those who believe are children of Abraham." The same concept is found in the Qur'an, which exhorts Muslims to "follow the religion of Abraham . . ." (Surah 3:95).

In Surah 16:123, Muslims are directed to ". . . follow the ways of Abraham, the true in faith . . ."

Abraham is an example of the *true religion* and a model for Muslims. Abraham is also a model for true Christians. All true believers of the Gospel are to have the same *saving faith* Abraham had. (See Galatians 3:8–9.) Abraham was a prototype of the true religion to come, through his faith in God. "Abram believed the LORD, and he [God] credited it to him as righteousness" (Genesis 15:6).

THE PROMISED SON—ISAAC OR ISHMA'IL?

God promised Abraham a son. Abraham was fully aware of the physical impossibility for him and his wife, Sarah, to have a son so late in life. She was barren. Yet Abraham believed God would fulfill His promise supernaturally.

Qur'anic references to the "promised son" and to Isaac

God commanded Abraham to sacrifice his son. The only reference to the sacrifice of the son of Abraham is in Surah 37:99–107, which reads, ". . . So We gave him the good news of a boy ready to suffer and forbear. Then, when (the son) reached (the age of) (serious) work with him, he [Abraham] said: 'O my son! I see in vision that I offer thee in sacrifice."

While this passage does not directly say which son it was, the Qur'an in this passage indicates that it is the same son whose birth is described as good news. Just two verses after the mention of the sacrifice, Isaac's birth is mentioned as good news: "Peace and salutation to Abraham . . . and We gave him the good news of Isaac . . . We blessed him and Isaac . . ." (Surah 37:109–113). Earlier, in Surah 11:71, Isaac's birth is foretold as good news: "But We gave her Glad tidings of Isaac, and after him, of Jacob." Angels announced Isaac's birth as good news, "And they [angels] gave him Glad tidings of a son . . . his wife came forward (laughing) aloud! She smote her forehead and said, 'A barren old woman!'" (Surah 51:28–29). Much attention is given to Isaac in the Qur'an.

At Tabari, the prominent Muslim-Arab historian and theologian, identifies Isaac as the boy to be sacrificed in Surah 37:101.[1]

Muhammad's companions believed that the son to be sacrificed was Isaac.[2]

Limited Qur'anic references to Ishma'il

The Qur'an actually contains no reference to the birth of Ishma'il, and it doesn't foretell that Abraham will be the father of Ishma'il. Nowhere in the Qur'an is it specifically stated that Ishma'il was promised to Abraham by name—yet Isaac was. Very little is said in the Qur'an about Ishma'il, and no attention is given to his mother or his sons. Ishma'il's birth is never announced as good news. It is apparent that the son about whom the good news was given and the one to be sacrificed, as mentioned in Surah 37:99–107, was not Ishma'il, but Isaac.

Abdullah Yusuf Ali, in his internationally acknowledged translation and commentary of the Qur'an, made a significant admission regarding Surah 37:99–107 (the only passage referring to the sacrifice of Abraham's son). Ali states, "The boy thus born was according to Muslim Traditions in the Hadith (which, however, are not unanimous on this point), the first born son of Abraham, viz., Ishma'il."[3] Ali's claim that the firstborn son to be sacrificed was Ishma'il is not based upon evidence from the Qur'an, but rather on Traditions of which he points out are not unanimous on this point.

Abraham's promised son is Isaac

Muslims and Christians agree that Sarah was Isaac's mother and Hagar was Ishmael's mother. It is important to note that the Qur'an never mentions Hagar, and yet Sarah is mentioned a few times. And the Qur'an presented Sarah as Abraham's wife. We read: "And his wife was standing (there) and she laughed: But we gave her glad tidings of Isaac . . ." (Surah 11:71).

One of the traditions confirms that Hagar was only a servant in Abraham's household. "When Sarah gave her to Abraham to bear him a son. Then he called Hagar who was the most trustworthy of his servants, and he bestowed her (Hagar) on her (Sarah) and gave her clothes. Subsequently Sarah made a gift of her (Hagar) to Ibrahim who cohabitated with her and she bore Ismail who was the eldest of his children."4

It is also significant that Hagar and Ishmael left Abraham's house many years earlier, before God commanded Abraham to sacrifice his son (Genesis 21:14). Isaac was Abraham's only son by his wife Sarah, who had the right to inherit from Abraham.

The Qur'an shows that because Abraham and his son had fully submitted themselves to obey God, God blessed them. We read first "They had both submitted their wills (to Allah)" (Surah 37:103).

Then we read, "We blessed him and Isaac" (Surah 37:113)

Clearly these two verses relate because both Abraham and Isaac had fully submitted themselves to God's will, making it reasonable for God's blessing to come on them both.

The Qur'an is silent and does not identify the son that God commanded Abraham to sacrifice. One of the most famous and explicit narratives in the Jewish and Christian Scriptures is God's command to Abraham to sacrifice Isaac (Genesis 22:2, Hebrews 11:17, and James 2:21). The Qur'an claims that it was sent by God to confirm the Holy Scriptures of the Jews and the Christians (Surah 5:48). If the Qur'an had come to correct any errors, as many Muslim scholars claim, it would clearly identify Ishma'il as the promised son that God commanded Abraham to sacrifice.

Surah 37, which is the only Surah to record the story of God's command to Abraham to sacrifice his son, mentions many of the prophets by name, such as Noah, Abraham, Isaac, Moses, Aaron, Elijah and Jonah. If Ishmael were the son to be offered as a sacrifice, why did this Surah not even mention him among the prophets, as it recognized Isaac?

The references from the Qur'an strongly suggest that Isaac—not Ishma'il—is the son announced by God to be sacrificed.

God bestowed "prophethood" on the children of Israel

God loves the Arabs, Jews, and all people equally. He desires to have a relationship with every one of them. While God promised Abraham He would bless his son, Ishmael (Ishma'il), God revealed that His blessings to the world would come through the descendants of Isaac. God told Abraham: "And as for Ishmael, I have heard you: I will surely bless him; I will make him fruitful and will greatly increase his numbers . . . But my covenant I will establish with Isaac, whom Sarah will bear to you . . ." (Genesis 17:20–21).

God chose to reveal prophecy to the Jewish people. It is important to read verses in the Qur'an that confirm the Biblical teaching that "prophethood" was confined to the children of Israel. For example, Surah 45:16 states, "We did aforetime grant to the children of Israel the Book, the Power of Command, and Prophethood . . . and we favored them above the nations." In this verse, "the Book" means the Holy Scriptures. "Prophethood" means the prophetic line was to come through Isaac's offspring alone.

The Qur'an's words are emphatic, and they point to the superiority of Isaac's role over Ishmael.

Surah 29:27 states, "And We gave (Abraham) Isaac and Jacob, and ordained among his progeny Prophethood and Revelation . . ." This verse and others in the Qur'an are in full agreement with God's words in the Torah: "Then God said, 'Yes, but, your wife Sarah will bear you a son, and you will call him Isaac, I will establish my covenant with him as an everlasting covenant for his descendants after him.'" (Genesis 17:19). Clearly, God's covenant was made through the line of Isaac.

Also found in the Torah (in Genesis 26:4; 28:14) is God's promise to Isaac and Jacob that through their seed all the families of the earth would be blessed. That promise was fulfilled by Jesus (the Messiah), who came through their lineage.

THE DIFFICULT TEST OF ABRAHAM'S FAITH

God tested Abraham's faith greatly, as recorded in the Torah:

> "Some time later God tested Abraham. He said to him, 'Abraham!'
>
> 'Here I am,' he replied.
>
> Then God said, 'Take your son, your only son, Isaac, whom you love, and go to the region of Moriah. Sacrifice him there as a burnt offering on one of the mountains I will tell you about.'" (Genesis 22:1–2)

Abraham must have thought deeply about God's shocking and unusual command. For God had promised Abraham that through his son, Isaac, he would have many descendants. His descendants were to be, "as numerous as the stars in the sky and as countless as the sand on the seashore" (Hebrews 11:12; Genesis 15:5 and 32:12).

Earlier in Genesis 21:12–13, God told Abraham to send Ishmael away. And now He asked him to sacrifice Isaac. Can you imagine how Abraham must have felt? Naturally Abraham would want to cling to Isaac because Isaac was now the only remaining son that he had.

Abraham trusted God

God told Abraham that through Isaac his offspring would be called (Genesis 21:12). Abraham believed God to be ever faithful. He believed God's promise would be fulfilled and that he would have many descendants through Isaac. Abraham no doubt pondered, "How can I have the descendants promised to me if I sacrifice my son, Isaac, as God has commanded?" Abraham believed in God's promises, His faithfulness, and His righteousness. He concluded that the only way Isaac could beget offspring—after being sacrificed—would be if God were to raise him from the dead. Abraham reasoned that since God gave him a son when it was naturally impossible to have one, then God could also raise that son back to life from the dead.

Abraham passed the test

The Bible makes it clear that Abraham passed this great test of faith by deciding to sacrifice Isaac. In obedience, he prepared his promised son Isaac to be sacrificed. "By faith Abraham, when God tested him, offered Isaac as a sacrifice. He who had received the promise was about to sacrifice his one and only son, even though God had said to him, 'It is through Isaac that your offspring will be reckoned.' Abraham reasoned that God could raise the dead, and figuratively speaking, he did receive Isaac back from death" (Hebrews 11:17–19).

The Qur'an shows harmony with Abraham's reasoning in Surah 2:260: "Behold! Abraham said: 'My Lord! Show me how Thou givest life to the dead.'"

Abraham's profound faith

Abraham's decision to obey God and sacrifice his son was not simply mindless or blind, uncomprehending submission to the will of God. Abraham believed that God would always be faithful to His word. He realized that the promise of descendants and blessings would be fulfilled through the sacrifice of his son. Abraham believed that God would raise Isaac from the dead. For that reason Abraham knew that sacrificing his son was not in any way the same as idolaters sacrificing their children to their gods.

Abraham discovered the harmony between God's shocking and apparently immoral command and God's goodness. Abraham trusted in the holy character of God.

9

THE GOSPEL PREACHED
TO AND THROUGH ABRAHAM

We see the prominence of Abraham in both the Qur'an and the Bible. The Qur'an states that God told Abraham, "I will make thee an Imam to the nations" (Surah 2:124). Pickthall's translation of this verse reads, "I have appointed thee a leader for mankind." As recorded in Genesis 12:3 and 22:18, God promised Abraham, "Through your offspring all nations [families] on earth will be blessed."

God's covenant with Abraham

As stated in the Bible, God told Abraham, "As for me, this is my covenant with you: You will be the father of many nations" (Genesis 17:4–6). Abraham considered why he was made a blessing for mankind and the father of a multitude of nations. So Abraham saw his chosen and high status as a reflection of God's great glory in heaven. Abraham realized that he resembled the heavenly Father as a *type*.

He surely also viewed Isaac's miraculous birth, expected sacrifice and resurrection from the dead, and his innumerable descendants as types of a greater reality yet to come.

Abraham foresaw the Good News of a greater sacrifice

Abraham understood that the heavenly Father also would have a Son born miraculously into this world. The Son would be offered as a sacrifice by the hand of His own Father. The Son would rise from the dead. And the risen Son would be the source of blessings to the world.

God revealed to His friend, Abraham, His plan of salvation and the coming blessing to mankind. Abraham foresaw the heart of the Gospel. Jesus told the Jews, "Your father Abraham rejoiced at the thought of seeing my day; he saw it and was glad." (John 8:56)

Prophetic conversation between Abraham and Isaac

The Bible states that Isaac spoke up and asked his father, Abraham, "The fire and wood are here . . . but where is the lamb for the burnt offering?" (Genesis 22:7–8). Abraham did not know God would provide a substitute in place of Isaac. Abraham truly believed that he would have to sacrifice his son. Abraham replied to Isaac, in part, "God himself will provide the lamb for the burnt offering, my son." The original words in Hebrew says in effect, "God will give the Lamb from His very own being." Abraham's answer to Isaac was in essence: My son, I must obey God and offer you as a sacrifice. I want you to know God will give of Himself a lamb as a sacrifice.

A foreshadow of the Lamb of God

Through this experience Abraham had some knowledge of the true religion to come. God revealed to His friend, Abraham, in some measure, that someday He would send His own Son to die for the sins of the world and that any person who trusts in God's saving grace will be blessed and saved. Note that after centuries of animal sacrificing in the Jewish Temple, John the Baptist (called the prophet Yahya in Qur'an) came and proclaimed the arrival of Jesus. John 1:29 states, "The next day John saw Jesus coming toward him and said, 'Look, the Lamb of God, who takes away the sin of the world!'"

How awesome it is to realize that 2,000 years after God asked Abraham to sacrifice his son Isaac on Mt. Moriah, God sacrificed His own Son. And Jesus was crucified on that same Mt. Moriah! Genesis 22, then, is a foreshadowing of the crucifixion of Jesus Christ according to God's plan of salvation for mankind. It is amazing and significant to find the Christian message, indeed the heart of the Gospel, written all over the Jewish Holy Scripture!

The righteousness of Abraham resulted from his faith

In spite of Abraham's sins, which are recorded in the Bible and in the Qur'an (Surah 26:82), God forgave Abraham and declared him to be righteous. Abraham's faith in God, and in His ability to perform what He had promised, was accepted by God as righteousness. Genesis 15:6 states, "Abram [Abraham] believed the Lord, and he credited it to him as righteousness."

Abraham's faith was an awesome example because he did not simply or merely bow to God's command but Abraham believed that God's command was consistent with God's faithfulness. Abraham depended on the righteousness, goodness, and trustworthiness of God. Thus his faith gave glory to God. Abraham's righteousness was not earned but a God-given righteousness.

Abraham's righteous status before God did not come from his own piety or merit earned by accumulating enough good works. Neither did it result from genetic lineage. God accepted Abraham as righteous because of his belief in God and faith in His power, His grace, and His faithfulness. The "faith" principle is explained in the Bible:

> Yet he [Abraham] did not waver through unbelief regarding the promise of God, but was strengthened in his faith and gave glory to God, being fully persuaded that God had power to do what he had promised. This is why it was credited to him as righteousness. The words "it was credited to him" were written not for him alone, but also for us, to whom God will credit righteousness—for us who believe in him who raised Jesus our Lord from the dead. He was delivered over to death

for our sins and was raised to life for our justification. (Romans 4:20–25)

Who are the true children of Abraham?

The true children of Abraham are those who have his faith, regardless of race or ancestry. The Bible makes this reality clear:

"Consider Abraham: 'He believed God, and it was credited to him as righteousness.' Understand, then, that those who *believe* are children of Abraham. The Scripture foresaw that God would justify the Gentiles [non Jews] *by faith*, and announced the Gospel in advance to Abraham: 'All nations will be blessed through you.' So those who have faith are blessed along with Abraham, the man of faith" (Galatians 3:6–9, emphasis mine).

Verses 13 and 14 further clarify that our identification with Abraham is based on faith. "Christ redeemed us . . . in order that the blessing given to Abraham might come to the Gentiles through Christ Jesus, so that by faith we might receive the promise of the [Holy] Spirit." In other words, just as Abraham was saved by faith, the real children of Abraham are those who have faith in God and His promises. They are not those who rely on their own ability to keep the laws of God.

Everyone who has this faith receives the blessing of justification. "Therefore, the promise comes by faith, so that it may be by grace and may be guaranteed to all Abraham's offspring—not only to those who are of the law but also to those who are of the faith of Abraham . . ." (Romans 4:16).

The Messiah came through Abraham's lineage

Abraham looked ahead to the coming of the greatest son, Jesus, whom he knew would be the Son of God. Jesus is called the son of Abraham in Matthew 1:1. Jesus is the seed of Abraham. "The promises were spoken to Abraham and to his seed. The Scripture does not say, 'and to seeds,' meaning many people, but 'and to your seed,' meaning one person, who is Christ" (Galatians 3:16).

The Bible clearly tells us that Jesus, the Messiah, descended from Abraham and came to earth to accomplish our salvation. Jesus' coming and sacrifice fulfilled God's promise to Abraham of the blessing to all people. By believing in Jesus, as Abraham did, people from all nations can receive salvation and be blessed with everlasting life!

Reconciliation is possible

Through faith in Jesus, the children of Ishmael and the children of Isaac can have a peaceful relationship with each other as part of God's blessing to all people. I believe God wants them to be united in one happy family with peace, love, joy and laughter.

God's sacrificial love for us

Have you ever wondered why God asked the father Abraham to sacrifice (give Him) his son rather than his sheep, land, or possessions? It was because a man's own son is more precious to his heart than anything else. If Abraham was willing to give up his own son to God, then he was prepared to give God anything and everything. Therefore, the best way for God to test Abraham's love for Him was to command him to sacrifice his son.

Abraham must have reasoned that what God commanded him to do was no more than what God was willing to do for him. Do you think God would ask a greater expression of love from man than He Himself would give to man? Would He require a deeper demonstration of love from us than that which He would demonstrate to us?

Abraham had to make a choice between his love for God and his love for his son. Abraham's willingness to sacrifice his son for God proved that he loved God more than his son and more than anything in life.

When God commanded Abraham to sacrifice his son, Abraham no doubt suffered deeply as a father. He was ripped at the depth of his being as he was taking his living son (who came from him) to be sacrificed.

Because his son was more precious to his heart than all the material possessions in the world, Abraham proved he had perfect, sacrificial love for God. It cost Abraham deeply to manifest his love for God because in his heart and mind he decided to sacrifice his son.

My precious reader, please allow me to ask an important question: Has God in Islam ever matched Abraham's supreme example of love? Has the Qur'an revealed the sacrificial love of God?

The significant question here is: Can a man's love for God (such as Abraham's) surpass God's love for mankind? The logical answer is, God never asked any man, including Abraham, to do more for Him than He was willing to do and more.

The Gospel gives us the perfect answer, "But God demonstrates his own love for us in this: While we were still sinners, Christ died for us" (Romans 5:8).

God bestowed on us the greatest form of love by giving His own Son, who was not created, and whose presence He enjoyed from all eternity. God sacrificed what was most precious to His heart. The Bible shows us that God's love for Abraham and for us, in Christ, far surpassed Abraham's love for God.

This truth is exactly what God wants you to discover, my dear Muslim friend. God expressed His perfect love for you: "He who did not spare his own Son, but gave him up for us all—how will he not also, along with him, graciously give us all things?" (Romans 8:32). Here we see God's heart aflame with love for mankind.

True followers of Jesus know God was willing to give His best and did not withhold His sacrificial love from us.

Leading with sacrificial love

I have read some true stories of World War II battles that illustrate different types of leaders. One of the military commanders leading a British unit ordered his troops to advance into the battlefield. While his soldiers were being killed, he stayed out of the fight having fun with an aloof attitude.

Another military commander leading a different British unit saw that his soldiers were surrounded by the enemy. He ordered them to engage in warfare, and he joined them on the front lines. He was able to lead them to victory against all odds. He was chopped to pieces in the process. However he saved the lives of most of his soldiers. This leader laid down his life for his men.

The second leader shows us a glimpse of how God has led His people to victory, even giving of Himself for their sake. God's love is perfect. The true test and measure of love is sacrifice.

When you look at the cross, at Jesus who hung upon it, you see the depth and intensity of God's infinite and eternal love for you.

Jesus is God's most precious gift to you. Would you receive His gift by opening your heart to Jesus by faith right now? Faith is the response God seeks to find in you.

10

GOD RANSOMED ABRAHAM'S SON

The Qur'an tells the story of Abraham. God had commanded Abraham to sacrifice his son; as he was about to perform this sacrifice, God intervened. We read these significant words in the Qur'an: "We called out to him, 'O Abraham! Thou hast already fulfilled the vision' . . . and We ransomed him [Abraham's son] with a momentous sacrifice"[1] (Surah 37:104–107).

God provided a substitute sacrifice

In the story of Abraham recorded in the Qur'an, Surah 37, Abraham was about to sacrifice his son but God set the son free. Did God then simply allow the prophet Abraham to take his son and leave? No, a sacrificial offering was still required. The only way God chose to free Abraham's son was by substituting another sacrifice. The principal of redemption is stated clearly in this story, for a ram was slain to redeem Abraham's son.

God loved Abraham's son, and therefore He rescued (ransomed) him. God provided a ram to be offered in his place (Genesis 22:13). Note that it was God who provided the alternate sacrifice. Surah 37:107 affirms, "And We ransomed him [Abraham's son] with a momentous sacrifice."

Likewise, my Muslim friend, it was God who ransomed us by a sacrifice that He Himself provided. And His motive was His love for us!

A sacrifice valuable beyond estimation

We read in the Gospel that when John the Baptist saw Jesus coming toward him, John proclaimed, "Look, the Lamb of God, who takes away the sin of the world!" (John 1:29). The Lamb of God is Jesus (AL-Masih Isa).

The prophet Isaiah, inspired of God, prophesied about the coming Messiah and recognized Him to be the sacrificial lamb: "He was oppressed and afflicted, yet he did not open his mouth; he was led like a lamb to the slaughter, and as a sheep before its shearers is silent, so he did not open his mouth" (Isaiah 53:7).

Again, Surah 37:107 states, "and we ransomed him with a momentous sacrifice." In this verse, "momentous" is worded in other universally recognized translations of the Qur'an as "mighty," "great," "tremendous," and "valuable beyond estimation."

The sacrificed ram represented a much greater truth

The logical question is: What kind of sacrifice deserves to be called "momentous," "mighty," and "valuable beyond estimation?" Obviously the simple animal (ram) that God provided for Abraham was not intended to fit this description. It was only a symbol of the greater sacrifice to come—Jesus Christ.

The answer is clearly stated in the Bible, "For you know that it was not with perishable things . . . that you were redeemed[2] from the empty way of life handed down to you from your forefathers, but with the precious blood of Christ, a lamb without blemish or defect" (1 Peter 1:18–19).

Biblical scholar D.C. Halverson poses a thought-provoking question: "If salvation is only a matter of rewarding those who do good, and if God's purpose was only to test Abraham's obedience, why then was there a need for a 'momentous sacrifice'?

Was it not sufficient that Abraham went as far as he did (by obeying God's command)?"[3]

Ultimate sacrifice on the cross

The Gospel tells us that because God loves us so much, He rescued us through the ultimate sacrifice of Jesus ("valuable beyond estimation"). The Qur'an describes AL-Masih Isa (Jesus) as "a Spirit proceeding from God" (Surah 4:171). Jesus took our place and was sacrificed on our behalf. He died on the cross as a ransom to free us from the penalty owed for our sins. Jesus said, ". . . the Son of Man did not come to be served, but to serve, and to give his life a ransom for many" (Matthew 20:28).

The most valuable sacrifice God could give us was of Himself. For this reason He came to our world in the person of Jesus to save us. The Lamb's sacrifice is "valuable beyond estimation" because it represents God's sacrifice of Himself, which is of infinite value and sufficient for our salvation!

Please allow me to illustrate this through a real life story. One day, a young man committed a murder. The police chased him on the ground and in the air, but he managed to get home to his family.

His father was shocked to see that his son's clothing was stained with blood. The son confessed to his father that he just killed someone and that the police sirens and helicopter were for him. The father told his son to take his clothes off quickly. The father put on his son's clothing and gave his clean clothes to his son and asked him to wear them.

The father surrendered himself to the police. They arrested him, because his clothes with stained with blood. The father paid for his son's crime.

WHO COULD PROVIDE THE PRICE FOR OUR RANSOM?

In Surah 10:54, we read: "Every soul that hath sinned, if it possessed all that is on earth, would fain give it in ransom . . ." A "ransom" is defined as the required price to pay for the release of a captive. God was the only One able to provide a ransom for our freedom from spiritual death and punishment.

In the Torah (Leviticus 4), God commanded the people to sacrifice an innocent animal, such as a lamb, sheep, or a goat that had no flaw or blemish, to cover their sins. The animal was brought to the priest, and the sinner would lay his hands on the animal's head (as a sign of identification) and confess his sins. The sins were thereby transferred onto the animal and its throat was slit. Then the priest would spread the animal's blood upon the altar for the remission of sins. Thus the penalty for sin was paid for by the innocent animal's death as a substitute for the sinful person. We read in the Bible: "The goat will carry on itself all their sins . . ." (Leviticus 16:22).

It is true that the clean, innocent animal was not guilty of any crime, but God desired to show the people how serious sin is in His eyes.

"The life is in the blood"

The Holy Scriptures of the Jews teach that forgiveness of sins must be by substitution. No person can be his own savior. The death of the sacrifice symbolizes the stroke of judgment due to sin and due to every person on account of his or her sin. The killing of the substitute represented the exercise of the divine wrath. God was wrathful towards sinful man; His wrath resulted from His holiness.

The Holy Scriptures of the Jews presented the foundation for the teachings of the Gospel. The Lord said, "For the life of a creature is in the blood, and I have given it [the blood] to you to make atonement for yourselves on the altar; it is the blood that makes atonement for one's life" (Leviticus 17:11). The term "atonement" means life for life.

How were people who lived before the time of Christ saved?

People have been saved through faith alone by the grace (unmerited favor) of God. The people who lived before the time of Christ looked forward to the future when God would send the Savior, who would be a sacrifice for them.

Old Testament believers offered sacrifices as an expression of their faith. The act of sacrificing animals could never take away sin, but God accepted it because it pointed to Jesus Christ (Hebrews 10:1–17).

Faith in God always involved confidence that God would somehow provide for the forgiveness of sins. Faith always anticipated the coming of Christ and His sacrifice on our behalf.

Incidentally your faith in God gives God the glory, Because God is glorified when you depend and count on His power to deliver and save you.

The Bible declares, "How much more shall the blood of Christ, who through the eternal Spirit offered Himself without spot to God, cleanse your conscience from dead works to serve the living God? And for this reason He [Jesus] is the mediator of the new covenant, by means of death, for the redemption of the transgressions under the first covenant, that those who are called may receive the promise of the eternal inheritance" (Hebrews 9:14–15 NKJV).

Do you see the significance of the Cross, my dear Muslim friend? Christ sacrificed His life in order to give us the right to live forever, freeing us from the debt we owe—the penalty for our sins. Jesus was our substitute. He paid the price for us.

Biblical scholar John Stott expressed the heart of the Gospel by saying: "Divine love triumphed over divine wrath by divine self-sacrifice."

Jesus said, ". . . This is my blood of the covenant, which is poured out for many for the forgiveness of sins" (Matthew 26:28).

His blood is the seal of the new covenant. Old Testament prophecy foretold that God would forgive the sins of His people through the new covenant (Jeremiah 31:31–34). Jesus' shed blood for the forgiveness of sins sealed the new covenant (Matthew 20:28).

When Jesus said "my blood . . . is poured out for many," He meant His life would be given for many. Jesus' death inaugurated the new relationship (which is called covenant or testament) between God and His people. This covenant would replace the old Mosaic covenant, which Moses sealed between God and the people by sprinkling the altar with the blood of animals (Exodus 24:6).

Significance of blood sacrifice in Islam

It is interesting to read in the Qur'an that Moses said to his people that God is commanding you to sacrifice a sound and unblemished heifer [animal] (Surah 2:67–71).

According to Muhammad (as recorded in Al-Bukhari), animal sacrifice was an acknowledged, divinely-appointed means of gaining God's acceptance.[4] Muslims celebrate an annual feast called "Feast of Sacrifice" (Id Al-Adha). On this day, animals are sacrificed. The Muslim world generally believes that this festival commemorates the willingness of Abraham to offer his son as a sacrifice to God.

The shedding of blood leads to forgiveness

The Gospel declares an important truth, "In fact, the law requires that nearly everything be cleansed with blood, and without the shedding of blood there is no forgiveness" (Hebrews 9:22). Christ forfeited His life in order to grant us forgiveness and the right to live forever. We can be redeemed because "in him [Jesus] we have redemption through his blood, the forgiveness of sins, in accordance with the riches of God's grace that he lavished on us with all wisdom and understanding. And he made known to us the mystery of his will according to his good pleasure, which he purposed in Christ" (Ephesians 1:7–9).

An illustration of God's ransom for us

It is difficult for many to understand why God would choose to rescue us through such a great sacrifice! I am reminded of a story I read about Shamuel, the Caucasian prince. He lived about two hundred years ago, and his people were constantly at war with the Turks. One night, he planned a surprise attack. But the enemy was ready and waiting because his secret plans had been revealed by someone to the enemy. Many of his soldiers lost their lives, and ultimately he lost the battle. Shamuel announced that the traitor would be punished—whipped with one hundred lashes.

In great secrecy, Shamuel's army launched another attack, but the same thing happened. Again his enemy was waiting to ambush. The prince lost another battle, but this time he discovered the traitor. It was Shamuel's own mother! She was having a romantic relationship with one of the enemy's soldiers.

What a difficult dilemma! What should Shamuel have done? If he exempted his mother from punishment, his followers would correctly accuse him of being unjust. The alternative would be even more difficult for Shamuel. Because he loved his mother, how could he mandate a just sentence that would result in the suffering and death of his beloved mother?

Shamuel addressed his people, "We have lost two battles because of treason. Many of our men have been killed. The law has been broken and punishment shall be executed—*one hundred lashes*! Righteousness and justice must be maintained."

The prince's mother was filled with great fear as she was led away to the circle where her punishment was to be administered. The executioner lifted his whip. But before the first blow was delivered, Shamuel shouted out, "Wait! Wait! I will take the punishment for her." He removed his royal clothes and commanded, "Executioner, you dare not strike me with less force than you would have used on the traitor. I am the person who will take her punishment. Do your duty—Strike on!"

Lash after lash struck the back of Shamuel until he collapsed to the ground unconscious. He did, however, survive the lashings contrary to all expectations. Prince Shamuel paid in full the penalty for his beloved mother's offense in order to set her free!

Likewise, Jesus came to pay a debt He did not owe because we owed a debt we could not pay. God's word says that, "He [Jesus] himself bore our sins in his body on the tree [cross] . . . by his wounds you have been healed" (1 Peter 2:24). Jesus Himself taught, "Greater love has no one than this, that he lay down his life for his friends" (John 15:13).

My precious Muslim reader, if you were to ask God "How much do you love me?" He would point to Jesus, who hung on the cross, and say, "I love you this much."

Jesus means "Savior"

The well-known Muslim scholar, Al-Qasemi, in his famous commentary *Mahasen at-Ta'aweel*, commented on Surah 3:45. He wrote, "The name Isa [Jesus] is an Arabic form from a Greek word, which means *Savior*."[5] Note that the Gospel, in Matthew 1:21, states, "She [Mary] will give birth to a son, and you [Joseph] are to give him the name Jesus, because he will save his people from their sins."

The animals sacrificed in Old Testament times were, of course, unequal in value to the human souls for whom they were offered. In fact, any one person was more valuable and precious than all of the animals offered. These sacrifices foreshadowed the valuable blood sacrifice of the divine Savior to come. The animal sacrifices only *covered* sins temporarily, whereas the sacrifice of Jesus *removed* sins once for all! Jesus was the only sacrifice acceptable to God as equal in value to all of the souls of mankind.

SECTION FOUR

JESUS IN THE QUR'AN
AND IN THE BIBLE

11

CHRIST JESUS (AL-MASIH, ISA) GOD'S ANOINTED MESSIAH

The Qur'an gives Jesus three distinguished titles: "Christ Jesus [*AL-Masih, Isa*], the son of Mary was . . . a messenger of Allah, His Word [*Kalimatuhuu*] . . . and a Spirit proceeding from Him [Ruhun Minhu] . . ." (Surah 4:171).

Jesus is the Messiah in the Qur'an and the Hadith

Jesus alone is referred to as AL-Masih (*The Messiah*) in the Qur'an. Its use of the definite article *the* positively distinguishes Jesus from all other prophets. Occasionally He is referred to solely by this title without using His name (as in Surah 4:172). Jesus is given the title, The Messiah, more than ten times in the Qur'an. For example, Surah 3:45 states that the angel Gabriel appeared to Mary and said the name of her son was to be "Christ Jesus" (AL-Masih, Isa, which is The Messiah, Jesus).

Jesus is called AL-Masih in the Hadith. Muslim scholars acknowledge that the title, AL-Masih, is not derived from an Arabic root. Scholar Al-Baidawi, commenting on Surah 3:45, says that the word *Christ* (AL-Masih) was originally a Hebrew word (*Mashih*). Note that the Qur'an does not explain the meaning of the title Messiah. By not giving an explanation of this title it implicitly agrees with what is written about the Messiah in the Bible.

The Gospel was written in the Greek language. The Greek word for AL-Masih or "The Anointed One" is *ho Christos*, from which comes the English word *Christ*. Therefore, whenever the word Christ is used in the English translation of the New Testament, it is the same as AL-Masih. Muslim scholars agree on this point.

Prophecies of the coming Messiah

The Old Testament was written between 400 and 1,500 years before Christ came to earth. It contains many inspired prophecies of One Glorious Savior, who would one day be sent by God and came to be called "Anointed One" (The Messiah) (Daniel 9:25).

Amazingly the Old Testament contains over 300 references to the coming Messiah, all of which were fulfilled in the life of Jesus.[1] And note that there are 61 major prophecies in the Old Testament about the coming Messiah, which Jesus fulfilled with 100 percent accuracy! Many books have been written on this subject. An outstanding reference book on Messianic prophecies is *All the Messianic Prophecies of the Bible*, by Herbert Lockyer.[2]

Fulfilled prophecies regarding Jesus could not have possibly been fabricated, as doubters might suggest, because many of the prophecies concerning the Messiah were totally beyond human control. Consider the following examples:

- His place of birth

  Jesus was born in Bethlehem, which was foretold by the prophet Micah about 700 years before the coming of Christ (BC) (Micah 5:2). The historical fulfillment of this prophecy is found in Matthew 2:1, 6 and John 7:42.

- His virgin birth

  Jesus was born of a virgin as prophesied by the prophet Isaiah seven centuries earlier, "Therefore the Lord himself will give you a sign: The virgin will be with child and will give birth to a son, and will call him Immanuel" (Isaiah 7:14). We see the historical fulfillment of this prophecy in the New Testament. "All this took place to fulfill what the Lord had said through the prophet: The virgin will be with child and will give birth to a son, and they will call him Immanuel which means God with us" (Matthew 1:22–23).

- His death by crucifixion

The Messianic prophecies foretold in Psalm 22 describe death on the cross. David wrote about the crucifixion 1,000 years before the coming of Christ. Verse 16 states, "a band of evil men has encircled me, they have pierced my hands and my feet." It is particularly significant that this prophetic Psalm was written nearly 600 years before crucifixions were even used as a means of execution.

The "piercing" of Jesus is also prophesied in Zechariah 12:10 and later fulfilled as written in John 19:34.

- His mission on earth

Details of Jesus' death and burial were prophesied by Isaiah around 700 BC (chapter 53). Verses five and six explain the Messiah's mission: "But he was pierced for our transgressions, he was crushed for our iniquities; the punishment that brought us peace was upon him, and by his wounds we are healed. We all, like sheep, have gone astray, each of us has turned to his own way; and the LORD has laid on him the iniquity of us all."

Messianic Psalms

My dear Muslim friends, note what the Qur'an informs us in Surah 2:136: "Say ye, 'We believe in Allah, and the revelation given to us, and to Abraham . . . and that given to Moses and Jesus, and that given to (all) Prophets from their Lord: We make no difference between one and another of them . . .'" David is one of the Prophets referred to in this verse. Most important is Surah 4:163, which states, ". . . and to David We gave the Psalms." Surah 21:105 notes, "Before this We [God] wrote in the Psalms." (See also Surah 17:55.)

The Psalms referred as much to the promised coming Messiah as they did to events at the time. Many of the passages in Psalms describe in detail events of Jesus' life and death. And they were written hundreds of years before Christ. Here are a few examples of astonishing Messianic prophecies and their fulfillments:

- Psalm 41:9

This Old Testament Prophecy foretold that the Messiah would be betrayed by a friend.

The New Testament fulfillment is recorded in Matthew 26:47–50 (which is when Jesus is betrayed by Judas and arrested).

- Psalm 110:1

This Old Testament Prophecy foretold the Messiah to be "Lord" and that He shall sit in honor at the right hand of God.

The New Testament fulfillment is written in: Matthew 22:41–45 (where Jesus recites the words of this Psalm and applies them to Himself).

Messianic prophecies in the Book of Isaiah

The Bible clearly declares that the predicted Messiah is a divine person. In one of the prophecies, the coming Messiah is given divine names: "For to us a child is born, to us a son is given, and the government will be on his shoulders. And he will be called Wonderful Counselor, Mighty God, Everlasting Father, Prince of Peace" (Isaiah 9:6).

The phrase "Everlasting Father" means that this child to be born is eternal and will have the heart of the perfect Father toward His people.

The prophet Isaiah foretold that the coming Messiah would be called *Immanuel*, which is a Hebrew name meaning "God with us." As written in Isaiah 7:14: "The Lord himself will give you a sign: The virgin will be with child and will give birth to a son, and will call him Immanuel." The fulfillment of this prophecy is recorded in Matthew 1:21–23 and Luke 7:16.

Another Messianic prophecy is written in Isaiah. It describes the Messiah's obedience and His humiliation instigated by His enemies. Hear the words of the Messiah as prophesied: "I offered my back to those who beat me, my cheeks to those who pulled out my beard; I did not hide my face from mocking and spitting" (Isaiah 50:6). This prophecy was fulfilled in Matthew 26:67: "Then they spit in his [Jesus'] face and struck him with their fists. Others slapped him. . . ."

Jesus is the Son of God and the Son of Man

Jesus called Himself "the Son of God." He said, "All things have been committed to me by my Father. No one knows the Son except the Father and no one knows the Father except the Son . . ." (Matthew 11:27). See also Matthew 26:63–64.

Jesus also called Himself "the Son of Man." He used these titles to make evident His humanity as well as His deity, which indicates that He is the Messiah.

The prophet Daniel used the Messianic title "Son of Man" and prophesied that the coming Messiah is divine:

"In my vision at night I looked, and there before me was one like a son of man, coming with the clouds of heaven. He approached the ancient of days and was led into His presence. He was given authority, glory and sovereign power; all peoples, nations, and men of every language worshiped him. His dominion is an everlasting dominion that will not pass away, and his kingdom is one that will never be destroyed" (Daniel 7:13–14).

In this passage Daniel saw in a vision a person like a Son of Man, referring to the fact that He was human in His appearance. He also saw that this person was given sovereign power and would be worshiped by all. His dominion is everlasting and He is the king of an eternal kingdom. Obviously, this One who is like a Son of Man was more than just a man! Clearly the prophets declared in the Holy Scriptures that the coming Messiah would be far superior than a mere prophet.

This verse is one of many Biblical references that predicted the coming of the great king who would rescue God's people and establish His eternal kingdom. This expected King came to be called the Messiah. Both Old and New Testament Scriptures teach the divine-human nature of the Messiah (Christ).

Jesus claimed to be the Messiah

The Gospel recorded a conversation between Jesus and a woman named Martha. Jesus said to her, "I am the resurrection and the life. He who believes in me will live, even though he dies, and whoever lives and believes in me will never die. Do you believe this?"

"Yes Lord," she told Him, "I believe that You are the Christ, the Son of God, who was to come into the world" (John 11:25–27).

In John 4:25–26, Jesus had a conversation with a Samaritan woman. "The woman said to him, 'I know that Messiah' (called Christ) 'is coming. When he comes, he will explain everything to us.' Then Jesus declared, 'I who speak to you am he.'"

In Luke 24:44–48, Jesus identified Himself as the Messiah and said to His disciples,

"This is what I told you while I was still with you: Everything must be fulfilled that is written about me [prophesied] in the Law of Moses, the Prophets, and the Psalms." Then he opened their minds so they could understand the Scriptures. He told them, "This is what is written: The Christ will suffer and rise from the dead on the third day, and repentance and forgiveness of sins will be preached in his name to all nations, beginning at Jerusalem. You are witnesses of these things."

In this passage, Jesus Christ confirmed God's revelation in the Old Testament to be authentic. He prepared His disciples for His future suffering and crucifixion. He told them about His resurrection.

Jews gathered around Jesus and said, "How long will you keep us in suspense? If you are the Christ, tell us plainly."

Jesus answered, "I did tell you, but you do not believe. The miracles I do in my Father's name speak for me but you do not believe because you are not my sheep. My sheep listen to my voice; I know them, and they follow me. I give them eternal life and they shall never perish; no one can snatch them out of my hand. My Father, who has given them to me, is greater than all, no one can snatch them out of my Father's hand. I and the Father are one" (John 10:24–30).

Prophecies of Jews rejecting the Messiah

Various prophecies even foretold of the Messiah's rejection by Jewish people (see Psalm 118:22 and Isaiah 8:14). Jesus referred to the prophecy in Psalm 118:22 when He spoke of being rejected by His own people (Matthew 21:42 and Mark 12:10–11). "He [Jesus] came to that which was his own [the Jewish people] but his own did not receive him" John 1:11.

The Messiah came for all people and all races

Unfortunately, in Jesus' time, many of the Jews thought the promises of God were only for them. They were incorrect. God declared in the Gospel that *all believers* are one in Christ. Faith in Christ transcends people's differences. The Bible assures us in Galatians 3:26–28, "You are all sons of God through faith in Christ Jesus. . . There is neither Jew nor Greek, slave nor free, male nor female, for you [believers] are all one in Christ Jesus." (Also see Romans 3:29–30.)

The Jewish religious leaders were mistaken when they expected the coming Messiah to elevate their nation. They were also mistaken when they believed the Messiah would establish Himself as an *earthly* king. Jesus declared, "My kingdom is not of this world" (John 18:36).

Announcement of the Good News

The prophets of the Old Testament looked forward to the appearance of the great Messiah. What a great moment in the history of humanity. The Good News was announced! AL-Masih, the Savior to all people, had finally arrived. God's Word proclaims His birth as *"Good News."* This account is recorded in the Gospel. An angel appeared to a group of shepherds in the fields of Bethlehem, and the glory of the Lord shone around them. The angel made this wonderful proclamation:

'Do not be afraid. I bring you good news of great joy that will be for all the people. Today in the town of David a Savior has been born to you; he is Christ the Lord. This will be a sign to you: You will find a baby wrapped in cloths and lying in a manger.' Suddenly a great company of the heavenly host appeared with the angel, praising God and saying, 'Glory to God in the highest, and on earth peace to men on whom his favor rests.' (Luke 2:10–14)

The Qur'an confirms this Good News as "Glad News"

It is clear that the Qur'an agrees with the Gospel regarding the identity of the Messiah. The Qur'an not only agrees with the Bible that AL-Masih (the Messiah) is Jesus, the son of Mary, but it also confirms the Biblical declaration that Jesus' birth is Good News. It declares in Surah 3:45, "Behold! The angel said: 'O Mary! Allah giveth thee Glad Tidings of a Word from Him: His name will be Christ Jesus the son of Mary, held in honor in this world and the hereafter and of (the company of) those Nearest to Allah.'" This Glad News is for you, my Muslim friend.

Opposition to the Good News

Many people in the world have never heard or understood why God declared the birth of Jesus Christ to be Good News. Of course the enemy, Satan (Shaitan in Arabic), does not want anyone to know about God's "Glad Tidings" for humanity. The Bible explains:

> Even if our gospel is veiled, it is veiled to those who are perishing. The god of this age [Satan] has blinded the minds of unbelievers, so that they cannot see the light of the gospel of the glory of Christ, who is the image of God. For we do not preach ourselves, but Jesus Christ as Lord, and ourselves as your servants for Jesus' sake. For God, who said, 'Let light shine out of darkness,' made his light shine in our hearts to give us the light of the knowledge of the glory of God in the face of Christ. (2 Corinthians 4:3–6)

Satan is working hard to prevent people from understanding Jesus' nature and mission, as it is revealed throughout the Bible. The Jewish religious teachers asked Jesus' disciples, "Why does your Teacher eat with sinners?"

Jesus Himself replied, "It is not the healthy who need a doctor, but the sick. I have not come to call the righteous but sinners" (Mark 2:17). Jesus came for sinners like you and me.

UNIQUE IDENTITY OF JESUS

We learn from the Bible that Jesus, AL-Masih, is the revelation of God's mercy, love, and salvation to humanity. It is very clear in the Scriptures that the coming Messiah would be nothing less than the Son of God and the Savior of the world. When Jesus appeared among the people, however, He was received with mixed reaction. Many people rejected Him. Some thought of Him as just a prophet. Others questioned His unique identity. For example, the high priest of the Jews inquired of Jesus, "I charge you under oath by the living God: tell us if you are the Christ, the Son of God" (Matthew 26:63).

On the other hand, there were many people who recognized Jesus as the anticipated Messiah (the Anointed One) and followed Him. The Gospel records the following account:

> When Jesus came to the region of Caesarea Philippi, he asked his disciples, 'Who do people say the Son of Man is?'
>
> They replied, 'Some say John the Baptist; others say Elijah; and still others, Jeremiah or one of the prophets.'
>
> 'But what about you?' he asked. 'Who do you say I am?'
>
> Simon Peter answered, 'You are the Christ, the Son of the living God.' (Matthew 16:13–16)

Jesus' miracles (signs and wonders)

During His mission on earth, Christ Jesus displayed great power and authority as no one had ever done. The miracles He performed were definite signs confirming that He was truly the Anointed One sent by God to be the Savior of the world. For example, His transforming purpose is stated in the Gospel, "Jesus did many other miraculous signs in the presence of his disciples . . . these are written that you may believe that Jesus is the Christ, the Son of God, and that by believing you may have life in his name" (John 20:30–31).

The book of Acts also references Jesus' supernatural abilities, "You know what has happened throughout Judea, beginning in Galilee after the baptism that John [*Yahya*] preached—how God anointed Jesus of Nazareth with the Holy Spirit and power, and how he went around doing good and healing all who were under the power of the devil, because God was with him" (10:37–38).

Jesus' miracles attest to His being the Messiah

The Bible prophesied that the coming Messiah would perform specific miracles (Isaiah 35:5–6). Hundreds of years later, when Jesus came to earth, He gave sight to the blind, He gave the lame the ability to walk, and He opened deaf ears. Thus, by His miracles, Jesus established that He is the promised Messiah, the Savior of the world.

References to Jesus' miracles in the Qur'an

The Qur'an says that the miracles performed by Jesus were "clear Signs" of God's power. These clear signs were not granted to all of the prophets. The Qur'an states in Surah 2:253, "Those Messengers we endowed with gifts, some above others: . . . to Jesus, the son of Mary, we gave clear (Signs) . . ." Commenting on this verse, Al-Baidawi said: "God made Jesus' miracles the evidence of his preferment (above all the prophets) because they are clear signs and great miracles. Together those miracles were not performed by anyone else."[3]

Jesus creates living beings and raises people from the dead in the Qur'an

According to the Qur'an, Jesus declares that He creates life, heals the blind, heals lepers, and even raises people from the dead! According to Surah 3:49, Jesus fashions a bird out of clay and gives it life by breathing upon it!

". . . I have come to you, with a Sign from your Lord, in that I make for you out of clay, the figure of a bird, and breathe into it, and it becomes a bird by Allah's leave. And I heal those born blind, and the lepers, and I quicken the dead, by Allah's leave; and I declare to you what ye eat, and what ye store in your houses. Surely therein is a Sign for you if ye did believe."

Jesus alone displayed the great power of God

The Gospel tells of the great multitude of people who had come to hear Jesus and to be healed of their diseases. "He [Jesus] went down with them and stood on a level place. A large crowd of his disciples was there and a great number of people from all over Judea, from Jerusalem, and from the coast of Tyre and Sidon, who had come to hear him and to be healed of their diseases. Those troubled by evil spirits were cured, and the people all tried to touch him, because power was coming from him and healing them all" (Luke 6:17–19).

It is surprising, and no doubt disappointing to many Muslim scholars, that the Qur'an nowhere states that Muhammad performed any miracle or sign. In fact Surah 28:48 addresses this absence, stating, "But (now), when the Truth has come to them [the Jews] from Ourselves, They say, "Why are not (Signs) sent to him [Muhammad], like Those which were sent to Moses?" The Qur'an records that many people did not believe in Muhammad because he did not perform any miracles. (Also see Surah 20:133 and 29:50.)

Jesus alone possesses the great power of God, and Jesus alone is able to heal spiritually and physically all who believe in Him! Perhaps you are feeling restless because of negative circumstances in your life. Perhaps you need healing or rest. Jesus says to you, "Come to me, all you who are weary and burdened, and I will give you rest" (Matthew 11:28).

12

JESUS CHRIST, "HIS WORD" (*KALIMATUHUU*)

In the Qur'an Jesus is called "His Word" (Kalimatuhuu), which means The Word of God. Surah 4:171 states "Christ Jesus the son of Mary was a messenger of Allah, and His Word . . ."

The Qur'an and the Bible agree that Jesus is the "Word of God"

The Qur'an records that the angel said to Mary, "Allah giveth thee Glad tidings of a Word from Him: his name will be Christ Jesus the Son of Mary . . ." (Surah 3:45). My dear reader, note that this "Word" which God gave to Mary was not a mere expression—it was the very Person of Christ Jesus.

Surah 3:39 states, "Yahya witnessing the truth of a Word from Allah." The famous Muslim scholar Al Razi comments on this verse. He explains the word of God to be Jesus (Isa). "What is meant by 'Word of God' is Isa, peace be upon him. This is the choice of the majority of the commentators."[1]

The Qur'an, in Surah 3:39, agrees with the Gospel record of John the Baptist (called the Prophet Yahya in the Qur'an) proclaiming that "The Word" (Jesus) would come from God.

According to the Bible, John the Baptist was sent by God to prepare the way and to announce the coming of Jesus Christ (John 1:23–27).

The Bible clearly gave Jesus the title "the Word of God" as stated in Revelation 19:13, "He is dressed in a robe dipped in blood, and his name is the Word of God."

In the Qur'an and in the Gospel, Jesus is the only person who is given the unique title "The Word of God." The emphasis of deity in this title is clearly visible and acceptable. The person of Jesus is the Word and the source of the Word is God Himself. Although the Qur'an gives no explanation for this title, the Bible explains it.

Jesus, the Word, is the full revelation of God to all humanity

Since God Himself calls Jesus "The Word of God" in the Bible and the Qur'an agrees, it is clear then that Jesus must be the One and only perfect expression of God's mind and will. The Bible declares in Colossians 1:15–19, "He [Jesus] is the image of the invisible God. . . ."

The Word of God (Jesus) indeed is the personal revelation of God to us all. To know Jesus is to know God. Jesus Himself said, "Anyone who has seen me has seen the Father" (John 14:9). Jesus does not only bring the revelation and words of God to men, but He Himself *is* the very Word who came down from heaven to earth (John 1:14).

Jesus' words are supernatural

It is clear throughout the Gospel that the words Jesus spoke were God's words. Note that the Qur'an acknowledges the heavenly effect of Jesus' words. Consider Jesus' powerful words in both the Qur'an and in the Bible.

- Jesus spoke to the leper, saying, "Be clean," and he was totally cleansed (Mark 1:40–45) and (Surah 3:49).

- Jesus told the paralytic, "Your sins are forgiven," and then gave him the ability to walk (Mark 2:5).

- Jesus raised a dead girl to life when He spoke to her; "Little girl, get up." (Mark 5:21–43) and (Surah 3:49; Surah 5:110).

- Jesus calmed the storm by saying, "Quiet! Be still!" showing authority over nature (Mark 4:35–41).

Jesus' supernatural words did what only God could do. The words of the historical Jesus healed the sick, forgave the sins of sinners, and raised the dead. The ascended Jesus still speaks such words today, for He is alive!

THE ETERNAL NATURE OF THE WORD OF GOD

Jesus is the Word of God, and the Word of God is eternal and uncreated. Therefore, God the Father and His Word, Jesus, are one. Jesus said, "I and the Father are one" (John 10:30). If someone denies that they are One, then that person must conclude that there are two separate entities who have existed for all eternity. Such a conclusion is blasphemy because only the one God is eternal.

"The Word" has always existed

The Gospel sheds some light on the title "The Word" given to Jesus in both the Qur'an and the Bible.

"In the beginning was the Word, and the Word was with God, and the Word was God. He was with God in the beginning. Through him all things were made; without him nothing was made that has been made. In him was life, and that life was the light of men" (John 1:1–4).

In these verses, the Bible specifies that in the beginning before creation the Word already existed. Jesus has been the Word of God throughout all eternity. The Word's very nature is of God, which shows that Jesus is divine.

The eternal Word became flesh

Jesus alone is the Word of God who came to earth in human form. The Word of God became the man Christ Jesus, the son of Mary. John 1:14 reveals, "The Word became flesh and made his dwelling among us. We have seen his glory, the glory of the One and Only, who came from the Father, full of grace and truth."

The Word having become flesh does not mean that the "Word" (*Logos*) ceased to be what He was. The verb "became" (*egeneto*) in this verse certainly does not mean the Logos changed into flesh, thus altering His essential nature. It means that He acquired an additional form (a human form) without changing His essential nature in any way. The word "flesh" (*sarx*) indicates human nature. The Word took on human nature or likeness (Philippians 2:7).

God communicates to us through His eternal Word

As stated in Hebrews 1:1–3, "In the past God spoke to our forefathers through the prophets at many times and in various ways, but in these last days he has spoken to us by his Son . . . The Son is the radiance of God's glory and the exact representation of his being." We have in Jesus the fullest possible expression of God toward man. It is through the Word, Jesus, that God expresses His character and communicates with us directly.

My dear reader, which is the better method of communication: to write a letter to someone or to personally go to the person? God chose to use the best method of communication.

John 1:4 reads: "In him was life, and that life was the light of men." Jesus, the Word of God, is the life and light God gave to humanity.

An eminent Muslim scholar Dr. Qaradawi wrote of God's nature, "If our hearing is through the sense of hearing that gets transmitted by air, God's hearing differs from ours. And if our sight comprehends things through the sense of seeing, and the rays (of light), God's seeing is not like ours."[2] The Qur'an states in Surah 42:11, "There is nothing whatever like unto Him." God's Word is totally different than anything else we know.

CHRIST IS LIKE "THE BOOK OF GOD"

In Surah 3:39, Jesus is called "a Word from God." AL-Baidawi, one of the most famous Muslim scholars, commented on this Surah: "Jesus is called the Word of God because he is like the Book of God." This is a very significant statement. According to the teaching of Muslim scholars and the Muslim beliefs, the book of God, the Qur'an, which is recited by tongues, and written in books (Masahif), and remembered in hearts, is eternal and exists in God Himself. It cannot be separated or parted from God by transferring it to hearts or by writing it on paper.[3]

Islam and Christianity are in agreement that God is eternal, His Word is eternal, and He is one. God bridged the gulf between the infinite and finite by revealing His eternal Word to His finite creation.

God's Word according to Islam

Muslims believe God expresses His eternal Word to His created beings through the Book called the Qur'an. For Muslims the Word resides eternally both within the being of God and within the pages of the Arabic Qur'an. Muslims also believe that the Qur'an was revealed to Muhammad at a particular place and time, almost fourteen centuries ago. Therefore, for the Muslim believer, the infinite and the finite meet within the Arabic Qur'an.

God's Word according to Christ followers

Followers of Christ believe God communicates His eternal Word to His created beings both in written form (the complete Bible) and through the living incarnate person of Jesus. For this reason the Bible speaks of the eternal Word of God "becoming flesh" as the man Jesus (John 1:14). Before the eternal Word became the man Jesus, the Word was residing eternally in the being of God. Jesus the Messiah is the eternal, living Word of God in human form.

IS THE WORD OF GOD CREATED OR UNCREATED?

God is eternal; He is uncreated. Therefore, His Word is also eternal and uncreated. Yet Muslims believe that God's uncreated Word can become a created book—namely the Arabic Qur'an. Prominent Scholar Ibn Hazm reports the leading scholar Ibn Hanbal as saying, "The Word of God is His eternal knowledge and hence it is uncreated."[4] Muslim scholars agree that the Qur'an has two aspects (natures)—human and divine. They claim the Qur'an has the following:

- Human (physical) nature because it is written in books by human hands, it appeared in human history, and it is subject to wear and tear.

- Divine (eternal) nature because the Qur'an is the knowledge of God. It exists in God Himself and cannot be separated and parted from God by writing it on paper.

One of the early leaders of the Muslim world, Caliph Ma'moun (AD 786–833), believed the Qur'an was created. Significantly he stated in a letter to the Governor of Baghdad, that those who believe that the Qur'an is uncreated are "like Christians when they claim that Jesus the Son of Mary was not created because he was the Word of God."[5]

God came in person and sent written instructions

My dear Muslim friend, I pray you will see that God, motivated by His strong love for spiritually dead mankind, was not satisfied to send only a Book. He also chose to present Himself as our personal Physician and Savior in the person of Jesus.

Imagine someone who is about to drown in the deep ocean. He can barely keep his head above the water. If you were that person, which would be your most urgent need? Someone to throw you a book of swimming instructions and ask you to try hard? Or someone to dive in the water and rescue you? In the gospel, God tells us that the human race is sinking in the depth of sin and He personally came to rescue us!

13

JESUS CHRIST, "A SPIRIT FROM GOD" (*RUHUN MINHU*)

Surah 4:171 states, "Christ Jesus the son of Mary was a Messenger of Allah . . . and a Spirit proceeding from Him (Ruhun Minhu) . . ." In another well-accepted translation of the Qur'an, the term *Ruhun Minhu* is translated as "a Spirit from God."

According to the Qur'an, Jesus is "a Spirit from God"

In the Qur'an, Jesus is the only one given the title "Spirit from God." Notice the Qur'an describes Jesus as a Spirit from God and not just a prophet. God is the source of the Spirit as He is the source of the Word. This title is not explained in the Qur'an. It is clear, however, that this title supports that Jesus was not a creature made from dust, but was an eternal Spirit who took on human flesh.

The Qur'an tells us that Jesus, the Messiah, Son of Mary, is "a Spirit from God." This statement affirms the pre-existence of Jesus before His miraculous conception on earth. In the Islamic *Traditions* (Hadith), which are a record of the words and deeds of Muhammad, Jesus is referred to as the "Spirit of God."

According to true Islam, Jesus is God's Spirit

In Al-Ahadith Al-Qudsiyyah (the highest revered group of Hadiths) it is stated, "Jesus (is) the servant of Allah, His Apostle, His Word and His Spirit."[1] In the introduction, the author highlights the divine authority of Al-Ahadith Al-Qudsiyyah as follows: "Hadith Qudsi, however, is a report of what God said, though not necessarily in His words. The Divine authority, explicitly stated or implicit in the context of the Hadith Qudsi, gives this group of Hadith a special character and significance to Muslims and non-Muslims alike."[2]

The "Spirit from God" is eternal

Abdullah Yusuf Ali defines the term "Spirit from God" in his internationally acclaimed translation and commentary, *The Meaning of the Holy Qur'an*. He comments on Surah 58:22, which states that God strengthens true believers with "a Spirit from Himself." In explaining what *Spirit from God* means, Ali says it is ". . . the Divine Spirit, which we can no more define adequately than we can define in human language the nature and attributes of Allah."[3] This is an amazing comment because it clearly and strongly indicates that the Spirit from God is the very Spirit of the Living God—uncreated and eternal.

Jesus is eternal

The words Abdullah Yusuf Ali used in his commentary are not vague. He interprets a "Spirit from God" to mean from the realm of Deity and not from the created order. "Spirit from God" is the very title that the Qur'an gives to Jesus in Surah 4:171. Therefore, Abdullah Yusuf Ali's interpretation of the term "Spirit from God" in Surah 58:22 leads us to conclude that Jesus is the *eternal* Divine Spirit who appeared in human flesh. My dear Muslim friend, the Qur'an calls Jesus the *Ruhun-Minhu* which in English means "Spirit from God."

My precious reader, you are far from where God is. You can't find the way to God's presence by yourself. You need a living person who came from heaven and knows the way to heaven. This person is Jesus. Jesus said,

"I am the way, and the truth, and the life. No one comes to the Father except through me" (John 14:6).

Jesus said to His disciples, ". . . the Father himself loves you because you have loved me and have believed that I came from God. I came from the Father and entered the world; now I am leaving the world and going back to the Father." (John 16:27–28).

John The Baptist (Yahya) said: "The one who comes from above is above all; the one who is from the earth belongs to the earth, and speaks as one from the earth. The one who comes from heaven is above all" (John 3:31).

SECTION FIVE

THE UNIQUE FEATURES OF JESUS

14

THE VIRGIN BIRTH OF JESUS CHRIST

As we investigate the uniqueness of Jesus Christ in the Qur'an and in the Bible, let us do this with the confidence that God guides us as sincere seekers of truth.

THE VIRGIN BIRTH ACCORDING TO BOTH THE QUR'AN AND THE BIBLE

Jesus' miraculous conception is taught in the Qur'an. We read in Surah 19:16–22:

> Relate in the Book (the story of) Mary. . . . We sent to her our angel [Ruhana] and he appeared before her as a man in all respects. She said: "I seek refuge from thee to (Allah) Most Gracious: (come not near) if thou doest fear Allah." He said, "Nay, I am only a messenger from thy Lord, (to announce) to thee the gift of a holy son." She said: "How shall I have a son, seeing that no man has touched me, and I am not unchaste?" He said: "So (it will be)": Thy Lord saith, "that is easy for Me: and (We wish) to appoint him as a Sign unto men and a Mercy from Us: It is a matter (so) decreed." So she conceived him, and she retired with him to a remote place.

Jesus was born of the virgin Mary

As previously indicated, an accurate translation of the Arabic Qur'anic word *ruhana* is simply "our spirit." (See Pickthall's translation of the verses above.) The Qur'an teaches that Jesus was conceived of a woman only. His mother was the "virgin Mary." The virgin birth of Jesus is also recorded in Surah 3:45–47. It is an amazing fact that Jesus' miraculous conception is taught in the Qur'an. Surah 21:91 clearly states: "And (remember) her who guarded her chastity. We breathed into her of Our Spirit and we made her and her son a Sign for all peoples."

According to the Gospel, Jesus was not conceived by human means, but by the power of the Holy Spirit of God. "Mary . . . was found to be with child through the Holy Spirit" (Matthew 1:18). (See also Luke 1:26–36.) Both the Bible and the Qur'an teach as a fact that Jesus was born of a virgin woman by the will of God through the power of the Spirit of God. Jesus was the only Man in all creation who was born in this unique, divine way. Many Muslims, during my conversation with them, tell me: "Adam's life was more unique than Jesus' because he came without a father and without a mother." I usually smile and remind my Muslim friends that Adam could not have had a father or a mother because Adam was the first man God created on earth.

Jesus' supernatural birth was a sign to all men

It is remarkable that in the Qur'an only the birth of Jesus is said to be a *sign* for everyone! It states twice that Christ's supernatural birth took place by God's purpose to give men a sign. Surah 21:91 states: "and We made her and her son a Sign for all people." In Surah 19:21 we read: ". . . and (We wish) to appoint him as a Sign unto men and a Mercy from us . . ." This distinction is not made concerning any other prophet's birth.

It is also significant to find that Jesus' mother is the only woman mentioned by name in the entire Qur'an. Surah 19 is named *Maryam* (Mary). In fact, Mary's name appears many times in the Qur'an while Eve, the first woman God created, is nowhere mentioned by name.

Mary was honored above all women

Both the Qur'an and the Bible teach that Mary is the most honored woman in the history of mankind. Surah 3:42 declares, "Behold! The angels said: 'O Mary! Allah hath chosen thee . . . above the women of all nations.'" And in Luke 1:42, Mary receives a prophecy: ". . . Blessed are you among women, and blessed is the child you will bear!"

One must wonder why Mary is honored above all women ever. The reason is clear. It is because God chose Mary to be the mother of the only perfect and divine Man who ever lived on the face of the earth!

Even Muhammad stated that Jesus' birth was the only birth in which Satan could not interfere.[1] My dear Muslim friend, are you beginning to see the uniqueness of Jesus?

THE REASON FOR THE VIRGIN BIRTH

The Gospel teaches that Jesus is the divine Son of God, who has existed throughout all eternity. Therefore, if the eternal Son of God came in the likeness of a man, He could not have been born as a result of a physical relationship between a man and woman. Because Jesus is the Son of God, it was absolutely necessary that Jesus be born of a virgin by the power of God's Spirit. Human life is typically passed on by the male seed.

Jesus' birth was the only exception to the normal process of procreation. In fact, when Jesus came into this world it was an entry, not a creation. All other people came through the union of a man to a woman. Jesus was conceived by the Spirit of God.

Teachings leading to the understanding that Jesus is the Son of God:

- Both the Bible and the Qur'an teach that Jesus was born of a virgin (His mother Mary) without a human father. According to the Bible and the Qur'an, Jesus is related to no human physical father.

- According to the Qur'an and the Bible, Jesus was conceived by the Holy Spirit.

- The Qur'an calls Jesus "a Spirit from God." And the Bible teaches that Jesus is the eternal Spirit and took on human flesh.

Keeping in mind that God's essence is a Spirit (He is present everywhere at the same time), these teachings help us understand that Jesus could not have been called anything other than the "Son of God."

Now we can see that Jesus' spiritual Sonship to the Father explains the necessity of the virgin birth and gives the reason for it. Please read and consider chapter 27 entitled, "Jesus is the Eternal Son of God in a Unique Spiritual Sense," for more details.

Jesus' virgin birth was prophesied in the Bible

Jesus was born of a virgin as prophesied by the prophet Isaiah seven centuries before Jesus was born (Isaiah 7:14).

The fact that Jesus had this unique beginning to His life on earth proves that He is unique. The virgin birth supports Jesus' divinity. The angel Gabriel told Mary when he came to explain Jesus' miraculous conception:

> "He will be great and will be called the Son of the Most High . . . The Holy Spirit will come upon you, and the power of the Most High will overshadow you. So the holy one to be born will be called the Son of God" (Luke 1:32–35).

15

THE SINLESSNESS OF JESUS CHRIST

No man or prophet had ever dared to claim himself infallible, but Jesus Christ had complete confidence in His perfection and purity. Therefore, He could boldly ask, "Can any of you prove me guilty of sin? If I am telling the truth, why don't you believe me?" (John 8:46). Jesus' sinlessness was taught throughout the Gospel:

"He [Jesus] committed no sin, and no deceit was found in his mouth." (1 Peter 2:22)

He ". . . was without sin." (Hebrew 4:15)

THE QUR'AN SUPPORTS THAT JESUS WAS SINLESS

The only person described as sinless in the Bible, the Qur'an, and the Hadith is Jesus Christ. Jesus was the only man who lived without committing a single sin throughout His life. The Qur'an, in Surah 19:19, states that an angel appeared to Mary and said, ". . . I am only a messenger from thy Lord (to announce) to thee the gift of a holy son." In another translation of the same Surah 19:19, Jesus is described as being "most pure" (Zakeyia).

AL-Baidawi described the Qur'anic phrase, "a boy most pure" as "pure from sins." In Yusuf Ali's translation of this verse, Jesus is referred to as "holy." In Arberry's translation He is referred to as "pure." And in Pickthall's translation, Jesus is referred to as "faultless." These are universally accepted translations of the Qur'an.

According to the Hadith, Jesus' sinlessness is very clear. He is the only person that was never influenced by Satan.[1]

Muhammad fell under the effect of evil magic

Al-Bukhari noted that even Muhammad fell under the effect of evil spirits.[2] Aisha (one of Muhammad's wives) reported an incident in which Muhammad was imagining he had performed sexual relations with his wives when actually he had not. Then Muhammad prayed to Allah regarding this problem, and Allah answered his prayer by sending two men to him in a dream. Muhammad heard one of them asking the other, "What is wrong with this man [Muhammad]?" The other replied, "He is under the effect of magic."

This Hadith reference goes on to say that Muhammad learned from his dream the identity of the person who performed the evil magic, as well as the material used and its location. Muslim scholars explain the implication of the dream. Because of the dream God gave to Muhammad, he was then able to recognize that he was under the effect of evil magic.

In the Gospel we see a contrast. Jesus displayed power over all evil spirits. For example, in Mark 5:1–12 Jesus met a man with an unclean spirit. With divine authority, Jesus commanded the unclean spirit, "Come out of the man, unclean spirit." The man was set free immediately. Therefore, my friend, Jesus is the only One who can protect you and me from the attacks of Satan and his evil spirits.

ALL HAVE SINNED

It is an easy matter to establish from the Bible, the Qur'an, and the Hadith that all people have sinned. Sin resides in every human being. Please consider a few examples:

In the Gospel: According to Romans 3:10–12, "There is no one righteous, not even one."

In the Hadith: One of the most reliable Hadith says, "Satan circulates in the human mind as blood circulates in it."[3]

In the Qur'an: We read in Surah 12:53, ". . . The (human) soul is certainly prone to evil . . ."

References to sins of the prophets

In order to show the unique sinlessness of Jesus, it is helpful to consider that the Qur'an and the Bible attributes sin to its other great prophets. Here are some references.

Adam

"So by deceit he brought about their fall when they tasted of the tree . . . and their Lord called unto them: 'Did I not forbid you that tree.' . . . They [Adam and Eve] said: 'Our Lord! We have wronged our own souls . . .'" (Surah 7:22–23).

Abraham

Abraham committed the sin of lying because he was afraid (Genesis 12:13).

Abraham asks, "And who, I hope, will forgive me my faults on the Day of Judgment" (Surah 26:82).

Jonah

Jonah disobeyed God (Jonah 1).

"Then the big fish did swallow him [Jonah], and he had done acts worthy of blame" (Surah 37:142).

Moses

Moses disobeyed God (Numbers 20:6–13).

Moses prayed: "O my Lord! I have indeed wronged my soul! Do thou then forgive me! . . ." (Surah 28:16).

Qur'an's references to Muhammad's sins

It is also significant that the Qur'an attributes sin to Muhammad. Here are several references to Muhammad's sins:

> ". . . that Allah may forgive thee thy faults of the past and those to follow." (Surah 48:2)

> ". . . and ask forgiveness for thy fault, and for the men and women who believe . . ." (Surah 47:19)

> "and ask forgiveness for thy fault . . ." (Surah 40:55)
> See also Surah 4:106; and 110:3.

It is recorded in the Hadith (Al-Bukhari) that Muhammad said: "By Allah! I ask for forgiveness from Allah and turn to him in repentance more than seventy times a day."[4] In the major works of Hadith there are examples of how Muhammad asked for forgiveness. Al-Bukhari recorded the following prayer by Muhammad: "O, Allah! Wash away my sins with the water of snow and hail, and cleanse my heart from all the sins as a white garment is cleansed from the filth, and let there be a long distance between me and my sins, as You made East and West far from each other."[5] Indeed he continued to ask forgiveness until the last breath.[6]

Who is most honored by God?

It is nowhere stated in the Qur'an, or in the Hadith, or in the Bible that Jesus needed to ask for forgiveness. Even Ayoub Mahmoud M., a noted contemporary Muslim writer, states that Jesus is free from sin. He writes, "Jesus is therefore free from the taint of evil and impurity . . . this purity, which Adam had until he was touched by Satan's finger and thus lost it, now remains exemplified in Jesus alone."[7]

God would certainly be most pleased with the One who is truly righteous, without sin. Surah 49:13 reads, "Verily the most honored of you in the sight of Allah is (he who is) the most Righteous of you." My dear reader, the most Righteous One is Jesus!

THE REASON FOR THE SINLESSNESS OF JESUS

In the Gospel, Jesus said, "I and the Father are one" (John 10:30). Jesus and the Father are not the same person, but they are One in essence and nature (which is explained in section nine). Since the Father and Son are one, as Jesus said, the Son always does the will of His Father. Jesus said, ". . . Whatever the Father does the Son also does" (John 5:19). Since God the Father would never sin, it follows that Jesus also would not sin.

Because Jesus is one with God, He always did the absolute will of God. He never did anything independently on His own accord. For this reason He never committed a single sin against God or against another human being. Jesus said, ". . . I always do what pleases Him" (John 8:29).

Jesus Christ was sinless throughout His earthly life because He was sinless in His nature. Jesus did not have the sin nature that is passed on from Adam to his descendants. Again, He was not conceived by the natural joining of man and a woman but by the Holy Spirit. We can see now why Jesus is the only Man in human history who lived a sinless life because He is the Son of God!

I am sure that you agree with me, that he who is able to live throughout his life without committing one single sin must be pure and sinless in his nature and essence.

Jesus cleanses us from all our sin

The Son of God demonstrated His authority to forgive sins. For example, in Mark 2:1–12, Jesus forgave the paralytic of his sins and healed him. And in Matthew 9:6, Jesus himself declared that He had the power on earth to forgive sin.

Please notice these significant words by Al-Baidawi regarding Jesus: "For by his words religion lives, the human soul lives eternally, and people are cleansed from sin."[8] Jesus is not only sinless, but also cleanses others from their sins. That is why He came to earth. Throughout the Bible we read that the blood of Jesus shed on the cross cleanses us from all sin! (See 1 John 1:7.)

Muslims believe that they should be ritually pure and clean. They wash with clean water before they pray. If they can't find clean water, then they can use sand. And if sand is not available, the person can reach out and touch a clean object to establish the intention that he be purified. My dear friend, clean water can clean only our physical body, but consider the transformation that happens when you reach out in a spiritual sense and believe upon the only pure Person—Jesus. At the moment you place your trust in Him and receive Him in your heart as Savior, His righteousness (purity) will be applied to you and you will be worthy to stand and kneel before God Almighty!

16

OTHER UNIQUE FEATURES
OF JESUS' LIFE

Jesus' ability to raise the dead is taught explicitly in both the Qur'an and the Bible. Raising the dead is a power belonging only to God.

Jesus has the power to raise the dead (as stated in the Qur'an)

The Qur'an confirms that no one can give life besides God (Surah 15:23; 36:12 and 50:43).

The Qur'an states in explicit language that Jesus actually raised people from the dead. We read in Surah 3:49 that Jesus stated: "And I quicken the dead, by Allah's leave . . . surely therein is a Sign for you If ye did believe." Surah 5:110 states that God Himself speaks of Jesus' power to raise the dead. According to the Qur'an, this power has been given only to Jesus. And significantly, all Muslim commentators on the Qur'an agree that the power to raise the dead belongs only to God. ". . . He [God] says, 'Who can give life to (dry) bones and decomposed ones (at that)?' Say, 'He [God] will give them life who created them for the first time!'" (Surah 36:78–79).

Jesus has the power to raise the dead (as stated in the Bible)

The Gospel teaches explicitly that Jesus has the ability to raise the dead. One example is when Lazarus, a close friend of Jesus, died. Jesus declared to Lazarus' sister Martha, "I am the resurrection and the life. He who believes in me will live, even though he dies; and whoever lives and believes in me will never die" (John 11:25–26). Then Jesus raised Lazarus from the dead.

Jesus came to conquer death and give eternal life to whoever believes in Him. Jesus proved that He possessed absolute power over life and death!

My dear Muslim friend, even though the Bible contains truths revealed by God, we are not *saved* by a written doctrine in a book; we are saved by the Redeemer, Jesus Christ! Now if you are sick, you need a doctor and not a medical book. If you are being sued, you need a lawyer and not a law book. Likewise, when you face your last enemy—death—you need the Savior. Jesus, by His resurrection from the dead, conquered the power of death. He provided the way for whoever would believe in Him to follow Him beyond the grave and into Paradise.

Jesus has power over death

In the Gospel, Jesus Himself declares that He has power over death. His words are recorded in the Gospel according to John:

> For just as the Father raises the dead and gives them life, even so the Son gives life to whom he is pleased to give it. (John 5:21)

> And this is the will of him who sent me, that I shall lose none of all that he has given me, but raise them up at the last day. (John 6:39)

> No one can come to me unless the Father who sent me draws him, and I will raise him up at the last day. (John 6:44)

Jesus has the ability to create life

The Qur'an clearly states that God is the one who creates all things. The Qur'an confirms that only the true and living God has the ability to create. This belief is noted in Surah

15:86; 16:17, 20; and 22:73. It is amazing to read in Surah 3:49 that Jesus created living beings (birds) out of clay the same way that God created Adam! (See also Surah 5:110.)

According to the Bible, Jesus has the ability to create life, something which no mere man could ever do. Two powerful scriptures indicating His creative power are Colossians 1:16 and John 1:3.

Jesus has the ability to know the unseen

Jesus has the ability to know the unseen, according to the Qur'an and the Bible. The knowledge of the unseen (that which cannot be seen by human eyes) is a divine quality. As the Qur'an states, "With Him are the keys of the unseen, the treasures that none knoweth but He" (Surah 6:59). The Qur'an also states: "Say: none in the heavens or on earth, except Allah, knows what is hidden . . ." (Surah 27:65).

Muhammad himself stated in the Qur'an that he did not possess the knowledge of the unseen: "If I had knowledge of the unseen, I should have multiplied all good, and no evil should have touched me" (Surah 7:188). (See also Surah 6:50 and Surah 11:31.)

According to the Qur'an in Surah 3:49, God granted the ability to know the unseen only to Jesus. Jesus had the ability to know even the small details of people's lives. According to the Gospel, Jesus even knows the thoughts and the intents of man's heart. John 2:24–25 states, "But Jesus would not entrust himself to them, for he knew all men . . . For he knew what was in a man."

We also learn from the Gospel that Jesus, as a prophet, knew unseen future events. The following are a few examples of events that came true as He predicted:

- His death and resurrection (Matthew 16:21)

- The Holy Spirit's arrival on Pentecost (John 16:7–15)

- The fall of Jerusalem (Luke 19:43–44)

Giving sustenance

The Qur'an states in Surah 51:58 that God is the only one who can give sustenance. A prominent early Muslim scholar, Ibn Kathir, explained that Christ had the ability to give sustenance to whomever He wished.

Clearly we see Christ's ability to give sustenance when he fed the five thousand people with a few loaves of bread and a couple of fish (Luke 9:12–17).

MORE UNIQUE FEATURES OF JESUS' LIFE AS RECORDED IN THE QUR'AN

Jesus was continuously accompanied by the Holy Spirit

Surah 2:87 says, ". . . We gave Jesus, the Son of Mary, clear (Signs) and strengthened him with the Holy Spirit." According to the Qur'an and the writings of Muslim scholars, Jesus was the only person who was continuously accompanied by the Holy Spirit from His conception to His ascension. We see that Jesus has the capacity to enjoy ongoing and total harmony and companionship with the Holy Spirit.

Jesus is forever eminent

Jesus is the only person described as being eminent in this world and in the next. In the Qur'an (in Surah 3:45), we read, "Behold! The angels said: 'O Mary! Allah giveth thee Glad tidings of a Word from Him: his name will be Christ Jesus, the Son of Mary, held in honor (*wajih*) in this world and the hereafter and of (the company of) those nearest to Allah.'"

The Arabic word *wajih* in the above verse is also translated "eminent" in other translations of the Qur'an. In commenting on this Surah 3:45, the well known Muslim scholar Shukani explains that "eminence is power and authority."[1]

Al-Razi, another prominent Muslim scholar, comments on Surah 3:45: "Jesus is distinguished (wajih) in this life, because his requests are granted, he raised the dead, healed the blind . . . He is distinguished in the life to come because He (God) made him intercede on behalf of his true people, and (God) accepts his intercession for them."[2]

Jesus is the intercessor

The Gospel assures that Jesus is continually interceding for His followers (believers) before God the Father. "because Jesus lives forever . . . he is able to save completely those who come to God through him, because he always lives to intercede for them" (Hebrews 7:24–25).

WHY WAS IT NECESSARY FOR JESUS TO COME?

17

THE PROBLEM OF SIN

In this chapter, my friend, we will observe the problem of our
sinful condition and God's solution to it. *Because sin is found
in every human heart*, there is no doubt that everyone needs
salvation.

Man's sinful condition

First, let us look at some of the passages in the Qur'an that
confirm the sinfulness of all human beings:

- "The (human) soul is certainly prone to evil . . ." (Surah
  12:53)

- "Verily, man is given up to injustice and ingratitude
  . . ." (Surah 14:34).

- "Truly man is, to his Lord, ungrateful" (Surah 100:6).

- Most men will not believe in God. ". . . most men believe
  not" (Surah 13:1). (See also Surah 12:103, 106; Surah
  15:10–11.)

- ". . . man doth transgress all bounds" (Surah 96:6)

- "He has created man . . . And behold this same (man)
  becomes an open disputer!" (Surah 16:4).

The Bible certainly confirms the fact that all of us have
sinned. It declares, "For all [people] have sinned" (Romans
3:23).

Prophet David said, "Surely I was sinful at birth, sinful
from the time my mother conceived me" (Psalm 51:5). David

also prayed, "Do not bring your servant into judgment for no one living is righteous before you" (Psalm 143:2).

The Hadith confirms this truth—the sinfulness of all human beings. It is recorded in one of the most acknowledged Hadith that Muhammad, the prophet of Islam, said, "Satan circulates in the human mind as blood circulates in it."[1] Muhammad also said, "Adam's every son is sinful . . ."[2]

Imam Khomeini, at his Inauguration as president in Iran on September 4, 1985, made some comments on man and said, "If the whole world is gathered and given to him, he will not feel satisfied. You see that the mighty who have great power seek more power . . . Arrogance should be stopped and ego should be controlled in everything. The downfall of man is that he wants absolute power" (i.e., the power of God).[3]

Khomeini confirmed his point by further saying, "You should pay attention and all of us should pay attention [to the fact] that man's calamity is his carnal desires, and this exists in everybody, and it is rooted in the nature of man."[4]

If people are essentially pure—as most Muslim scholars teach—how can we ignore all the evidence that proves the opposite?

Those who teach that man is fundamentally good and pure creature are not teaching the truth.

I encourage you, my dear Muslim reader, to examine the evidence.

What is sin?

Sin is like a disease that destroys people from within. We were all born with the effects of that horrible disease (sin) in us. This causes external symptoms to appear. The symptoms do not make the disease but the disease creates the symptoms.

One never has to teach a baby or young child how to be disobedient because disobedience and selfishness come naturally.

Sin is the breaking of God's law, but it is much more than that. Our words and actions reflect what is deep in our hearts. Jesus said, "For out of the overflow of the heart the mouth speaks" (Matthew 12:34). Our sinful nature is manifested through our natural inclination (desire) to live independent from God.

If sin is merely a choice which a person makes then why is no one able to keep a promise to God to do all according to His will and submit to Him always through perfect obedience. I am sure you would agree that no one is able to live up to a perfect commitment and never sin again.

The unfortunate reality is that human nature's tendency to sin is a compelling force. Obviously it is naive to think that people are basically good and pure.

Sin is disobeying God by committing acts against His will and it begins with evil thoughts. Jesus said, "For out of the heart come evil thoughts, murder, adultery, sexual immorality, theft, false testimony, slander. These are what make a man unclean . . ." (Matthew 15:19–20). Jesus taught us that it is far more important to be clean on the inside than just on the outside (Matthew 23:25–28).

The Bible explains that the root of all sin is selfishness. Sin is a condition of our human nature that is not in harmony with the will of God.

An illustration of sin

Our sinful nature manifests itself through our thoughts, actions, and words. Our entire being (including the mind, heart, mouth, eyes, etc.) is infected by the sin virus that makes us impure before God.

My dear Muslim friend, imagine, for example, that you are at the market. You are given a choice of three meat mixtures. The first has 50 percent beef and 50 percent pork. The next has 90 percent beef and 10 percent pork. The third has 99 percent beef and 1 percent pork. Which one would you buy? As a devout Muslim, you would refuse them all because Islam teaches that any amount of pork, no matter how insignificant, makes the meat *haram* (unlawful to eat). That is how sin is; no matter how small we think our sins are, they put us in a state of defiance to God and His will. Thus we become *unacceptable* in God's eyes! Sin makes us unable to obtain God's approval and unworthy to enter paradise.

A life containing many good works mixed with bad deeds is like an omelet that contains good eggs and bad eggs. You could not serve your guests that omelet. In the same way, God will not accept a life stained with sin.

No person can depend on self to become clean before God. One cannot count on enough good works to gain God's favor. It is really arrogant to think one can be good enough for God.

Even tiny sin is sin

According to the Islamic teaching and beliefs, if someone were to wash all his body in preparation to pray, and before he started his prayer some dust fell on him, then ritually he would be considered unclean. God would not accept his prayers. As a Muslim, if you believe that some dust on your physical body will disqualify you from praying, then you should be able to accept the Biblical truth that the dirt of sin within us makes us unclean. Even a tiny speck of sin disqualifies us from approaching the holy God. Remember, Adam and Eve were banned from the presence of God because of one single sin.

If a man's wife were to sleep with a man other than her husband, just once, she would be considered unfaithful. There is no such thing as "partial fidelity." In the same way, God considers "partial obedience" as disobedience.

My dear Muslim friend, would you accept a glass of water if I added one drop of ink to it? You would likely refuse. In the same way, the pure, just, and holy God cannot accept us into heaven on the basis of our good works. Our lives contain various selfish and sinful deeds that good works cannot erase. God will not allow any defiled or impure person to enter Paradise.

The Bible declares, "All of us have become like one who is unclean, and all our righteous acts are like filthy rags . . ." (Isaiah 64:6). Human efforts to be clean always fall short. Even tiny sins make us unclean. God cannot accept us in our unclean or sinful state.

Qur'an's reference to "hell fire"

The Qur'an mentions hell fire in Surah 19:71, "Not one of you but will pass over it [hell fire]: this is, with Thy Lord, a Decree which must be accomplished." In a different Qur'anic translation of the same verse, the expression "pass through it" is used. Many Muslims ask whether this verse refers just to the wicked or includes all men. The Suyuti tells us that Muhammad himself answered this question by saying, "There is no righteous or debaucher who would not enter hell."[5]

The Qur'an offers no eternal security

Tragically, according to the Qur'an and the Hadith, no Muslim can be sure of what to expect after death. According to Al-Bukhari, Muhammad, the prophet of Islam, said, "By Allah, though I am The Apostle of Allah, yet I do not know what Allah will do to me."[6]

The God of the Qur'an does not guarantee the Muslim forgiveness of sins, acceptance, or the promise of eternal life. For example, Abu Bakr Al-Sadik, the first Caliph, is regarded by all Muslims as one of the best Muslims. Even Muhammad acknowledged that Abu Bakr Al-Sadik was the closest to him (by being a faithful Muslim), and he told the believers to emulate Abu Bakr Al-Sadik as a model. Therefore, the Muslims elected him as Caliph after the death of Muhammad. (*Caliph* is the title for the primary leader of the Muslims.)

However, consider Abu Bakr's insecurity regarding his eternal destiny. Tragically, he was quoted as saying: "I swear to God that I do not feel safe from God's cunning (deceitfulness) even if one of my feet is already inside paradise."[7]

What an acknowledgment spoken by Abu Bakr! He feared that God might change His mind, and push his foot outside of paradise. Abu Bakr Al-Sadik also said, when resurrection, paradise, or hell were mentioned in his presence, "I wish I were a tree eaten by an animal; I wish I had never been born."[8] Obviously, he was frightened of God.

This kind of fear is not surprising. God as described in the Qur'an, does not bestow on the believer any assurance concerning eternal life.

Muslim teachers emphasize that good deeds must outweigh bad ones in order to have a chance to enter paradise. Unfortunately, according to Islam, God never gave clear instructions as to His scoring system for good deeds. This makes God resemble an employer who conceals the job description from His employees and then judges them according to an unknown standard.

What should a righteous judge do?

Our sins violate the will and law of God. They are an insult to God and harmful to those He created and loves. Since God is holy and just, the sinner deserves His judgment. God would not be fair and just unless He was to punish the sinner. Repentance alone, which is a return to the place of obedience, cannot remove past sins, nor can it satisfy the holiness and justice of God even if we were to add our good works to it.

Mere sorrow or repentance and good works cannot earn God's forgiveness. Imagine a young man brought before a judge and convicted of rape. The man pleads, "I repent and I am very sorry for what I did and I will never do it again. Your Honor, I promise to be nice and respectful toward all the women I meet for the rest of my life. I will donate much of my time and money to help victims of rape. As a matter of fact, Your Honor, I can prove I did many, many good deeds before and after this crime. Your Honor, I am really sorry for the wrong I did, and I am sorry I broke the law. Since I have done many good deeds and I plan to do more, I am asking you to grant me a pardon. Forgive me and set me free."

How do you think the judge should respond? The judge should say, "Although I appreciate your good deeds and apology, I must deal with your crime by issuing a punishment."

God will judge each person for his or her sins

My beloved Muslim reader, it will be the same when we stand before God on the Day of Judgment. Because of His holiness and justice, He has to deal with our sins. Eternal punishment is certain for those whose sins are not forgiven.

Again, repentance and good works do not eradicate the effect of sin or guilt. While obedience requires good works, we cannot use them to offset our bad deeds. In other words, good works are a requirement of obedience but not a solution to sin!

It is recorded in Al-Bukhari that Muhammad said to a group of people, "The deeds of any one of you will not save you (from the hell fire)." Then they asked him, "Even you (will not be saved by your deeds), O Allah's Apostle?" He responded, "No, even I (will not be saved) unless and until Allah bestows

His mercy on me."[9] Muhammad also said, "The good deeds of any person will not make him enter Paradise."[10] It is a fact that there is nothing man himself can do to prevent the judgment of God. God's justice demands that the penalty for sin be paid, and that the sinning person deserves to pay that penalty.

The Qur'an states, ". . . Allah called them to account for their sins. For Allah is strict in punishment" (Surah 3:11).

Sin requires payment

Dishonoring the mayor is a big mistake. Dishonoring the president is certainly a bigger mistake. Dishonoring the perfect God is an infinite mistake that places us in a state of infinite debt. We cannot pay such a debt.

If you are wronged, naturally you want whoever wronged you to pay for what he has done to you. God also requires payment for all the offenses (sins) we committed against Him.

If I wronged a colleague with whom I worked, another colleague could help me to reconcile with the one I wronged.

If I wronged the president and owner of the company for whom I worked, my colleague could not intercede between the president and me. He could not help me. I would need someone very influential, someone to whom the president would consider it important to listen.

If you or I sin against God, we need Jesus to intercede for us.

Jesus saved us from the condemnation of the law

God said, "cursed is everyone who does not continue to do everything written in the Book of the Law" (Galatians 3:10; Deuteronomy 27:26). The glorious Good News of the Gospel is that the Messiah, Jesus, has paid the debt for our sins with His own shed blood. His sacrificial death on the Cross satisfied God's judgment on sin and fulfilled the demands of His just

Law. "Christ redeemed us from the curse of the Law by becoming a curse for us . . ." (Galatians 3:13).

Obedience to the law can never bring salvation because no one can obey perfectly. The law merely shows the sinner that he is guilty before God. The law demands perfect obedience, but man is not capable of perfection. Under the Law, we are condemned. However there is good news, "but when the time had fully come, God sent his Son, born of a woman, born under the law, to redeem those under the law, that we might receive the full rights of sons" (Galatians 4:4–5).

GOD MADE IT POSSIBLE FOR US TO BECOME RIGHTEOUS THROUGH FAITH

The Bible tells us,

> . . . the whole world [is] held accountable to God. Therefore no one will be declared righteous in His sight by observing the law; rather, through the law we become conscious of sin. But now a righteousness from God, apart from law, has been made known, to which the law and the prophets testify. This righteousness from God comes through faith in Jesus Christ to all who believe. There is no difference, for all have sinned and fall short of the glory of God, and are justified freely by His grace through the redemption that came by Christ Jesus. (Romans 3:19–24)

This passage contrasts the righteousness gained by observing the law—which no one is able to obtain—and the righteousness provided by God apart from keeping the law.

God's law is a reflection of His perfect standard. God's law declares us guilty. Just as we recognize a bent line when we place it next to a strait line, in a similar way the law shows us how far from perfect we really are.

We will not be able to plead innocence because we are not innocent of sin. In the just courtroom of heaven, before God the righteous and just Judge, we stand. The verdict? Guilty. We deserve eternal punishment.

Followers of Christ and Muslims agree on the basic meaning of the word "sin" in that it is any word, thought, or deed that falls short of God's perfect standard. Sin can be:

- Violation of the law of God

- Lack of obedience to the revealed will of God

- An absence of righteousness by not submitting completely to God

- Human nature, which is not in harmony with the will of God

Jews (followers of Moses), Christians (followers of Jesus), Muslims (followers of Muhammad), and, as a matter of fact, all humanity failed to keep God's law. Therefore, no human being can be regarded or treated as righteous; we all have sinned.

The Bible addresses the act of people relying on their own efforts to gain God's favor, "For I can testify about them that they are zealous for God, but their zeal is not based on knowledge. Since they did not know the righteousness that comes from God and sought to establish their own, they did not submit to God's righteousness. Christ is the end [fulfillment] of the law so that there may be righteousness for everyone who believes" (Romans 10:2–4).

This passage reminds me of many of my dear Muslim friends who rely only on their works to establish their own righteousness and are hoping to gain righteous status before God. My wife was one of them, born and raised as a devout Muslim. She graduated from an Islamic University, majoring in Islamic study and Arabic language. She was always trying to gain God's favor through her works. Her life changed when she put her faith in what God has done for her through Jesus Christ.

My wife's faith is genuine. She suffered and was thrown in prison because she refused to deny Jesus Christ. She almost lost her life, but Jesus was protecting and comforting her during her time in prison. She met three other ex-Muslims in prison. They joined my wife in prayers and singing praise songs to God every day. God used all of them to help many prisoners experience God's love and salvation.

Knowledge of sin

God gave the law not to justify people but to produce knowledge of sin. God gave the Torah to show us how desperately we need His salvation.

The law reveals our sin like the mirror shows us exactly how we look. The mirror cannot fix or improve our appearance. In a similar way, the law shows us God's standard and our inability to live up to it. But the law cannot make us righteous.

No single human being has ever or will ever be accepted by God on the basis of his or her own merit. God sent Jesus on our behalf to fulfill every requirement of the law. Jesus paid the penalty for every law we broke or sin we committed.

True submission to God is to humble ourselves before Him, realizing His holiness, and confessing our sins and shortcomings. Honoring God is knowing our unworthiness and accepting His provision.

God is offering all people the chance to be justified and declared righteous through faith in Jesus. God is offering you, my dear reader, His unmerited favor and grace. If you reject His offer and refuse to believe in Jesus and instead continue to rely on your own efforts, you will eventually have to suffer the penalty for all of your sins.

God is offering you salvation through faith. Faith in itself does not save you. God is the One who saves you. Placing your trust in Jesus is the means by which you accept God's grace. If you reject God's gracious offer now, you will one day have to face His righteous judgment according to His law.

Salvation through faith is relying on the living Lord Jesus Christ as your only Savior from sin. Jesus' sacrifice is sufficient for the whole world, but is only effective for those who put their trust in Him.

God inspired David to write, "Blessed is he whose transgressions are forgiven, whose sins are covered. Blessed is the man whose sin the lord does not count against him . . ." (Psalm 32:1–2).

A verse in the Qur'an shows our need for God to make us righteous and that we do not have the solution to our sin problem, "Our Lord! We have heard the call of one calling (us) to faith, 'Believe ye in the Lord,' and we have believed. Our Lord! Forgive us our sins, blot out from us our iniquities, and take to thyself our souls in the company of the righteous" (Surah 3:193).

God gave you free will and freedom of choice. You have made wrong choices and disobeyed Him. You sinned willfully. The cost of the damages you did is more than you can pay. Divine rescue is necessary. God, the heavenly Father, paid the price Himself. The moment you trust Christ as your Savior, you are granted immunity from punishment and the case against you is closed.

All the penalty and death we deserve for our sins fell upon Jesus. Through God's divine self-sacrifice, God manifested His divine love for you and me, which triumphed over His divine wrath towards us (sinners).

God will justify you only when you accept His own payment for all of your sins. It is extremely important to realize that Jesus' crucifixion is not just a Biblical doctrine; it is also a personal and spiritual experience you can enjoy when you believe in it. You will feel His forgiveness, I guarantee it!

I clearly remember struggling as if I were climbing a mountain with a heavy backpack. In February 1976, I repented and put my faith in Jesus Christ as my Savior. I felt so light, so free, so forgiven. Forgiveness, like medicine, is not effective until taken.

Jesus paid the penalty for our sins

Jesus Christ removed the barrier between man and God. The Bible notes, "This is love: not that we loved God, but that he loved us and sent his Son as an *atoning sacrifice* for our sins" (1 John 4:10). Out of matchless love for us, God placed our sin debt on Jesus, who willingly took our place as the sacrifice for us. Therefore, the sinner will be saved immediately if he accepts, by faith, this gift of mercy and grace from God.

God's grace is a free gift

Remember, my friend, that none of us can say with a clear conscience, "I am not a sinner." It only takes one sin to become a sinner. In addition, as previously expounded, our fallen sinful nature guarantees that everyone will sin again to some degree. Trying to deal with difficult situations, trying to enjoy moments of pleasure, and simply living with a sinful nature leads you to commit sin.

Are you willing, like me, to admit that you have sinned and you are a sinner who cannot earn your way to heaven? Will you acknowledge that you are in need of God's mercy and grace?

The fantastic news is that Jesus dealt with our problem of sin and provided the solution for it once and for all. "For all [people] have sinned and fall short of the glory of God, and are justified freely by his *grace* through the redemption that came by Christ Jesus" (Romans 3:23–24, emphasis added). We can only be considered good or pure by the grace and mercy of God.

Illustration of God's gift of grace

God wants you to obtain and enjoy His salvation—as a gift. If you tried to earn it by your efforts, you could not because you do not deserve it. But if you ask God to save you because of your trust in who Jesus is and in His finished work on the cross, He will do so gladly because He loves you.

The following story demonstrates God's gift of grace:

There once was a poor and hungry woman. While she was tired from walking, she saw a garden full of fruits. She tried to pay the gardener some money to sell her some fruit. But he refused the money.

Each time she attempted to buy the fruit, her offer was refused. But the woman continued to plead with the gardener to take her money. Then one day the prince, the king's son, overheard the woman begging. After he learned the situation, the kind prince told the woman, "My father the king owns this garden. He is not a merchant and does not need your money. You cannot buy his fruit, but he will give it freely to you if you merely ask and believe in his free gift. The woman joyfully accepted the king's gracious offer. Then the prince picked an abundance of the most perfect fruit and gave the woman all she needed!

God knows we are unable to save ourselves. Because of His deep and amazing love toward us, He offers us salvation as a gift. "For it is by *grace* you have been saved, through faith—and this not from yourselves, it is the gift of God—not by works, so that no one can boast" (Ephesians 2:8–9).

Realizing that we are desperately in need of God's grace humbles us, and receiving God's grace uplifts us.

JUSTIFICATION THROUGH FAITH

God will justify (declare "not guilty") the sinner who believes Jesus died on the cross for his or her sins. The moment sinners trust in Jesus as their Savior, all of their sins are forgiven and removed.

You—a sinner—can be justified by faith in Jesus Christ. "Since we have been justified through faith, we have peace with God through our Lord Jesus Christ" (Romans 5:1). God is asking you to respond in faith so you can experience His grace and forgiveness to save your soul.

Salvation by God's grace, not good works

Salvation is a gift of God's grace obtained through faith. To be justified by faith means God considers you righteous—not on the basis of your good works—on the basis of your faith and trust in Christ's sacrifice. God accepted the sacrifice of Christ as the payment for your debt according to divine justice. Your own human works cannot acquire God's favor or access to heaven.

My dear reader, what does God see when He looks at you? Does He see religious deeds mixed with sin? Or does He see His own righteousness credited to you through your faith in Christ? The only standard of righteousness God accepts is the righteousness of Christ.

I remember when I was a child I would occasionally get into trouble. My father owned the building where we lived in Egypt. His legal practice was on the ground floor while we resided upstairs. Many times I invited my friends over to play soccer in the hallway on the ground floor. On one occasion, our ball broke a light bulb. And another time, it hit one of my father's clients. Sometimes the ball would even hit the glass door of my father's office. These disturbances, along with the joyful yelling and screaming, often interrupted his business conversations.

When my father finished work and entered our home with that certain look that told me I was in trouble, I would run to my mother crying. I would hide behind her, trusting that through her I would be safe and forgiven. Although he was angry, many times he would see my mother's beautiful face and my repentant heart and let me go unpunished. Other times, my mother would gather me in her arms and shield me with her big body. When my father reached out to spank me, his newspaper, belt, or hand would fall on her instead of me.

This memory always reminds me of when I ran to Jesus in February 1976 and put my trust in Him; I experienced God's forgiveness. Jesus covered me with His righteousness, shielding me from punishment.

My friend, that glorious moment when you receive Jesus Christ as *your* Lord and Savior, God will credit the righteousness of Christ to your account.

The Bible states, ". . . It is by the name of Jesus Christ . . . Salvation is found in no one else, for there is no other name under heaven given to men by which we must be saved" (Acts 4:10–12).

My dear reader, you need to drink from God's grace so your soul can be satisfied. Then you will have an unimaginable inner peace filling your innermost being. God knocks softly on the door of you heart. If you were to ask me, Samy, how do you know? I would answer, He knocked on the door of my heart years ago and I invited Him in. I have not been the same since because He continues to fill me with peace and love. Can you hear Him knocking? He desires to have fellowship with you. Will you open the door for Him by faith and allow Him to enter your life and be your Lord and friend? God is inviting you to cast yourself on His grace, mercy, love, and forgiveness.

Salvation is immediate!

Even if you are one of the worst sinners, you can be forgiven and saved today! You can begin to enjoy knowing you have eternal life with God. God as described in the Gospel gives wonderful hope even to the sinner who lives all his life without faith in Him, and who never accumulated good works.

While Jesus hung on the cross, He told the thief, a sinful criminal hanging on the cross next to Him, "Today you will be with me in paradise" (Luke 23:43). God knew this sinner (who expressed his faith in Jesus) would die with no time left to complete any good works. God knew his believing and repentant heart. God accepted the thief on the cross even though his sins far outweighed his good works—because of his faith in Jesus.

The Gospel message here is not that those people who accumulated enough good works make it to heaven, but rather those whose sins are forgiven through faith in Jesus Christ.

True Christians do not want to continue in sin

There are many people today who claim to be Christians. They call themselves Christians but live a sinful lifestyle. These people are deceived, for the true believers and followers of Jesus Christ obey His teaching and submit completely to God. The Bible instructs us to "become blameless and pure, children of God without fault in a crooked and depraved generation" (Philippians 2:15).

The forgiveness of sin does not give Christians the right to continue in sin. No true follower of Christ purposely continues to live in sin. Paul the Apostle, inspired by the Holy Spirit, explained God's instructions for Christians:

What then? Shall we sin because we are not under law but under grace? By no means! Don't you know that . . . you are slaves to the one whom you obey—whether you are slaves to sin, which leads to death, or to obedience, which leads to righteousness? But thanks be to God that, though you used to be slaves to sin, you wholeheartedly obeyed the form of teaching to which you were entrusted. You have been set free from sin and have become slaves to righteousness. (Romans 6:15–18)

Christ gives His true followers the desire and power to do good. Titus 2:14 notes that Jesus "gave himself for us to redeem us from all wickedness, and to purify for himself a people that are his very own, eager to do what is good."

Some Muslims incorrectly teach that Christians do not care about doing good works because of their dependence on what Jesus has done for them. Islam teaches Muslims to pray five times a day. The Gospel, on the other hand, teaches believers to "pray continually" (I Thessalonians 5:17). Thus, all true Christians who follow the teachings of the Bible know they are to remain in fellowship with God, surrendering their lives to Him and submitting to His will continually.

Regarding prayer Jesus Himself taught, "When you pray, do not be like the hypocrites, for they love to pray standing in the synagogues and on the street corners to be seen by men. I tell you the truth; they have received their reward in full. But when you pray, go into your room, close the door and pray to your Father, who is unseen. Then your Father, who sees what is done in secret, will reward you" (Matthew 6:5–6). Jesus taught a similar message about fasting (in verses 16–17).

Spiritual growth for the Christian is a process

Just as infants grow physically, people who are "born again" (through faith in Jesus) grow spiritually. Followers of Christ stumble and fall short of the perfect standard of their holy God. They struggle against sin, the flesh, and Satan. Gradually they mature in their spiritual lives. When Christians grieve about their sins, they can take comfort in God's promise to always forgive them when they confess and repent. This glorious promise is found in 1 John 1:9: "If we confess our sins, he is faithful and just and will forgive us our sins and purify us from all unrighteousness."

Believers in Christ rejoice that God does not leave them to struggle alone. The Holy Spirit empowers them to overcome temptations and changes their character to be more like Jesus. Thus they become more loving, forgiving, and willing to obey and serve God. "For it is God who works in [them] to will and to act according to his good purpose" (Philippians 2:13).

The Bible assures us that God, who starts a good work in each believer, is faithful to complete it (Philippians 1:6). The Holy Spirit within the believer produces good works and wonderful traits. We read in the Bible, "The fruit of the Spirit is love, joy, peace, patience, kindness, goodness, faithfulness, gentleness and self control" (Galatians 5:22).

The Bible tells us that God is constantly working in us, to change us to be the people He created us to be.

Farid Esack, a renowned Muslim scholar and currently the Brueggeman Chair in Interreligious Studies at Xavier University in Cincinnati, Ohio, wrote, "One can be totally committed to Islam and yet not have it touch one's inner being . . . Our lives as Muslims are largely devoid of an ongoing and living connection with Allah."

Muslim scholars agree that Islam's focus is upon what the Muslim person must do for God to achieve the status of being a good Muslim. The Muslim person is commanded to perform repetitive rituals and act according to prescribed religious regulations without a personal relationship with God.

18

GOD HIMSELF CAME TO US IN THE PERSON OF JESUS, THE MESSIAH

According to the Bible, God Himself came to us in the person of the Messiah. The Gospel teaches that God chose to enter our world in the person of Jesus, who was conceived by the Holy Spirit in the body of a virgin. Jesus remained pure and sinless as He expressed God's wonderful love for the human race.

God is both mighty and humble

Many Muslims say that Jesus ate, drank, and slept while He lived on earth. They reason, "How can Jesus be God, since God does not need to do any of these activities that humans do?"

It is true that God does not have to do any of these human activities, just like a king does not have to sleep where his servants sleep or eat with them. He certainly does not have to go through such humbling experiences. However, he can choose to do so if he wants to get close to his servants to experience their feelings and ultimately solve their problems. He can choose to spend time with them in their environment. A king also can wear the clothes of a soldier and yet remain the king.

Likewise, the God of the Bible is the servant-King. The Bible states, "For you know the grace of our Lord Jesus Christ, that though he was rich, yet for your sakes he became poor, so that you through his poverty might become rich" (2 Corinthians 8:9).

Would we dare to place boundaries upon God's power and will? Are we not limiting God by saying He is unable to express Himself in human form? Man certainly could not become Almighty God. But God certainly could come to our world in the form of a man and manifest Himself through the perfect man, Jesus Christ.

Spirit beings can take on human form

Take note: the Qur'an states that the Spirit of God can appear in human form. An example is in Surah 19:17, ". . . We sent to her Our Spirit (Ruhana), and he appeared before her as a man in all respects." The original Arabic word *ruhana* in this verse means "Our Spirit." (Unfortunately it was mistranslated into English by Yusuf Ali as "our angel.")

The Bible and the Qur'an both acknowledge that God at times sends His angels, who are spirit in form (*ruh*), in the exact likeness of human appearance. So there is no reasonable argument against the possibility that Jesus, who likewise is Spirit in form, took on actual human form.

God desires to associate closely with people

Many Muslim scholars, such as Assfy, point out that: "God does not have to be associated in any way with men."[1] Of course this statement is true. God, however, reveals Himself in the Gospel to be a God of love who desires to meet us at our level and graciously identify with us closely. He is a God who longs for us to come to Him so He can embrace us and communicate with us through His Spirit, which He will send to dwell within us. He wants to adopt us as children and become our loving, heavenly Father.

God is almighty and present everywhere

The Qur'an states in Surah 55:14: "He [Allah] created man from . . . clay like unto pottery." This verse indicates that God made Adam at a specific time by holding in His hand clay from a specific place on the earth. And in the Bible, we learn that God walked in the Garden of Eden and communicated with

Adam (Genesis 3:8). These events did not confine Him, because God is almighty and ever-present. In the same way, God's incarnation (coming in the form of a man) at a specific time and place did not confine Him. He remains the almighty, sovereign God who fills the whole universe with His presence and yet desires to fellowship with us one-on-one.

Our loving God desires to relate to us personally

Islam agrees with the Christian faith that, ultimately, God can only be known through His self-revelations. The Bible declares that God came to us through the person of Jesus Christ, taking on human nature to reveal the infinite in a language the finite can understand.

Please consider this hypothetical situation: If you desired to communicate with a bird and you have unlimited power and authority, what would be the best way for you to do so? The answer is that you would become a bird! Then you could communicate on the same level.

Please consider another illustration: During the Vietnam war, a Vietnamese family was separated. While the wife and two boys were able to move to the United States, the father was forced to stay in Vietnam. For seventeen years they communicated with each other only through letters and pictures. The father could watch his boys grow up only from a distance. Then, finally, the governments of Vietnam and the United States signed an agreement that allowed the father to come to the U.S. to be with his family.

What if the father had said to his family, "I don't really see any need to visit you in person? Communicating through letters and pictures has been sufficient for seventeen years, so it will continue to be sufficient for me." What would you think of such a father? Likewise, what would you think of a God who was able to communicate with and visit His creation in person, but refused to do so?[2]

Our loving God chose to relate directly to us by coming in a human form, in the person of the Messiah.

God's divine nature is never lessened

My dear Muslim reader, Almighty God is able to appear in the person of the Messiah and to personally relate to mankind without lessening His essence or staining His divine character. According to the Gospel, Jesus' life on earth was a perfect demonstration of God's love, forgiveness, holiness, healing, and salvation.

Also remember that all the bodily functions of a human being are God's design and are pure as long as they are used according to His will.

Jesus Christ, the Word of God, did not lose His divine nature when He became a human. According to both the Qur'an and the Gospel, He raised the dead, healed the lepers, and gave sight to the blind. He had many other divine characteristics that cannot be attributed to a mere human being. Many of these are introduced in later chapters.

Could the Creator of all things and the human body visit our world and present Himself to save us without being impaired in any way? Of course He could! On one occasion, "Jesus told His disciples, 'with man, this is impossible, but with God all things are possible'" (Matthew 19:26).

Please, allow me to share with you a real life story.

Before the Labor Day holiday, the President of the United States left the White House wearing the clothes of a factory worker. He spent most of the day visiting and working in a factory.

The President was not less honorable because of what he did. On the contrary, his humble spirit and actions honored him, the factory workers, every worker in America, and also America itself.

The Incarnation of Jesus

Some Muslims ask, "If Jesus Christ is God, how was it possible for Him to be killed? Can God die?" The answer is that God cannot die. God the Father is without visible form. But Jesus Christ assumed a tangible form on earth as a man. Jesus, of divine nature, took on an additional human nature—which was put to death on the cross. Death, however, could not keep Him in the grave. After He died, He rose from the dead and walked the earth for forty more days. Then He ascended into heaven. He went to heaven in a new form, in His glorified body.

In His divine nature, the Son is an infinite eternal Spirit. This same divine Being became personally united with human nature and yet retained His divinity.

God entered His creation in a new way and experienced it while still remaining God overall. He did not only walk among us; He *became* one of us—in a true human form.

The humanity of Jesus

The Gospel contains many statements showing us that Jesus' body on earth was a real human body. His humanity was obvious in that Jesus was hungry, tempted, and crucified. He walked and talked with His disciples and others. He suffered mental anguish and physical pain. He was fully human.

The deity of Jesus

The Gospel includes many statements indicating the deity of Jesus. For examples, Jesus is

- Eternal (everlasting): He existed before the world was formed (John 8:58; 17:5).

- Ever-Present: He is present everywhere at all times (Matthew 18:20).

- All-Knowing: He demonstrated knowledge of things that could only be known if He were divine (Matthew 9:4; Matthew 11:27; Luke 6:8; John 4:29).

- All-Powerful: He demonstrated unlimited, supernatural power and authority (Matthew 8:23–27; 28:18; Mark 5:11–15).

Indeed, Jesus had the attributes of a man and also the attributes of God. Christ acted in accordance with His humanity and in accordance with His deity.

Jesus, fully human and fully divine

Some people ask, "How is it possible for the divine nature to be united with the human nature?" I answer, "Whatever the Almighty God decides to do according to His infinite wisdom, He is able to accomplish."

This dual nature of Jesus is incomprehensible to our limited human intellect. There are many other things we don't fully understand. How is it possible for spirit and flesh to be united in us? The creation of the first human was also a mystery. God made man (His vice regent on Earth) by using mud and His divine Spirit or breath. Therefore, we should not consider it a strange thing that the second man whom God sent to be our savior, the Messiah Jesus, was also both fully divine and fully human.

The union of the divine with human form took place in Christ for the purpose of satisfying God's justice, manifesting His love for us, and accomplishing our salvation.

Man was created in God's image

My dear Muslim friend, God chose to save us. He accomplished this goal by appearing in the form of a perfect, sinless man to be our personal Savior. God did not become incarnate in a plant, bird, or animal because they do not bear His image. But we know from the Torah that God created us in His image. "God said, 'Let us make man in our image'" (Genesis 1:26). The Qur'an in Surah 15:29 states, "When I have fashioned him and breathed into him [only into man] of My Spirit . . ."

Biblical scholar, Bedru Kateregga, explains that "man created in the image of God does not mean that God looks like man or that man looks like God. But it does mean that man has profound God-like qualities."[3] For example, God created man with the ability to be loving, just, and compassionate. It is interesting that all of us are aware that we should act better and that we can become better humans. Kateregga continues, "This is the witness of our God—likeness within our conscience. It is a persistent voice in the conscience that we should become better people, that we do not always do what we know we should do, that we really should be more kind, true, reliable, pure, more God-like."[4] It is also God-like to be humble and to love sacrificially.

John Gilchrist, a respected Biblical theologian, writes concerning God appearing in human form:

Man was so made that he could possess and manifest all God's characteristic attributes: holiness, love, purity, etc. . . . The question is not whether God can be confined in human form, it is purely whether humanity can bear the divine image. The answer is an unqualified yes. Jesus Christ manifested every one of God's perfect attributes to the full when he lived on earth as a man. There is no reason why the Son of God could not become the Son of Man. In no way was his Divine character blurred while he walked among us. On the contrary, God's love, grace, forgiveness and compassion were all revealed to the full when he laid down his life to redeem us from all iniquity and prepare us for a heavenly dwelling.[5]

In harmony with what I just mentioned, Muhammad said, "Allah created Adam in His picture."[6]

JESUS IS THE PERFECT MEDIATOR

Jesus, the Messiah, is the perfect Mediator between God and man. The Bible declares, "This is good, and pleases God our Savior, who wants all men to be saved and come to a knowledge of the truth. For there is one God and one Mediator between God and men, the man Christ Jesus, who gave himself as a ransom for all men" (1 Timothy 2:3–6). Only Christ could be called the perfect and acceptable sacrifice to God. In Him we see all the necessary characteristics that must be found in the Mediator (Savior).

The Savior must be human

How could God—who is Spirit—pay the penalty for the sins of man who is flesh? It was a human penalty He wanted to bear. Therefore God acquired human form, became a true member of humanity, and in humility died for us while in human form.

It was necessary for the Savior to be born as a human under the same law that was broken by every human being. Since man is the one who sinned, it follows that the one who pays the penalty had to be a man. It was essential that a human being take our place (die as a sacrifice on our behalf) to pay the penalty for all of our sins. As a man, Christ could represent humanity. No one else, even an angel, would qualify.

The Bible declares that Jesus "shared in [our] humanity" (Hebrews 2:14). Jesus understands our struggles because He faced them as a human being on earth.

Jesus mediates between God and people. As humanity's representative, He intercedes for us before God. As God's representative, He brings us God's salvation and assures us of God's love and forgiveness.

The Savior must be without sin

In the Torah (Leviticus), the Law of God required the sacrifice offered on the altar to be without blemish. Only the sinless could qualify as a substitute for the guilty. Because Jesus did not sin, He qualified as the sacrifice without blemish for our sins. The Savior could not Himself be a sinner. If He were a sinner,

- He would not have been an acceptable sacrifice.

- He would be dying as a penalty for His own sins and certainly not for the sins of others.

- He could not be the Source of righteousness and eternal life to His followers.

The Savior must be Divine

To take away the sins of the world, the Savior had to pay the full price. Who but a wholly righteous One could satisfy the demand of God's justice? The sacrifice had to be of a value equivalent to the number of souls to be redeemed. Nothing but the blood of God's Perfect Lamb was sufficient to wash away all the sins of mankind committed against God! So God sent perfection personified. Christ died so that we could be forgiven and have eternal life.

Only God in the flesh could defeat Satan and set free those whom Satan held captive. Everything Jesus did derived unique significance from His divine identity. The Savior descended to us from God so He could lift us up to God.

The Savior must have the fullness of God

Jesus shares the very nature of God. This mystery is described in the Bible: "For in Christ all the fullness of the Deity [Godhead] lives in bodily form" (Colossians 2:9).

Jesus said, "I am the life" (John 14:6). The moment you believe in who Jesus is and invite Him to enter your life; Jesus will enter your life and give you the abundant and eternal life God created you to enjoy. You will be full of life.

Jesus alone qualified as the connecting link between God and man. The gulf between heaven and earth was bridged by the coming of Jesus. None but Jesus Christ could give spiritual life to all those who believe in Him.

The union of Godhead and manhood—in the person of Jesus—made it possible for man and God to be united forever! Jesus promised He would enter (through His Spirit) the life of every believer in Him when He said, "Here I am! I stand at the door [door of your heart] and knock. If anyone hears my voice and opens the door, I will come in . . ." (Revelation 3:20).

The awesome truth is that the moment you believe in Jesus, you become united to God. Jesus prayed, ". . . I pray also for those who will believe in me . . . Father, just as you are in me and I am in you. May they also be in us . . . I in them and you in me . . ." (John 17:20–23). A marvelous transformation and inheritance awaits those who believe in Jesus.

19

THE INCARNATION OF JESUS

According to the teaching of most Muslims, God is completely transcendent—distant physically, spiritually, and emotionally from the created world. According to the Bible, God is not entirely separated from His people. Christ's miraculous *incarnation* (God coming in the form of man) was God's plan to redeem all people.

The union of deity and humanity in Christ

God took on human nature alongside His divine nature without ceasing to be God. Christ has always existed. He came in a tangible form when He was born in Bethlehem. In a prophecy of the Messiah, Isaiah foretold the union of deity and humanity in Christ, "For to us a child is born, to us a son is given, and the government will be on his shoulders. And he will be called Wonderful Counselor, Mighty God, Everlasting Father, Prince of Peace" (Isaiah 9:6). A Child would be born (a reference to His humanity) who would also be Mighty God (a reference to His deity).

In the Gospel presented by Luke, we read that the angel Gabriel (*Jibraile*) appeared to the Virgin Mary and spoke these words: "Do not be afraid, Mary, you have found favor with God. You will be with child and give birth to a son, and you are to give him the name Jesus. He will be great and will be called the Son of the Most High" (Luke 1:30–32).

The Bible explains, in Philippians 2:5–11:

> Your attitude should be the same as that of Christ Jesus: Who, being in very nature God, did not consider equality with God something to be grasped, but made himself nothing, taking the very nature of a servant, being made in human likeness. And being found in appearance as a man, he humbled himself and became obedient to death—even death on a cross! Therefore God exalted him to the highest place and gave him the name that is above every name, that at the name of Jesus every knee should bow, in heaven and on earth and under the earth, and every tongue confess that Jesus Christ is Lord, to the glory of God the Father.

These passages in Philippians reveal truths about the nature and work of Christ. "Being in very nature God" refers to Christ's divine nature. He shares the very essence of God; Christ is united to God in one spirit throughout eternity. When Christ came to earth, He humbly took on an additional nature (a human nature) and appeared in our world as a man. He had two natures—one divine and one human—that were unified in one body.

Jesus submitted to the Father's will

The passage continues by saying Jesus "made Himself nothing," which does not mean He gave up or surrendered His divine nature. It means He voluntarily submitted Himself to serve the will of the Father. And "taking the very nature of a servant."

This passage in Philippians reminds me of a true story of a noble King whose kingdom was invaded by an evil enemy. The enemy captured many of his people and used them as slaves in a remote place. The king's only son, the prince, agreed with his father's desire to be sent to this remote place. The prince wore the cloth of a common person and went where his people suffered as slaves. Then at the right time the prince used his power and influence and set his people free from the captivity of the enemy. The son restored the honor of his father and his kingdom.

We read in the Bible about Jesus: "For you know the grace of our Lord Jesus Christ, that though he was rich, yet for your sakes he became poor, so that you through his poverty might become rich" (2 Corinthians 8:9).

Note that while He lived on earth, Christ's glory remained veiled to most people. He used His divine power only according to the will of the Father. He did not use His supernatural powers to alleviate His own human suffering or for any personal gain (Matthew 8:20).

The verses in Philippians 2:5–11 convey God's immeasurable love for humanity and encourage us to have humility of mind and to follow the example of Christ. The Son of God sacrificed greatly when He voluntarily left glory (relinquished His pre-incarnate position of glory) and acquired a human body. He lived as a servant and then died on the cross for our sins. Therefore, "God exalted him to the highest place and gave him the name that is above every name!" (Philippians 2:9).

THE PURPOSE OF JESUS' INCARNATION

1) It proved God's supreme love for us even in our fallen condition because He did not abandon the human race when it was infected by sin. Instead, He sent the Savior.

2) It accomplished God's plan by providing an acceptable sacrifice of Himself on our behalf to remove our sin.

3) It showed God's intense condemnation of sin.

4) Jesus destroyed the work of Satan (1 John 3:8; Colossians 2:15).

Consider these other important aspects of the incarnation:

- God revealed Himself to us in Jesus, so we can know Him and relate to Him (John 17:26). It takes God to reveal God.

- Jesus provided an example for our lives by His living in total submission to God's will. We are told in the Bible to "walk as Jesus did" (I John 2:6).

- Jesus demonstrated how we are to love our neighbor as we love ourselves, and even to love our enemies (Matthew 5:44). He taught, ". . . Love your enemies, do good to those who hate you, bless those who curse you, pray for those who mistreat you. If someone strikes you on one cheek, turn to him the other also . . . Give to everyone who asks you . . . Do to others as you would have them do to you. Forgive those who sin against you" (Luke 6:27–31).

- Jesus taught us to serve one another. For example, when He washed and dried the feet of His disciples, He said to them, "I have set you an example that you should do as I have done for you" (John 13:15).

God's amazing grace toward us

The incarnation of Jesus opens our eyes to the value God places on human life. It assures the powerful, deep love God has for you and me. He even came for us while we were still in our sinful and fallen state.

The life of Jesus Christ was so precious that it qualified to pay what was owed for the sins of the whole world. That is God's amazing grace toward us!

Man could never pay his own debt

Man attempts to save himself. He knows that he has sinned and tries to make right the wrong he has done against God.

However, man's debt is so great that he can never pay it. Only God could satisfy His own demand for the payment of our sin.

Man's sin resulted in separation from God because a sinful man cannot stand before a holy God. So the love of God extends grace to sinful man through the only vessel that God can use—Jesus Christ. Salvation is accomplished by God, for no mere man has the power or the right to earn it by works.

Jesus Christ fulfilled the Law's requirements

Jesus assumed our human position, and in the form of man took the entire burden (judgment) of our sin upon Himself. He fulfilled the requirement of the Law by never committing a single sin and then dying as a man, shedding His blood for all our sins against God. Christ fulfilled the will of God on our behalf. In relation to our sins, we see in Christ both the judgment and the mercy of God. We see God as both the *Just* and the *Justifier*.

God is just. The Judge of all the earth had to do right. Sin was a violation of the holy Law of God according to God's moral order. Therefore, it was impossible for God to deal lightly with sin. Forgiveness of sin had to be on basis that would satisfy the perfect standard of the holiness and justice of God. Through the sacrifice of Jesus Christ, God satisfied His righteous justice.

God made it possible for our sins to be pardoned without endorsing them. God cannot condone our sins, for He cannot compromise or lower His holy standard.

Since all men are sinners, God Himself had to provide the sinless man. Jesus paid the price for us when He willingly bore the punishment in our place. God is still God and the consequence of sin is still death. Through Jesus, however, we can be saved and have eternal life. God is greater (Allah akbar). Glory to God!

Jesus traded our sins for His righteousness

To emphasize, we sinners could never erase our debt. The holiness and the justice of God demands payment that has always been humanly impossible. So God Himself paid the debt by offering the ultimate sacrifice. He was motivated by His perfect love for you and me. The price was paid on the cross where Jesus Christ bore our sins.

Jesus suffered greatly to redeem us

Jesus suffered not only the excruciating physical pain of crucifixion, but the spiritual agony of separation from God. Their fellowship was broken because God's wrath against sin fell upon Jesus while He hung on the cross. This time of separation between the Son and the Father is beyond our human understanding.

God did not refrain from the ultimate sacrifice. Jesus endured death on the cross. His purpose was—and is—that we could be saved from hell, where there is eternal separation from God. Jesus accepted a temporary separation from God to rescue us from our destined eternal separation from God.

The awesome wonder of the Incarnation

The incarnation of Christ leads us to an awesome wonder. ". . . Great is the mystery of godliness: God was manifested in the flesh" (1 Timothy 3:16 NKJV). What a wonder! The eternal One entered time, became a man, and walked among us! The Gospel reveals, "The Word became flesh and dwelt among us, and we beheld His glory" (John 1:14 NKJV).

Before you read more Glad News, please stop and say a prayer. Ask God to guide you to His truth, to an understanding of His Word. Believe that God desires to pour out His love on you. You might be thinking you don't deserve God's love. None of us deserves God's awesome love. The Bible declares that in spite of our unworthiness, God loves us with an everlasting love. God wants you to receive His love by opening your heart to Him and letting Him show you how much He loves you.

God is waiting for you to give Him your burdens. He promises to take good care of you. God wants you to feel comfortable. The Bible tells us "Cast all your anxiety on him because he cares for you" (1 Peter 5:7).

Remember that the more you believe Jesus' words and obey God by faith, the more you will sing and jump with joy.

THE CRUCIFIXION AND RESURRECTION OF JESUS CHRIST

20

THE CRUCIFIXION OF CHRIST
ACCORDING TO ISLAM

In this chapter we will address the question of whether Jesus
was crucified and if God foresaw and allowed His crucifixion.

**Muslims teach Jesus is an honorable prophet; therefore, He
could not have been crucified**

Many Muslims say that God would never have allowed the
Jews to crucify Jesus, who is honored in the Qur'an as a great
prophet. I would like to remind these beloved Muslims of verses from the Qur'an that teach of *messengers* (prophets) of God
who were killed:

. . . in that they [the Jews] broke their covenant; that
they rejected the Signs of Allah; That they slew the
messengers in defiance of right . . . (Surah 4:155)

. . . that whenever there comes to you [the Jews] a
Messenger with what ye yourselves desire not, ye are
puffed up with pride? Some ye called impostors, and
others ye slay. (Surah 2:87) (Also see Surah 2:91 and
Surah 3:183.)

I just thought about an interesting observation. Muslims
and Christians agree that God's prophets represent God's feelings and thoughts. If we also agree that many of them suffered in the process of representing God and communicating
God's message, then Muslim teachers should not think that it
is strange that God, who sent the prophets, also suffered for
our sakes through the person of Jesus Christ.

I know that Muslim teachers view a prophet killed at the hand of his enemies as a defeat. For this reason, I'd like to present to you this question: which of the following choices honors Jesus most and brings glory to God?

1. If Jesus used violence to attack the people that were trying to arrest Him,

2. If Jesus escaped, or

3. If Jesus took the worst His enemies could inflict on Him (death on the cross), then publicly conquered death by resurrecting from the dead.

Obviously this third action will bring the most glory to God, and it is exactly what the Bible declares that Jesus did.

The Qur'an's vague account of Jesus' crucifixion

In the entire Qur'an, there is only one passage that mentions the crucifixion. Surah 4:157–158, states: "That they said (in boast), 'We killed Christ Jesus the son of Mary, The Messenger of Allah'—But they killed him not, nor crucified him, but so it was made to appear to them . . . For of a surety they killed him not, Nay, Allah raised him up unto Himself. . . ."

The subject of this passage is not Jesus; it is actually the Jews. This passage is not dealing with whether or not Jesus was killed, but rather with who killed Him.

To whom was the Qur'an referring when he said, "They killed him not, nor crucified him"? The answer from the context is, of course, the unbelieving Jews. The purpose of this verse is not to deny that Jesus was killed or crucified. It merely states that "they" (the Jews) did not kill or crucify Him. This verse denies the proud Jewish boast that they killed Jesus.

Jesus' crucifixion and God's master plan of salvation

The Gospel teaches that the crucifixion of Jesus was according to God's "set purpose and foreknowledge" (Acts 2:23). The cross was the centerpiece of God's work of salvation for us! Let us consider the words of Jesus the week before His self-sacrifice. According to the Gospel account, Pilate claimed to have the power of life or death over Jesus. However, Jesus declared that Pilate was only carrying out the will of God the Father when he gave Him over to be crucified. Jesus answered Pilate saying, "You would have no power over me if it were not given to you from above" (John 19:11).

Christians know and believe, based on the Bible, that God was the primary cause for Jesus' crucifixion. It is revealed throughout the Bible that Christ's coming, crucifixion, and resurrection were planned by God before the world began. It was a glorious plan out of God's great love and grace for fallen man to be redeemed and reconciled to Him! Concerning God's salvation plan, the prophet Isaiah foretold:

> Yet it pleased the Lord to bruise Him; He has put Him to grief. When You make His soul an offering for sin, He shall see His seed, He shall prolong His days, and the pleasure of the Lord shall prosper in His hand. (Isaiah 53:10 NKJV)

The Qur'an also states that God allowed Jesus to die and then raised Him up after His death. ". . . Allah said: 'O Jesus! I will take thee and raise thee to Myself And clear thee (of the falsehoods) of those who blaspheme; I will make those who follow thee superior to those who reject faith to the Day of Resurrection . . ." (Surah 3:55). The words, "I will take thee," in the original Arabic are *Innii mutawaffiika*, which means "I will cause you to die." This verse clearly confirms that it was God who caused the death of Jesus.

"THE SUBSTITUTION THEORY"

Muslim scholars generally teach that Jesus was substituted when He faced arrest and death. They believe God changed the face of someone else making that man look like Jesus. So when the Jews and Romans tried to arrest Jesus, they thought the substitute was Jesus and arrested and crucified him by mistake. Most of the Muslim scholars believe that at the very moment of this substitution, God lifted Jesus up bodily into heaven. Note that the Muslim scholars are not in agreement as to the identity of the substituted person who supposedly replaced Jesus.

"The Substitution Theory" challenged

The Muslim scholars base their belief in the substitution theory upon this one unclear verse that states: "but so it was made to appear to them" (Surah 4:157). Christian scholar E. E. Elder comments on this verse and clarifies:

> There is no mention of a substitute here, or anywhere else in the Qur'an. It seems obvious that "it" cannot refer to Jesus. It certainly must refer to something else that has been mentioned. Now the phrase could be translated, "it was made a misunderstanding—a perplexity to them." In that case the subject understood would refer to His crucifixion. The verse could then be properly translated, "yet they slew him not, and they crucified him not—but it (Jesus' crucifixion) was made a misunderstanding to them." His crucifixion perplexed them. They saw the event, but failed to appreciate its inner meaning. They even thought that they had power over his life.[1]

Therefore, it is not possible to reach a definitive conclusion based on this single and ambiguous verse in the Qur'an. One possible way to interpret Surah 4:157–158 is that the unbelieving Jews intended for the crucifixion of Jesus to shame Him in the eyes of the world. The ridicule He would suffer would then destroy Him in the hearts and eyes of the people. Also, His death would invalidate His mission. However, the Jews failed to accomplish that goal. On the contrary, by the crucifixion, the name and person of Jesus was glorified when God later raised Him up to be with Him.

Ironically, what Satan (through unbelieving Jews) used to kill Jesus, God the Father used to exalt the Christ. The Gospel notes that on the cross Jesus "disarmed the [evil] powers and authorities, he made a public spectacle of them, triumphing over them by the cross" (Colossians 2:15). Again, the crucifixion actually fulfilled God's plan. God won the victory by the cross by raising Jesus from the dead!

"The Substitution Theory" examined

Not only is the Qur'an's teaching about the crucifixion brief and vague, but the substitution theory itself cannot be believed on moral and logical grounds for the following reasons:

- What kind of God would take a person and change his appearance to look like Jesus so that he would be subject to arrest and then crucifixion in place of Jesus? The substitution theory portrays God as guilty of misrepresenting one man as another, which is misleading and dishonest. We know that God does not lie.

- Why should anyone innocent of a capital crime suffer crucifixion? Why would God cause an innocent substitute person to be killed? He did not have to give someone else to the Jews to crucify. That isn't consistent with the character of a loving, just, and merciful God.

- Some Muslims believe that the crucifixion was God's way of rescuing Jesus. However, if God's motive had been merely to rescue Jesus, He could have displayed

His power using a less complicated miracle and one not involving the agony of the cross—such as angelic intervention.

- Based on teachings in the Qur'an and the Bible, Jesus could have saved Himself because He had the ability to know the unseen and the power to raise the dead. He was capable of performing incredible miracles, and He dwelt in the continuous company of the Holy Spirit.

- The Gospel records the words of Jesus while on the cross. All of the verses confirm that the person on the cross could only be Jesus. One example is Jesus' prayer for His enemies in Luke 23:34: "Father, forgive them, for they do not know what they are doing." Can you imagine an innocent person hanging on the cross while having an attitude of forgiveness toward those who were crucifying him? Only the holy and humble Servant Jesus could do this!

- Based on the teachings of the Qur'an and the Bible about the pure character of Christ, He would never permit another man—even Judas—to take His place on the cross and suffer the consequences of His own teachings and mission.

- What kind of God would allow Mary, the mother of Jesus, and His beloved friends to suffer in such a way? For they stood at the cross watching the agony of the one whom they thought to be Jesus (John 19:25–27). Would God allow His followers to go through this torturous experience because of an illusion that He Himself had orchestrated?

- Is it reasonable to believe that the faithful and true God would mislead Jesus' devoted disciples by casting Jesus' likeness upon someone else, making another man look like Jesus? It is because the man who hung and died on the cross looked exactly like Jesus that the disciples of Jesus believed and proclaimed Jesus' crucifixion and death.

- More than 2 billion people today all over the world base their faith on the historicity of the crucifixion and the resurrection of Jesus!

My Muslim friend, is it logical to believe that God would allow the foundation of the Christian faith to be based on a misidentification that God Himself orchestrated? Such a theory would make God the author of the biggest hoax in human history. This cannot be. By nature, He is a just and holy God who does only what is right! (1 Peter 1:15).

Islam does not deny the crucifixion

I ask you, my friend, to please recognize that Islam *does not entirely* deny the story of the crucifixion, as people usually think. According to the teachings of the Muslim scholars:

- Islam accepts that the Jews plotted to crucify Jesus.

- Islam accepts that Jesus was present on a certain day and that the Jews were seeking to arrest Him.

- Islam accepts that Jesus remained unwavering in loyalty to His mission. He did not escape and was ready to face His arrest.

- Islam accepts that the man arrested appeared to the Jews to look exactly like Jesus, and that the man who died on the Cross looked exactly like Jesus. Everyone present at the cross recognized him to be Jesus.

Significantly, the only part of the crucifixion event which most Muslim scholars deny is that the person who died on the cross was actually Jesus!

Various Muslim beliefs concerning Jesus' death

In view of Surah 4:157–158, the majority of the Muslim scholars believe Jesus did not die at all, but that God lifted Him up bodily into heaven—that He ascended alive to heaven. They believe this is how His life on earth ended.

On the other hand, well-regarded Muslim scholars disagree. They point out Surahs in the Qur'an that record Jesus' death. One such passage is Surah 19:33, which clearly records the death of Jesus. In this passage, Jesus is quoted as saying, "So peace is on me the day I was born, the day that I die, and the day that I shall be raised up to life (again)." Clearly these are successive days: The day of birth, the day of His death and the day He shall be resurrected. According to the interpretation of these Muslim scholars, this verse reveals that Jesus died prior to being brought back to life.

Two contradicting Muslim views exist. While the Qur'an frequently refers to the death of Jesus, other teaching indicates that He ascended into heaven without dying at all. Some Muslim scholars, in an attempt to reconcile these views, teach that Christ will come back to this world some day to do many great and wonderful things, and then He will die.

The evidence disproving this teaching is Surah 19:33 which does not describe the sequence of Jesus' life as first, birth ("The day I was born"); second, resurrection ("The day I shall be raised up"); third, death ("The day that I die").

Nowhere does the Qur'an state that Jesus is yet to die!

Other verses in the Qur'an that discuss the death of Jesus use the past tense, indicating it has already happened.

For example, we read an identical passage in Surah 19:15 about Yahya (John the Baptist): "So peace on him the day he was born, the day that he dies, and the day that he will be raised up to life (again)!"

It is a recognized fact that Yahya died and was buried. And the reference to being "raised to life again" refers to the Day of Resurrection. Abdullah Yusuf Ali comments on this passage: "This is spoken as in the lifetime of Yahya. Peace and Allah's Blessings were on him when he was born; they continue when he is about to die an unjust death at the hands of the tyrant; and they will be especially manifest at the Day of Judgement."[2] Therefore, according to the meaning of the parallel verse, Jesus likewise died.

Muslim scholar A. H. Obaray also comments on Surah 19:33. He believes Jesus did die and He will not return to die. He writes: "No Muslim will shift the death of John to the future. All know that John died . . . Since no one can now shift the death of John to the future, therefore no one can now shift the death of Jesus to the future. In fact there is not one single passage throughout the Qur'an showing that Jesus will return to die. The parallel statement with regard to John, who died, clearly shows that Jesus also died."[3]

Other such passages that speak of the death of Jesus include Surah 3:55 and Surah 5:117, which states: ". . . when thou didst take me up . . ." Other translations of this verse in the Qur'an read: "take me to thyself" and "cause me to die" (tawaffaitani).

The expression tawaffaitani is explained by Dr. Mahmud Shaltut, one of the previous presidents of Al Azhar University:[4] "(It) is entitled in this verse to bear the meaning of ordinary death . . . there is no way to interpret 'death' as occurring after his return from heaven . . . because the verse very clearly limits the connection of Jesus . . . to his own people of his own day and the connection is not with the people living at the time when he returns."[5]

Many Muslim scholars continue to struggle with these verses that refer to the death of Jesus.

Various Muslim theories concerning Jesus' death

Abdullah Yusuf Ali commented on Surah 4:157, which states: "But they killed him not, nor crucified him." Ali said, "The end of the life of Jesus on earth is as much involved in *mystery* as his birth."[6] And regarding Surah 4:158, which states: "Nay, Allah raised him up unto himself," Ali writes:

> There is difference of opinion as to the exact interpretation of this verse. The words are: The Jews did not kill Jesus, but Allah raised him up to Himself. One school holds that Jesus did not die the usual human death, but still lives in the body in heaven, which is the generally accepted Muslim view. Another holds that he did die but not when he was supposed to be crucified, and that his being "raised up" unto Allah means that instead of being disgraced as a malefactor, as the Jews intended, he was on the contrary honored by Allah as His Messenger.[7]

Distinguished Muslim scholars and commentators such as Zamakshari, Ibn Abbas, and others state that Christ remained dead for several hours before being raised to heaven. In addition, Al-Razi records that some Muslim theologians believe Jesus was dead for three hours and others say seven hours.[8]

Maududi, a renowned modern Muslim scholar in Pakistan, comments on Surah 4:157: "After this, God who can do any and everything He wills, raised Jesus to Himself and rescued him from crucifixion and the one who was crucified afterwards was somehow or other taken for Christ."[9] Note the vagueness in his statement.

Daryabadi, another noted Pakastani Muslim theologian says, "It was not Jesus who was executed but another, who was miraculously substituted (how and in what way is another question, and is not touched upon in the Qur'an) for him."[10] This statement regarding the crucifixion also is obscure.

The Qur'an does not disqualify the Biblical account

Because of the vague, limited, and apparently contradictory verses in the Qur'an, Muslim scholars are unsure about the end of the life of Jesus on earth. They disagree about whether He died on earth or was raised alive to heaven without dying at all. Since these scholars have no definitive evidence or specific information regarding the circumstances of the crucifixion, their differing conclusions involve speculation and theory.

My dear reader, since there is confusion among Muslim scholars about Jesus' death, Islam does allow for the possibility that the Biblical account is accurate. As previously stated, the Qur'an does recognize the Bible as the primary source of enlightenment, as clearly indicated in Surah 10:94. Now let us go to the next chapter and examine the Biblical account of Jesus' crucifixion and resurrection.

21

THE CRUCIFIXION AND RESURRECTION OF JESUS ACCORDING TO THE GOSPEL

All of the accounts in the Gospel are specific and consistent that Christ was crucified, He died, and He rose from the dead.

Foundational faith of followers of Christ

For nearly two thousand years, all true followers of Christ throughout the world have believed in the crucifixion, death, and resurrection of Jesus Christ because of the clear testimonies in the Bible to these facts.

We can trust the Bible and what it says about Jesus' crucifixion because it records the testimony of eyewitnesses. The Bible records what took place in public.

For example, the Apostle Peter, speaking to the Jews after the healing of a crippled man, boldly stated, "Then know this, you and all the people of Israel: It is by the name of Jesus Christ of Nazareth, whom you crucified but whom God raised from the dead, that this man stands before you healed" (Acts 4:10).

Seven weeks after Jesus' crucifixion, Peter said to a great multitude of Jews: "Men of Israel, listen to this: Jesus of Nazareth was a man accredited by God to you by miracles, wonders and signs which God did among you through him, as you yourselves know. This man was handed over to you by God's set purpose and foreknowledge; and you, with the help of wicked men, put him to death by nailing him to the cross. But

God raised him from the dead, freeing him from the agony of death, because it was impossible for death to keep its hold on him" (Acts 2: 22–24).

When Peter said these words to the Jews that were there, they never denied that they crucified Jesus. The Bible records that 3,000 of them put their faith in Jesus after Peter finished speaking to them. Would they have believed in Jesus if they had any doubt that he was really crucified?

It was the mission of Jesus to die on the cross as the final and perfect sacrifice, once and for all! As Jesus approached His crucifixion, He said: "Now my heart is troubled, and what shall I say? Father, save me from this hour? No, it was for this very reason I came to this hour. Father, glorify your name!" (John 12:27).

And in the Gospel, Jesus predicts His own death and resurrection to His twelve disciples:

"Jesus took the twelve aside and told them, "We are going up to Jerusalem, and everything that is written by the prophets about the Son of Man will be fulfilled. He will be handed over to the Gentiles. They will mock him, insult him, spit on him, flog him and kill him. On the third day he will rise again." (Luke 18:31–33). See also John 2:19–21.

OLD TESTAMENT PROPHECIES REGARDING JESUS' CRUCIFIXION

The New Testament was written after the crucifixion and contains details of it; the Old Testament was written hundreds of years before the crucifixion and contains amazing prophecies about it. Two of these amazing specific prophecies are found in Isaiah 53 and Psalm 22.

Jesus' death and burial

Isaiah 53:9 gives specific details in advance about the death of Jesus: "He was assigned a grave with the wicked, and with the rich in his death . . ." No one at the time of the prophet Isaiah could understand the meaning of this prophecy. It did not make sense at face value. The account of His burial appeared to be a contradiction. Was He buried with the outcasts or was He buried with the noble and rich?

Both seemingly contradictory statements regarding Jesus' burial in Isaiah 53:9 came to pass. First of all, Jesus "was assigned a grave with the wicked," fulfilling the first part of the prophecy, because He was crucified between two thieves. According to Roman law, criminals that were crucified were assigned to be thrown into a burning pit and cremated. However for Jesus, this was not carried out.

The second half of this prophecy was fulfilled when Jesus was buried in the tomb of a rich man, Joseph of Arimathea. In the Gospel, Matthew 27:57–60 reads: "As evening approached, there came a rich man from Arimathea, named Joseph, who had himself become a disciple of Jesus. Going to Pilate, he asked for Jesus' body, and Pilate ordered that it be given to him. Joseph took the body, wrapped it in a clean linen cloth, and placed it in his own new tomb that he had cut out of the rock." Thus, what seemed an unexplained paradox in Isaiah 53 was easily understood when Jesus came and fulfilled the prophecy!

The dividing of Christ's clothes

Other prophetic words of Christ's crucifixion are found in Psalm 22:18: "They divide my garments among them and cast lots for my clothing." This verse was a mystery to the people at that time. It seemed as though the prophecy contained a contradiction. Did they take the clothes and divide them among themselves, or did they cast lots to see who would get them?

The fulfillment of this prophecy is documented in John 19:23–24. When the soldiers crucified Jesus, they took His clothes and divided them into four shares, one for each of them. But the undergarment remained. It was seamless and woven in one piece from top to bottom. In effect, the soldiers said to one another, "Let's not tear it, let's decide by lot who will get it." Then, not realizing that they were doing what the prophet predicted, they gambled to see who would win it. This action happened that the Scripture might be fulfilled which said, "They divide my garments among them and cast lots for my clothing." So that is what the soldiers did. The prophecy of Psalm 22:18 was explained and fulfilled to the letter at the foot of the Cross.

Incidentally, the Jews in the first century who rejected Jesus as the Son of God and their Savior dared not delete from their sacred Scripture any one of the numerous Messianic prophecies that were fulfilled in Jesus. If they did not delete scripture at this crucial time in their religious history how could they be suspected of altering it 600 years later when Islam appeared on the scene?

Historicity of the crucifixion

The crucifixion of Jesus is a well-attested event in history. Modern historians agree that Jesus was a historical character and that He was crucified. Even one of the most acclaimed Muslim writers in the history of Egypt, Abaas Mahmood Al Akad, (who lived in the 19th century) wrote a book about the life of Christ, in which he confirmed that we can depend on the four Gospels (the books of Matthew, Mark, Luke, and John) as historical evidence to know what happened in Jesus' life.[1]

Jesus' death is directly mentioned more than a hundred and fifty times in the New Testament. For example, see Matthew 27:50, John 19:30, John 19:33–35, and Luke 23:46.

Again, it is not rational to believe the claim, made more than 600 years after Christ's crucifixion, that the person crucified was not Christ but rather a look-alike replacement. An analogy would be if a man were to come hundreds of years from now and tell the world that the person assassinated in America in the twentieth century was not Martin Luther King, Jr. himself, but rather someone who looked exactly like him.

Furthermore, if the biblical and other historic records of the crucifixion had been untrue, we would expect the Qur'an to have many verses stating that Jesus did not die on the cross. However, the amazing truth is that in more than 6,000 Qur'anic verses there is not a single one that clearly refutes Jesus' crucifixion. Not one verse indicates that the Gospel was incorrect on this point.

Jesus, a perfect example of what the word "Muslim" means

The word Muslim means one who surrenders and submits. If you want to know what a man looks like who is absolutely submitted to God, look to Jesus. Jesus was a perfect man. His crucifixion actually demonstrates the meaning of the word *Muslim*.

Jesus obeyed God the Father to the end. Note that Jesus submitted Himself to the will of His Father (leading Him to the cross to be sacrificed), just as Abraham's son submitted himself to the will of his father (leading him to the altar to be sacrificed). The crucifixion of Jesus represents the ultimate surrender to the will of God! Jesus said, "I have come down from heaven not to do my will but to do the will of him who sent me" (John 6:38).

With humility, we as followers of Christ view the crucifixion as the reason for giving the greatest honor to Jesus, who willingly took our place and punishment on the cross (Hebrews 12:2). We also stand in awe at the power of God in raising Jesus from the dead and accomplishing our salvation!

Jesus taught His followers what true submission to God really is. For example, Jesus taught us to pray that God's kingdom come and God's will be done here on earth as it is done in heaven (Matthew 6:10).

Also, Jesus taught us that the most important commandment is to love God with all our heart, soul, mind, and strength (Mark 12:28–31). Jesus taught us to give God all our hearts, our intellects, our will, our emotions, and our deeds and to live for God every day of our lives in full submission.

Records from Jewish historian Josephus (AD 37–100)

Regarding the crucifixion, most Muslims ignores not only the records of Matthew, Mark, Luke, and John, but the entire New Testament. Unfortunately, Muslim scholars also disregard the historical evidence. There are extensive writings by non-Christians since the time of Christ that have discussed Jesus and His crucifixion as a historical fact. Consider the non-Christian historian, Flavius Josephus. Born with the name Joseph ben Matthias, Josephus was a Jewish historian born of a priestly family, who descended from the Judaic royal lineage. He became a Pharisee devoted to the study of the Law of God and became a Roman citizen named "Flavius Josephus."

Josephus lived in the area of Jerusalem where he gained access to first hand information. He documented Jewish history and traditions for Rome.[2] With no ties to the Christian sect, there was no reason for him to fabricate his records. His background and qualifications validate his writings as valuable and objective documentation of the events in the life of Jesus (i.e., His crucifixion and resurrection). Regarding Jesus Christ, Josephus wrote:

> Now, there was about this time, Jesus, a wise man, if it be lawful to call him a man, for he was doer of wonderful works . . . a teacher of such men as receive the truth with pleasure. He drew over to him both many of the

Jews, and many of the Gentiles. He was "the" Christ; and when Pilate, at the suggestion of the principal men amongst us, had condemned him to the cross, those that loved him did not forsake him, for he appeared to them alive again the third day, as the divine prophets had foretold these . . . and the tribe of Christians, so named from him, are not extinct at this day.[3] (emphasis mine)

Josephus had access to individuals (both Christian and non-Christian) who had been eyewitnesses to the events surrounding the life, death, and resurrection of Jesus Christ. As a modern historian of his day, he was held responsible for the facts reported in his journals. His reports were under the scrutiny of diametrically opposed factions. To this day he is considered to be a reputable historian. Josephus also documented accounts of individuals who witnessed Jesus' miracles, His teaching, His arrest and trial, and His crucifixion and resurrection.

JESUS CAME BACK FROM THE DEAD!

Jesus' disciples believed in His resurrection because they actually saw Him alive after His death by crucifixion. One account of Jesus' resurrection is found in the following passage: "The angel said to the women, 'Do not be afraid, for I know that you are looking for Jesus, who was crucified. He is not here; he has risen, just as he said. Come and see the place where he lay. Then go quickly and tell his disciples: He has risen from the dead and is going ahead of you into Galilee. There you will see him. Now I have told you'" (Matthew 28:5–7).

The resurrection of Jesus was in bodily form. Jesus' body, which had been buried, was resurrected as a glorified body.

Jesus appears to His disciples

We read in the Bible: ". . . When the disciples were together with the doors locked for fear of the Jews, Jesus came and stood among them and said, "Peace be with you." After He said this, He showed them His hands and side. The disciples were overjoyed when they saw the Lord" (John 20:19–20).

Jesus Christ showed Himself to His disciples that they might see that He resurrected from the dead. Christ showed His disciples His hands and side that still had the marks and wounds of the cross in order that they might know that this man before them truly was Jesus who had been crucified. Jesus gave them unquestionable proof of His identity.

After Jesus rose from the dead, he personally spoke to Thomas who was doubting His resurrection, and said to him, "Put your finger here: see my hands. Reach out your hand and put it into my side. Stop doubting and believe" (John 20:27).

Because Thomas saw the physically resurrected Christ, he was inspired and compelled to preach the Gospel even in India. It is recorded that wherever he went he spoke about Jesus' death and resurrection. Thomas became a martyr because of this message that he proclaimed.

Hundreds of witnesses saw the risen Christ over a forty-day period in various locations and at various times. For example, Jesus was seen in His resurrected body by over 500 brethren at once (1 Corinthians 15:1–6). Please see other accounts of Jesus' resurrection in John 21:1–23, Mark 16:9–13 and Acts 1:3.

When you read John 20, you will know that there were eyewitnesses that Jesus' tomb was empty. The resurrection proclamation could not have been believed in Jerusalem if the emptiness of the tomb had not been established. Please read the testimony of Jesus that the Apostle Peter recorded in Acts 10:38–43.

The Holy Scriptures foretold Jesus' resurrection

God inspired David to foretell the resurrection of the Christ: "Therefore my heart is glad and my tongue rejoices; my body also will rest secure, because you will not abandon me to the grave, nor will you let your Holy One see decay" (Psalm 16:9–10).

The apostle Peter applied this prophecy to the resurrection of Jesus when he said to the Jews:

Men of Israel, listen to this: Jesus of Nazareth was a man accredited by God to you by miracles, wonders and signs, which God did among you through him, as you yourselves know. This man was handed over to you by God's set purpose and foreknowledge; and you, with the help of wicked men, put him to death by nailing him to the cross. But God raised him from the dead, freeing him from the agony of death, because it was impossible for death to keep its hold on him.

David said about him: ". . . because you will not abandon me to the grave, nor will you let your Holy One see decay . . ." Brothers, I can tell you confidently that the patriarch David died and was buried, and his tomb is here to this day. But he was a prophet and knew that God had promised him on oath that he would place one of his descendants on his throne. Seeing what was ahead, he spoke of the resurrection of the Christ, that he was not abandoned to the grave, nor did his body see decay. God has raised this Jesus to life, and we are all witnesses of the fact. (Acts 2:22–32)

Two credible professors speak out on historical evidence

Professor Thomas Arnold, the Lord Master of Rugby University, author of *The History of Rome* and the holder of the Chair of Modern History at Oxford University, was well equipped to evaluate evidence to determine historical fact. After carefully sifting the ancient documentation for the crucifixion and resurrection of Christ, this renowned, modern-day scholar wrote:

> I have been used for many years to study the histories of other times and to examine and weigh the evidence of those who have written about them. I know of no one fact in the history of mankind which is proven by better and fuller evidence of every sort, to the understanding of a fair inquirer, than the great sign which God has given us that Christ died and rose again from the dead.[4]

John Singleton Copley, a professor at Cambridge University, and Attorney General of Great Britain in 1824, rose to the highest office as judge in England. He was recognized as one of the greatest legal minds in British history. After his death, a document was found among his private papers in which he had written: "I know pretty well what evidence is and I tell you, such evidence as that for the resurrection has never been broken down yet."[5]

Historicity of the resurrection

Note that certain facts are undisputed even by secular (nonreligious) historians and they include:

- Jesus Christ was crucified and died.

- Jesus' tomb was empty after His burial. (John 20)

- There was a proclamation that Jesus had risen.

According to the Gospel, after Jesus Christ died by crucifixion, His body was taken down from the cross and laid in the tomb of Joseph of Arimathea. A large stone weighing between one and two tons was placed at the front of the tomb, and the Roman seal was placed on that stone. Well-trained Roman guards constantly watched and guarded the tomb. On the third day, the tomb was empty.

Following Jesus' arrest, His disciples were afraid. We read: "Then all the disciples deserted him and fled" (Matthew 26:56). However, several days after the resurrection, this same group became courageous. Their transformation occurred not only because they had seen an empty tomb, but because they had seen and experienced the risen Christ.

Credibility of Jesus' disciples

If someone were to ask, "Did the disciples lie?" the answer would be simple. What could they possibly gain by proclaiming that Jesus had risen and that they had seen Him alive? Prestige? Wealth? According to recorded tradition, Jude and Simon Peter were crucified; Luke was hanged from an olive tree; Paul was beheaded; Philip was scourged and crucified; James (son of Zebedee) was killed by the sword; Mark was dragged through the streets by his feet and then burned alive; James (half brother of Jesus) and Barnabas were stoned to death. This treatment was their earthly "reward" for proclaiming the Good News:

Jesus is risen, He is alive, He offers forgiveness of sins, and He gives eternal life to those who believe in Him!

Here I'd like to express an observation from my personal experience. I was a lawyer in Egypt. I worked for my father who had been a lawyer for about fifty years. My grandfather was also a lawyer for about fifty years. My older brother is currently a judge in the Supreme Court in Egypt. Most of my extended family is in the legal profession. We had never seen or heard of a witness who allowed himself to go to prison or to suffer for something that he knew was a lie.

SECTION EIGHT

THE ASCENSION AND RETURN OF JESUS CHRIST

22

THE ASCENSION OF JESUS

The ascension of Jesus is recorded in the Qur'an and is clearly explained in the Bible.

The ascension of Jesus in the Qur'an and in the Bible

It is clear from the Qur'an that Jesus was lifted up to be with God and is alive today. For example, Surah 4:158 states: ". . . Allah raised him unto Himself . . ."

In addition, there are many Hadiths supporting the ascension of Jesus. Generally, the Muslim world believes that God lifted up Jesus bodily into heaven and that He went up alive to heaven.

The Gospel records the ascension of Jesus in Mark 16:19: "After the Lord Jesus had spoken to them [His apostles], he was taken up into heaven . . ." See His ascension accounts also in Luke 24:49–53 and Acts 1:9–11.

We see that both the Qur'an and the Bible teach that Jesus ascended not just into heaven, but indeed into the ultimate presence of God. The Qur'an and the Bible agree on the fact that Jesus Christ is alive in heaven to this day.

Purpose of the ascension offered by Muslim scholars

Contrary to the Biblical records, many Muslim scholars claim that God raised Jesus to Himself in order to save Him from crucifixion by the Jews.

Again, it is difficult to accept the theory that ". . . God took Jesus up to Himself . . ." (in Surah 4:158) just as an escape route to rescue Him from the hands of the Jews. First of all,

God could have used a less severe way to deliver Jesus. An example is in the Gospel according to Matthew 2:13: When Herod wanted to kill Jesus, an angel warned Joseph in a dream and told him to take the Child and His mother and flee to Egypt.

Furthermore, Jesus could have saved Himself from the hands of the Jews. For according to the Bible (and the Qur'an agrees):

- Jesus had the ability to know the unseen (Surah 3:49).

- Jesus had the ability to perform miracles (Surah 5:110).

- Jesus had the ability to raise the dead (Surah 3:49 and 5:110).

The reason that Muslim scholars give is not sufficient to explain the fact that God chose to enjoy the presence of Jesus for nearly two thousand years since His death and ascension.

My dear Muslim friend, the logical conclusion is that God the Father desired to raise Jesus to be with Him. He certainly did not have to raise Him to save Him from the "murderous intentions of the unbelieving Jews."

Jesus abides in heaven with God the Father

The Qur'an does not explain why God desired to have Jesus leave earth to abide with Him in heaven in glory for the last 2,000 years. According to the Qur'an, Jesus was the only human (only prophet) to be raised off the earth into the very presence of God Himself. Note that this teaching leads us to wonder: How could a mere man be lifted up to be with God and withstand the majesty, the power, and holiness of the Most High?

The Bible explains the reason for Jesus' ascension

According to the Gospel, Jesus is the eternal Son of God, and heaven is His permanent home. Therefore, it was impossible for Him, after He accomplished His mission on earth, to return to dust like all other prophets and men naturally do. Rather, He returned to heaven. Jesus stated His mission when He said, "For I have come down from heaven not to do my will but to do the will of him who sent me" (John 6:38).

In John 3:13, Jesus spoke of Himself, saying, "No one has ever gone into heaven except the one who came from heaven— the Son of Man." And in John 8:23, we read that Jesus told the Jews, "You are from below; I am from above. You are of this world; I am not of this world."

The eternal Son of God returned to heaven

Remember, my dear Muslim reader, the Qur'an said in Surah 4:171 that Jesus is a "Spirit proceeding from God." It seems fitting then that only He who came from God could go back to be with God. And, of course, Jesus' ascension to heaven is logical if He is the eternal Son of God.

According to the Bible, after Jesus died and completed His work on the cross, He was reunited with the Father. The ascension of Christ meant the end of His earthly ministry and the beginning of His heavenly ministry. It also meant that God accepted Jesus' service and sacrifice on our behalf. Motivated by love, "Therefore he [Jesus] is able to save completely those who come to God through him, because he always lives to intercede [praying to the Father] for them" (Hebrews 7:25).

My dear friend, Jesus Christ is without a doubt, higher than all creation. He is alive with the Heavenly Father today! Isn't it amazing, my dear reader! Jesus' divine nature makes Him at home with the Majesty and Holiness of God the Father.

23

THE SECOND COMING OF JESUS

While Islam and Christianity differ on the details, both acknowledge that Jesus is coming back to earth. This event is referred to as the "Second Coming of Jesus."

The Qur'an and the Bible refer to Jesus' Second Coming

In the Qur'an, Surah 43:61 states: ". . . [Jesus] shall be A Sign (for the coming of) the Hour (of judgment) . . ." Abdullah Yusuf Ali commented on this verse in his translation of the Qur'an: "This is understood to refer to the second coming of Jesus in the Last Days before the resurrection when he will destroy the false doctrines that pass under his name."[1]

Throughout the centuries, most Muslim commentators have interpreted Surah 43:61 as a prophecy of Jesus' second coming. It is interesting, my dear Muslim friend, that this event is prophesied in the Old Testament. Daniel recorded:

> In my vision at night I looked, and there before me was one like a son of man [that is a human figure], coming with the clouds of heaven. He approached the Ancient of Days [Almighty God] and was led into his presence. He was given authority, glory and sovereign power; all peoples, nations and men of every language worshiped him. His dominion is an everlasting dominion that will not pass away, and his kingdom is one that will never be destroyed. (Daniel 7:13–14)

This passage in Daniel is a clear prophecy of the second coming of Jesus Christ that is confirmed in the Gospel in Mark

13:26, which reads: "At that time men will see the Son of Man coming in clouds with great power and glory."

According to Muslim theologians, Jesus will return from heaven heralding the climax of human history and will assume control over the whole world. Jesus alone is to herald the hour of judgment. Ibn-Atya, a distinguished Muslim commentator, states that "Muslim theologians are unanimous in contending that Jesus Christ is physically alive at present in heaven and is destined to return to this world . . . towards the approach of the Last Day."[2]

Certainly the Hadith teaches that Jesus will return from heaven in the last days. There are approximately seventy Traditions in support of the doctrine of the return of Jesus to earth. All of them are considered to be of unquestioned reliability.

Who is the Judge?

The Qur'an states clearly that God controls the Day of Judgment. "In the name of Allah . . . Master of the Day of Judgment" (Surah 1:1, 4).

Significantly, Muhammad said, "Surely (Jesus), the son of Mary will soon descend among you and will judge mankind justly (as a just ruler)."[3] Now, who exactly is this "man" who can judge every person justly? Don't you wonder, my friend?

Jesus is going to judge the world

It is logical that the One chosen to descend from heaven to bring the judgment of God will be the Son of God.

The Bible teaches that the Son of God, by coming in the likeness of man, has revealed God to men and has brought men face to face with God. He shall return to judge the earth. Jesus Himself declares, "Moreover, the Father judges no one, but has entrusted all judgment to the Son, that all may honor the Son just as they honor the Father. He who does not honor the Son does not honor the Father, who sent him" (John 5:22–23).

Jesus goes on to say, "For as the Father has life in himself, so he has granted the Son to have life in himself. And he has given him authority to judge because he is the Son of Man" (John 5:26–27).

When Jesus comes back to earth, He will be shining with all the brightness of His heavenly glory. A glimpse of Jesus' divine glory is recorded in the Gospel account of Matthew when He was momentarily *transfigured* on earth. On a high mountain (before three of His disciples), Jesus' "face shown like the sun, and his clothes became as white as the light" (Matthew 17:1–13). In harmony with this revelation, Suyuti comments on Surah 6:158: "Then the earth will shine with the light of its Lord and Jesus, Son of Mary, will descend." Jesus will appear from heaven in power and glory.

Jesus will be the most glorious sight that humans have ever seen. The Suffering Servant will come back as the Conquering King. He will put an end to evil and will rule with holy justice!

True believers will be transformed into Jesus' image

When Jesus comes back, He will transform His true followers (true believers) into His image, to share His glory with them forever. We read about this glorious promise in the Gospel: "But our citizenship is in heaven. And we eagerly await a Savior from there, the Lord Jesus Christ, who, by the power that enables him to bring everything under his control, will transform our lowly bodies so that they will be like his glorious body" (Philippians 3:20–21).

Jesus will give us new, glorified bodies suited for heaven. At Jesus' first coming He made Himself like us, whereas at

Jesus' second coming He will make us like Him. We read in the Bible:

"We know that when he appears, we shall be like him, for we shall see him as he is." (1 John 3:1–3)

"As was the earthly man [Adam], so are those who are of the earth; and as is the man from heaven [Jesus], so also are those who are of heaven. And just as we have born the likeness of the earthly man, so shall we bear the likeness of the man from heaven." (1 Corinthians 15:48–49)

Jesus will take believers to heaven to be with Him

My dear Muslim friend, the purpose of Jesus' coming into our world was to save us and give us eternal life. A part of the Good News of the Bible is that when Jesus descends from heaven, He will gather all people who believe in Him. Then we will join Him, ". . . and so we will be with the Lord forever . . ."! (1 Thessalonians 4:17)

We look forward to this glorious day when we will be with Jesus. He has promised us:

Let not your heart be troubled; you believe in God, believe also in Me. In My Father's house are many mansions; if it were not so I would have told you. I go to prepare a place for you. And if I go and prepare a place for you, I will come again and receive you to Myself; that where I am, there you may be also. (John 14:1–3 NKJV)

Islam teaches that Jesus alone will defeat the false christ

According to the Hadith, a false christ (*Dajjal*) will appear before the Hour of Doom. The Dajjal ("the deceiver" in Arabic) will pretend he is the Christ. (Note that the Bible identifies this individual as the Antichrist.) He will perform many miracles. According to the Hadith, the false christ will be the ultimate manifestation of evil. He will cause the greatest assault against the only true God. He will attempt to cause the greatest harm to mankind.

Muhammad said, "There would be no creation (creating more trouble) than the Dajjal right from The creation of Adam to the Last Hour."[4] We read in one of the Hadiths that Muhammad frequently prayed, "O Allah! I seek refuge with you from the punishment in the grave and from the punishment in The Hell fire and from the afflictions of life and death, and the afflictions of Al-Masih Ad-Dajjal."[5]

In the Hadith, it is recorded that Ayisha said: "I heard Allah's Apostle [Muhammad] in his prayer seeking refuge with Allah from the affliction of Al-Masih Ad-Dajjal."[6] Also in the Hadith, Christ (Isa) is the only One whom God will send to defeat the false Christ, save mankind, restore faith in the true God, and establish peace on earth!

According to the Hadith, Muhammad said, "Jesus, Son of Mary, will descend . . . and will lead them in prayer. When the enemy of Allah (the Dajjal) sees him, he will dissolve just as salt dissolves in water."[7] His statement is very thought-provoking, my dear reader! Only Jesus, without the assistance of other prophets or angels, is supposed to win the most tremendous and final battle in the history of humanity.

Muhammad also stated: "Then a people whom Allah had protected would come to Jesus, Son of Mary, and he would wipe their faces and would inform them of their ranks in Paradise."[8] How amazing! Who is this man who is supposed to tell people their degrees in Paradise before the day of judgment? Here Muhammad's teaching harmonizes with the Christian belief that Jesus knows the eternal destiny of all people. This parallel is just another example showing that Jesus is unique and more than a mere prophet!

Regarding the Dajjal, Muhammad said, "I warn you of him and there is no prophet who has not warned his people against the Dajjal."[9] Isn't it interesting, my dear Muslim reader, that according to Muhammad, every prophet came to warn his nation of the deception of the Dajjal, but Christ alone is supposed to come again to earth to destroy the *false christ* without even the assistance of an angel or prophet?

We read in the Bible: ". . . while we wait for the blessed hope—the glorious appearing of our great God and Savior, Jesus Christ, who gave Himself for us to redeem us from all wickedness and to purify for Himself a people that are his very own, eager to do what is good" (Titus 2:13–14).

24

THE UNIQUENESS OF JESUS COMPELS
A CONCLUSION

My dear Muslim friend, I hope you will continue to ask God to guide you to the straight path that leads to Him. God desires us to be sincere in evaluating and accepting the truth He reveals to us.

Jesus, more than a mere prophet

While Muhammad perceived Jesus Christ only as a prophet, the Qur'an and the Bible attributed to Him characteristics that only belong to God. The unique features of Jesus' life prove that He is more than a mere prophet. The prophets we have heard or read about were ordinary men. Each one was born of a father and a mother. They lived a normal life. Sometimes they did good things and other times they sinned against God and against fellow human beings. When their lives ended, they returned to the dust from where they came.

Consider again that both the Qur'an and the Gospel attribute three similar titles to Jesus that are consistent with the Christian belief that Jesus is Lord and Savior. These divine titles are: the *Word of God*, *Messiah*, and *Spirit from God*. According to the Bible, the eternal Spirit took on human flesh as Jesus Christ.

We learn from the Qur'an and the Bible that Jesus' life was unique. He was set apart even before conception. Jesus' virgin birth tells us that God made the only exception to the natural process of procreation, in having Jesus conceived by the power of God's Spirit. Jesus was also unique in His sinlessness, His ability to create life and raise the dead, perform the greatest miracles, His ascension, and His inevitable return to judge the world. Thus, His abilities and traits compel the conclusion that Jesus is more than just a prophet. He is the unique, eternal Son of God who came to save us!

There is considerable commonality between the Bible and the Qur'an regarding the person of Jesus Christ (AL-Masih, Isa). When you examine the parallels within them, God certainly will guide you to the complete truth.

The glorious and supernatural Person of Jesus

My beloved Muslim friends, please ask yourselves, why were all these unique and heavenly features found only in Jesus Christ?

Jesus' uniqueness is totally the result of the will and power of God. It was God that gave Jesus an exceptional life on earth.

When you prayerfully consider the unique features in Jesus' life, you will certainly discover that there is something majestic and heavenly about the Man Jesus. There is something particularly glorious and supernatural about the Person of Jesus! The idea that Jesus Christ was merely a prophet and messenger surely is unreasonable in the light of the evidence surrounding His life. My appeal to you, my Muslim friend, is to ponder and evaluate all the facts about Jesus presented in this book before making any judgment on the theological issue of His divine nature and divine mission!

Jesus was born and raised in a small village. He worked as a carpenter until He was 30. He never had a position in government. He had no money and never owned a house. He never had an army. He never fought a war or commanded His disciples to fight. He ministered only for three and a half years then His enemies arrested Him and crucified Him.

There has never been a prophet, military leader, educator, or king who has made a more positive impact on humanity than Jesus. Jesus Christ is superior to all others in His moral influence and in His promotion of human welfare.

Jesus was unique and superior in His teaching. For example, He taught:

"Love your enemies." (Matthew 5:44.)

"Love your neighbor as yourself." (Matthew 22:39.)

"Bless those who curse you, pray for those who mistreat you." (Luke 6:28.)

Humans are indeed weak, but God is able to empower us to live up to His highest standard.

If you read Jesus' teachings recorded in the Bible, you will discover that if people only obeyed what Jesus taught, all the problems in the world would be solved.

Two thousand years have passed since the death of Jesus, and He is still the most loved and honored person who ever lived. My precious reader, by the time you have finished reading this book you will discover that Jesus is unique and had a superior, positive impact on humanity because of who He is and because God sent Him to rescue us.

All these unique features in Jesus' life find their very meaning and significance in two essential doctrines of Christianity: First, Jesus is the eternal and unique Son of God. Second, Jesus is the Savior of mankind. After discovering the divine uniqueness of Jesus Christ, you can invite Him into your life as Savior and receive the free gift of eternal life!

THE MYTH OF THE THREE GODS
OF CHRISTIANITY

25

DO CHRISTIANS WORSHIP THREE GODS?

The Bible consistently reveals in at least 28 verses that there is only one God (Tawhid). Jesus Christ Himself quotes the famous passage in the Torah, Deuteronomy 6:4–5: "Hear, O Israel: The LORD our God, the LORD is one. Love the LORD your God with all your heart and with all your soul and with all your mind and with all your strength" (Mark 12:29–30).

The Bible teaches there is only one God

The first commandment God gave to Moses was, "You shall have no other gods before me" (Exodus 20:3). The Apostle Paul wrote, "There is no God but one" (1 Corinthians 8:4).

Numerous explicit statements in the Old and New Testaments declare that there is only one God of the entire universe. The Bible emphasizes monotheism and that God is one.

Old Testament examples include:

Deuteronomy 4:35, 39; 2 Samuel 7:22; 1 Kings 8:60; Isaiah 43:10–11; 45:5–6.

New Testament Examples include:

Romans 3:30; 1 Corinthians 8:4; Ephesians 4:6; Jude 25.

God is one essence revealed in three Persons

The Gospel recorded words Christ spoke to His disciples before He ascended:

"Therefore go and make disciples of all nations, baptizing them in the name of the Father and of the Son and of the Holy Spirit, and teaching them to obey everything I have commanded you. And surely I am with you always, to the very end of the age." (Matthew 28:19–20)

This passage refers to the Tri-unity of the one God. Note that Jesus used "in the name" (singular) not "in the names" (plural). Notice also that Jesus gave equal honor to the Father, the Son, and the Holy Spirit. Throughout the Gospel, the Son and the Holy Spirit are not associates or partners with God, but rather the three Persons constitute only one God.

My dear reader, it is important to know that the author of the Trinity (Tri-unity) is Jesus. Jesus' disciples and the early church arrived to faith in the Triune God as an understanding of what Jesus Christ had revealed.

Jesus talked about the Holy Spirit and told His disciples: "And I will ask the Father, and He will give you another Counselor to be with you forever—the Spirit of truth. The world cannot accept him, because it neither sees him nor knows him. But you know him, for he lives with you and will be in you" (John 14:16–17). Jesus also told them:

". . . The Counselor, the Holy Spirit, whom the Father will send in my name, will teach you all things, and will remind you of everything I have said to you" (John 14:26).

"When the Counselor comes whom I will send to you from the Father, the Spirit of Truth who goes out from the Father, he will testify about me" (John 15:26).

"But I tell you the truth: It is for your good that I am going away. Unless I go away, the Counselor will not come to you; but if I go, I will send him to you. When he comes, he will convict the world of guilt in regard to sin . . ." (John 16:7–8)

"I have much more to say to you, more than you can now bear. But when he, the Spirit of truth comes, he will guide you into all truth. He will not speak on his own; he will speak only what he hears, and he will tell you what is yet to come. He will bring glory to me by taking from what is mine and making it known to you. All that belongs to the Father is mine . . ." (John 16:12–15)

It is also clear throughout the Gospel that Jesus talked about Himself as the Son of God and of God as His Father. Jesus also said, "All things have been committed to me by my Father. No one knows the Son except the Father, and no one knows the Father except the Son and those to whom the Son chooses to reveal him" (Matthew 11: 27). Again, this statement would be blasphemy if Jesus were just a human being.

Jesus claimed absolute equality with the Father when He said: "I and the Father are one." Again the Jews picked up stones to stone him, but Jesus said to them, "I have shown you many great miracles from the Father. For which of these do you stone me?" "We are not stoning you for any of these," replied the Jews, "but for blasphemy, because you, a mere man, claim to be God" (John 10:30–33).

All these words that Jesus said clearly present to us God the Father, God the Son, God the Holy Spirit. The Holy Spirit is the person of God who lives within the believer.

GOD'S REVELATION OF HIMSELF

I noticed that Jesus made no serious attempt to explain the Tri-unity of God or to prove it to the people to whom He was speaking.

We read in the Gospel that Jesus said, "My teaching is not my own. It comes from him who sent me. If anyone chooses to do God's will, he will find out whether my teaching comes from God or whether I speak on my own" (John 7: 16, 17).

My dear reader, God reveals the Trinity to those who desires to know Him and do His will. This is something that God does not easily allow to be projected to the world and trampled on. Through understanding the Trinity, God is inviting sinners into an intimate relationship with Him, to experience Him as Father, and to be united to Him forever based on His grace and mercy. We read in the Bible: "For through him [Jesus] we both have access to the Father by one Spirit [Holy Spirit]" (Ephesians 2:18).

The Bible reveals to us that God wants us to relate intimately to Him through Father, Son, and Holy Spirit.

One day Jesus was alone with His disciples and asked them a question: "Who do people say the Son of Man is?" (Matthew 16:13) They replied, people are not sure who you are, but they agree that you are a Prophet. Then, Jesus asked them, "'But what about you? Who do you say I am?'" Simon Peter answered, 'You are the Christ, the Son of the Living God.' Jesus replied, 'Blessed are you, Simon son of Jonah, for this was not revealed to you by man, but by my Father in heaven . . .'" (Matthew 16:15–17).

Note, Jesus did not tell Peter that he was smarter than the others, but that he was blessed because his insight came only from God.

Any revelation of God's truth is a manifestation of His grace. The Tri-unity of God is the highest revelation God makes of Himself to His people as they sincerely and wholeheartedly seek Him.

My dear reader, I will do my best in this book to help you understand. But without a special revelation from God to your heart, mind, and soul, you will never believe.

The Bible teaches that the nature of God is compound, which means there is plurality in the oneness of God. In the book of Genesis we read: "Then God said, 'Let *Us* make man in *Our* image, in *Our* likeness, and let them rule over the fish of the sea and the birds of the air, over the livestock, over all the earth, and over all the creatures that move along the ground.' So God created man in *His* own image, in the image of God *He* created him; male and female *He* created them" (Genesis 1:26–27, italics added). The italics added in these verses emphasize the combination of singular and plural pronouns revealing the compound unity of God.

The Bible confirms the following truths:

1. God is one. He is also unique and undivided.

2. Within this one being there are three divine persons.

3. These divine persons are the Father, the Son, and the Holy Spirit.

4. The relationship among these divine persons is eternal. They have eternally existed in this unique relationship.

The Tri-unity of God is not based on philosophy. It is a revealed truth.

The Gospel teaches that within God (who is one being), there are three co-eternal and co-equal persons, they are the Father, the Son (Jesus, AL-Masih, the Word), and the Holy Spirit. They exist eternally within the being of God.

Note that when we refer to three Persons in the One Triune God, this word "person" is used in a different sense from its normal use in relation to human beings. Again, God is infinite.

Of course, the word "persons" is not adequate to express the divine concept. We must get out of our minds any human analogy. However, each possesses intelligence, emotion, and will.

Note that all true Christians believe in one God (Tawhid), and they regard *polytheists* (those who believe in more than one God) as unbelievers. God is one. This oneness of God is the most essential characteristic of the Trinity. According to the Christian belief in the absolute unity of one God, the Father is divine, the Son is divine, and the Holy Spirit is divine. The unity of God allows for the existence of three personal distinctions in the divine nature.

God is not merely one; He is the only God. God does not consist of parts. His unity is consistent with His Tri-unity. His oneness and unity is not a mere single unit as a table or a chair.

Misunderstanding of the Christian doctrine of the Trinity

Many Muslims mistakenly think that Christians believe in three gods: Mary, Jesus, and God. On this issue, Ibn Abbas writes: "What is meant by the Trinity is God the most high, His consort, and His Son."[1]

I will briefly mention some of the reasons behind this misunderstanding:

The Arabic word "thalatha" is mistranslated as "Trinity"

Thalatha appears nineteen times in the Qur'an where it is correctly translated as "three." Unfortunately, the word thalatha was mistranslated as "Trinity" by Abdullah Yusuf Ali. His translation of Surah 4:171 (from Arabic to English) reads, "Say not 'Trinity'" (The Qur'an in Arabic states "say not thalatha"). Again, thalatha only means "three," and it is certainly different from the word "Trinity," which means three in the unity of one (Pickthall's translation to this verse is accurate).

Also, in Yusuf Ali's translation of the Arabic Qur'an (Surah 5:73), he mistranslated the simple Arabic words "Thaalithu thalatha." He made them mean "one of three in a Trinity," instead of the obvious and only meaning "The third one of three."

Consider the problem that the majority of the Muslim world has by not understanding the Arabic language of the Qur'an. When they read this verse in English, they automatically assume that the Qur'an rejects the Biblical belief in the Triune God (Trinity). Abdullah Yusuf Ali's translation is widely distributed all over the world.

The Arabic Qur'an contains no reference to the Christian doctrine of the Triune God

Neither the *word* Trinity nor the *concept* of the Trinity appear at all in the original Arabic Qur'anic text (which we will discuss briefly in the next chapter). The Qur'an never mentions that Christians believe in God as Father, Son, and Holy Spirit. The Qur'an never mentions the word "Three in one."

The Qur'an just rejects the belief in three separate gods

The Qur'an misrepresents the Trinity as a family of Allah, Mary, and Jesus. For example, Surah 5:73 states: "They do blaspheme who say: Allah is one of three in a Trinity." The Qur'an named these three gods as Jesus, His mother Mary and Allah as we read in Surah 5:116, which states: "O Jesus the son of Mary! Didst thou say unto men, 'Worship me and my mother as gods in derogation of Allah?'"

We read in Surah 5:75: "Christ, the son of Mary, was no more than a Messenger . . . His mother was a woman of truth. They had both to eat their (daily) food." The Qur'an explains that Jesus and Mary couldn't be gods because they needed to eat food to survive. So, like everybody else, they were both humans, because God does not need any sustenance.

The famous Muslim commentator Zamakhashari commented on the word thalatha in Surah 4:171: "According to the evidence of the Qur'an, the Christian maintains that God, Christ, and Mary are three gods and that Christ is the Child of God by Mary . . ."

Although the Qur'an denounces the doctrine of the existence of three gods, this should not be confused with the Christian doctrine of the Holy Trinity. The Holy Trinity is one God, and within this Divine Unity there are three eternal Persons of one substance and power.

There is no evidence that Christians actually believed that the Trinity consisted of God, Jesus and Mary.

Unfortunately, the excessive prayers given to Mary by some misguided Christian sects, which are contrary to the teaching of the Bible, led Muhammad to misconceive the true meaning of the Trinity. Muhammad mistakenly thought that Christians believe and teach that the Virgin Mary is one of the persons of the Triune God. Muhammad did not have adequate information for correct understanding of the doctrine of the trinity.

Apparently, Muhammad was unable to recognize the vast difference between the Christian belief in Jesus as the unique eternal Son of God and the pagan Arab belief in their goddesses as daughters of God. He assumed both beliefs to be identical in character.

We read in the Qur'an: "The Jews call Uzayr a son of God, and the Christians call Christ the Son of God . . . (In this) they but imitate what the Unbelievers of old used to say . . ." (Surah 9:30).

It seems that Muhammad was completely unaware that the God of the Bible, whom all true Christians worship, is Father, Son, and Holy Spirit in one eternal, Divine being.

The Qur'an misrepresents the Biblical and historic Christian position on the Trinity and only presents Mohammad's limited knowledge and misconception of it.

My precious Muslim reader, please allow me to ask a sincere and serious question: If the Qur'an indeed came from God, how can we explain such a mistake of not even remotely representing the true Christian doctrine of the Tri-unity of God?

Regarding the Qur'anic verse: "They do blaspheme who say: Allah is one of three . . ." (Surah 5:73). Christians agree with this statement because we believe that God is one and only one. He cannot be one of three.

The Qur'an also states: "They do blaspheme who say: Allah is Christ the son of Mary" (Surah 5:72). It is not stated anywhere in the Bible that God is Christ the Son of Mary. The Bible states instead, "That God was reconciling the world to himself in Christ" (2 Corinthians 5:19). There were heresies in the early Christian centuries that taught that Christ was God the Father. Although the word of God reveals that Christ is God because of His divine nature, the Bible never confined God to the person of the Son (Christ) alone.

The Qur'an teaches that Christians are monotheistic

On the other hand, the Qur'an actually testifies that Christians ("people of the Book") are monotheistic (they worship one God) and they are not infidels (idolaters). The following passage from Surah 29:46 is an example:

And dispute ye not with the people of the Book, except with means better (than mere disputation) . . . but say, "We believe in the Revelation which has come down to us and in that which came down to you; our God and your God is One; and it is to Him we bow (in Islam)."

This verse affirms that Christians worship the true God. (Read also Surah 2:139.)

Surah 2:62 and Surah 3:113–114 also confirm that the revelation that the Jews and Christians received was from the only true and living God.

Note that Arab Christians called God "Allah" centuries before the time of Muhammad. Today, Arab Christians all over the world still call God "Allah." The word Allah is not found only in the Qur'an, but also in all Arabic Bibles. Incidentally, the Arabic word for God is *Ilah*, which is similar to the word for God in other Semitic languages (Aramaic: *Elah*; Syriac: *Alaha*; Hebrew: *El, Elohim*).

So *Ilah* is the Arabic word for God. *Allah* is this same word combined with the definite article, meaning "the God," which means "the One and only God."

I am sure that you know that Islam forbids the Muslim man to marry an idolatress, but it does not forbid him to marry a Christian because Christians are people who know the one God and worship only Him.

It is important to mention here that although the Roman Catholic, Orthodox, and Protestant denominations disagree on some secondary doctrines, they have never disagreed about the doctrine of the Trinity, not even in its slightest details. The reason is because the entire Bible clearly teaches this fundamental Christian belief in the Triune nature of God.

The revelation of the "Tri-unity" doctrine

The Old Testament presents plurality within God's unity and the New Testament teaches the concept of the Tri-unity of God.

The Old Testament

The Old Testament contains a clear emphasis on God's oneness and unity as an emphatic declaration to the pagan nations surrounding the people of Israel (Deuteronomy 4:35).

The Old Testament also contains some references to the persons of the Tri-unity. Regarding the Son, see Isaiah 7:14. Examples of references to the Holy Spirit are found in Genesis 1:2 and Nehemiah 9:20.

The New Testament

The New Testament emphatically revealed the Triune God to us and made this doctrine crystal clear. A Tri-unity of Father, Son and Holy Spirit is consistently presented throughout the New Testament. For example:

"For through him [Jesus Christ] we both have access to the Father by one Spirit [Holy Spirit]" (Ephesians 2:18).

"May the grace of the Lord Jesus Christ, and the love of God, and the fellowship of the Holy Spirit be with you all" (2 Corinthians 13:14).

". . . Who have been chosen according to the foreknowledge of God the Father, through the sanctifying work of the Spirit, for obedience to Jesus Christ and sprinkling by his blood . . ." (1 Peter 1:2).

"For this reason I kneel before the Father . . . I pray that out of his glorious riches he may strengthen you with power through his Spirit in you inner being, so that Christ may dwell in your hearts through faith. And I pray that you, being rooted and established in love, may have power, together with all the saints, to grasp how wide and long and high and deep is the love of Christ, and to know this love that surpasses knowledge—that you may be filled to the measure of all the fullness of God" (Ephesians 3:14–19).

"How much more, then, will the blood of Christ, who through the eternal Spirit offered himself unblemished to God, cleanse our consciences from acts that lead to death, so that we may serve the living God!" (Hebrews 9:14).

"Do not get drunk on wine, which leads to debauchery. Instead, be filled with the Spirit. Speak to one another with psalms, hymns and spiritual songs. Sing and make music in your heart to the Lord, always giving thanks to God the Father for everything, in the name of our Lord Jesus Christ" (Ephesians 5:18–20).

"Keep watch over yourselves and all the flock of which the Holy Spirit has made you overseers. Be shepherds of the church of God, which he bought with his own blood" (Acts 20:28).

26

UNDERSTANDING THE TRI-UNITY (TRINITY) OF GOD

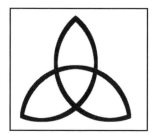

The knowledge of the Triune God is something that has to be spiritually discerned.

There isn't any symbol in the physical universe that can adequately portray the Tri-unity of God as taught in the Bible. However, the symbol that appears above is made of one continuous line, attempting to convey the one eternal Godhead with three distinct Persons. All three—the Father, Son, and Holy Spirit—are distinct yet interconnected.

The Triune God is infinite and indescribable

The impossibility of explaining the Tri-unity of God indicates that humans did not invent this doctrine. No one can give an illustration of the Trinity that truly explains the God who created the heavens and the earth. Consider how long it took mankind to discover and understand simple facts about the universe, the earth, the human body, etc. And we are still very far from knowing everything that relates to our world.

Therefore, it is not surprising that it is impossible for us to explain the God who created and controls the world. God's nature and essence cannot be completely understood by mere humans. We are unable to comprehend an infinite God with our finite minds. God's nature lies outside our experience and knowledge. God is transcendent.

Whereas the oneness of God in Islam is described in finite terms, the oneness of God in Christianity is described in complex terms. The early church did not invent the doctrine of the Trinity. It just accepted it from what God had revealed about Himself throughout the entire Bible.

The moment a person tries to understand God through human analogies, he makes the mistake of reducing God to mankind's level. It is the height of arrogance for anyone to think that he can understand everything about God's nature and essence. No human can have exhaustive knowledge of God.

Because God is Spirit, infinite and eternal, His being is beyond our comprehension. God is completely unique. He is God and there is no other.

There is complexity within unity

God's oneness is not merely a simple, single unit. Consider that each human is one, but his unity is more complex than that of a one-celled bacteria. If the oneness of man involves spiritual aspects as well as physical, surely the concept of the oneness of God is not diminished by its complexity. In fact, when the Bible says that we are created in the image of God, it means we are each a trinity in the sense that we are body, soul, and spirit.

Since we know that God is infinite, we must agree that His potential is unlimited. The possibilities of His complex nature are inconceivable to our earthly mind. Who are we to say that God cannot exist in a Tri-unity?

Trinity means three in the unity of one

Father, Son, and Holy Spirit are one in essence, will, and nature. Christians believe in one God, eternally existing as Father, Son, and Holy Spirit.

Many of my Muslim friends think that this doctrine of the Trinity contradicts itself. They ask, "How can something be three and one at the same time?" In response, Biblical scholar Dean Halverson explains:

> For a statement to contradict itself it must both affirm and deny the same thing in the same respect. Does the doctrine of the Trinity do that? The answer is no, because the doctrine states that God is one essence (or being) and three in person. Essence and personhood are different. God is three in person, in that each person of the Trinity is distinct within the Godhead. God is one, in that each person of the Godhead shares the same self-existing essence and other qualities unique to God. This simultaneous distinction and sameness is seen in John 1:1.[1]

Each Person in the Trinity is called "God"

One of my Muslim friends told me $1 + 1 + 1 = 3$, but in Christian mathematics $1 + 1 + 1 = 1$.

Expressed mathematically, the concept of the Trinity is not $1 + 1 + 1 = 3$. Rather, it is $1 \times 1 \times 1 = 1$. I usually share with my Muslim friends that God is Spirit, and numbers apply only to the physical world. We cannot use material thoughts to try to comprehend God who is a Spiritual Being. It is impossible to understand all the facts related to the infinite God through the forms of finite thought.

While each of the three Persons within the one God performs specific functions (more than the other two Persons), nonetheless all three are continuously involved in everything together. The Father, Son, and Holy Spirit are bound together in such a close unity that the life of each flows through each of the others.

Again, The Bible teaches that each of the three distinct Persons is called *God*. First, the Holy Spirit is called God. For example, in Acts 5:3–4 we see that the Holy Spirit is identified as God and also is seen as a distinct Person. (See also Acts 13:2; John 3:5–6; Romans 8:9; 1 Corinthians 2:10–11; 2 Corinthians 3:17–18.)

The Father is repeatedly called God (1 Peter 1:2; Galatians 1:1; Ephesians 1:3; and 1 Corinthians 8:6).

Jesus is called God as well (Romans 9:5; Titus 2:13; Acts 20:28; Matthew 1:21–23). Considering all the revealed Biblical teachings on the nature of God, the clear conclusion is that there are three Persons in the one Godhead.

Each one of us is one finitely. God is one infinitely. Within the infinite realm of God there are three distinct personalities, they are named the Father, the Son, and the Holy Spirit. The Bible does not explain how the one God can be three distinct persons.

Helpful Muslim explanations

Al-Ghazzali answered a similar question about Tri-unity. He is one of the most respected Muslim theologians in the history of Islam. He wrote:

> How can the many be one? Know that this is the goal
> of all revelations, and the secrets of this science should
> not be penned down in a book, for the people of knowl-
> edge said, the unveiling of the secret of Lordship is
> blasphemy . . . the thing can be many in one sense,

but also can be one in another sense. And so, as man is many in one sense if you look at his spirit and body and limbs and blood vessels and bones and members, but in another sense, he is one man.[2]

Even the famous Muslim, Imam Shaarani, acknowledges: "Conventional plurality does not preclude essential unity, such as the branches of a tree in relation to its root or the fingers in relation to the palm."[3]

Three can be in one

Through an experiment known as the triple point of water, it is possible for water (one substance) to exist simultaneously as ice (solid), steam (gas) and water (liquid). The sun consists of material, light and heat.

Heat and light will come out of the flame of the fire, wherever there is a flame, light and heat exist. The flame, the light and the heat are three manifestations of one fire, they are not three fires.

The nature of God's oneness

Although the word *Trinity* is not in the Bible, the concept is clearly Biblical. Also, the word *tawhid*, which Muslims usually use to describe God, is not in the Qur'an.

Christians agree with Muslims that God is one—entirely distinct from all created beings. But we have not yet begun to deal with the issue of what mysteries the Divine Nature may contain within itself. Mysteries are inherent in the supreme divine nature of God. Therefore, whatever our beliefs, whether we hold onto the Muslim belief about the *singular oneness* of God's nature or the Christian belief in the *compound unity* of God's nature, neither conflict with oneness. We are dealing simply with the *inner* nature of that essence. Muslims are taught that God's nature is a single unity. The Bible teaches us that it is a complex unity.

Christianity, Judaism, and Islam are all monotheistic. They firmly and equally teach that God is one. The conflict deals with understanding and defining God's divine unity. Again, God's nature surpasses the capacity of our minds to fully imagine. To argue that the Christian belief in God is against reason is simply to make oneself the judge of what God can or cannot be, which is blasphemy. After all, God is the Potter and we are but the clay!

God's nature cannot be fully expressed or imagined

The non-Christian reader must agree that in using such words as "Father," "Son," and "Holy Spirit," God is using human terms for our benefit. It is God through His grace accommodating Himself to human limitations and ignorance, just as, for example, a human father must use simple language when trying to explain something very complex to a child.

So there is no human language suitable to express the realities of the Divine Nature. The relationship between the Persons of the Godhead so transcends all human thought and language that we can neither comprehend nor express it fully. Many Muslims state that they cannot believe in the doctrine of the Trinity because they are unable to understand it. In their minds, it has not been proven. However, again, the problem is not in the doctrine itself but in the limitations of the human mind.

Even though we are able, for the most part, to accurately describe everything that we can see, the truth is we cannot use finite human standards to define the unseen infinite Creator.

It is wrong to conclude that because three persons on earth cannot be absolutely one in essence and nature, therefore Father, Son, and Holy Spirit cannot be one. We must acknowledge that because God is infinite, His unity must be of a character different from that which we see or expect.

We must admit that no matter how wise and intelligent we are, we cannot define or limit the extent of God's eternal oneness. Because God is infinite, it is expected that His unity is more complex than human minds can anticipate.

Many of my dear Muslim friends tell me that Islam's concept of God is simple and easily understood. Therefore, it is more reasonable and acceptable than the Christian's incomprehensible concept of the trinity. My answer to them is that a doctrine of God that can be imagined in the human mind most likely was invented by the human mind in the first place. The very fact that no human can imagine the Tri-unity of God is not evidence to the weakness of the Christian doctrine. Rather, it is evidence that it is true because the essence of the true God is beyond human description.

Biblical scholar Kenneth Cragg has said, "A doctrine of God does not commend itself by its ability to be reduced to a statement on a postage stamp."

The doctrine of the trinity is not contrary to reason; it is above the realms of finite human reasoning.

God desires for us to love Him and obey Him. He did not create us to analyze Him. It is wrong for anyone to try to put God in a laboratory in order to examine Him. It is also impossible to try to reduce God to fit a formula.

Spiritual revelations are considered truth even when not provable

Let me pose a question: If an atheist asked for proof for the many beliefs Muslims hold as truths, would it be possible for you as a Muslim to prove them? For example, consider the Muslim belief in the resurrection of the dead. If an atheist asked you how it would be possible for the dead to be raised back to life, could you satisfactorily explain and prove it? It is not possible to do so through human logic or intellect alone.

My point is that if you allow yourself to reject the Tri-unity of God because Christians cannot absolutely prove it with intellectual arguments, then you cannot blame the atheist for rejecting the belief in God's revelation that cannot be proven. God's essence is not material but spiritual. Mankind must accept by faith what God has revealed in the Bible about His nature.

Note that according to the Qur'an and the Hadith, Allah has a face, hands, fingers, feet, and eyes (Surah 55:27 and Surah 38:75). The highly influential Muslim scholar and jurist, Imam Abu Hanifah, teaches: "The most high has a hand and face and soul without asking how."[4]

My dear Muslim reader, "Do you believe that Jesus performed miracles?" I am sure that your answer is "yes." You believe that Jesus preformed miracles even though you never saw Him perform one, but you believe because the Qur'an stated that Jesus performed many great miracles.

We followers of Christ also submit and believe in the Triune God because that is what the Bible revealed God to be.

Human logic and reason alone are insufficient to lead to the full knowledge of God's nature. As we read in the Bible, "Can you fathom the mysteries of God? Can you probe the limits of the Almighty? They are higher than the heavens—what can you do? They are deeper than the depths of the grave—what can you know?" (Job 11:7–8).

I know of a devout follower of Jesus Christ who was thinking hard trying to understand everything about the Tri-unity of God. He became very frustrated, even angry at times, because he was not able to figure out everything about the Tri-unity of God.

One day, he was walking on the beach and again thinking hard about the Trinity. He saw a child running back and forth trying to carry in his hands water from the ocean and put it in a hole in the sand. God guided the man's thoughts through what he saw. He realized the futility of his attempts to contain the complexity of God in his mind, as it is impossible for the child to bring the ocean into a small hole by his hands.

Functions of the Persons within the Trinity

The purpose of God's revelation to us in the Gospel is:

- To guide us to know Him as our Heavenly Father,
- To be forgiven by Him through Jesus Christ, and
- To enjoy His divine presence through the Holy Spirit.

God wants us to have the right relationship with Him in order to worship, love, obey Him, and know that we are going to heaven. And that should be good enough for all of us. Biblical scholar G. Parrinder explains:

God as creator and provider is seen in the Father who cares for mankind. The essential nature of God as love manifesting Himself in action is seen in the 'Son,' . . . [while on earth] his loving actions and words, his suffering and death. The ever-present nature of God is seen in the [Holy] Spirit. Yet these three are one, the threefold revelation of God to men.[5]

You can know God's love, power, and salvation experientially

It grieves my heart that Muslim theologians, based only on the Qur'an (and ignoring Biblical revelation), teach that God is one and singular. This leaves people with an empty and incomplete concept of God. By rigidly insisting on simplicity in God's nature, they tragically and unknowingly sacrifice experiencing the salvation, love, and power of God personally. Beloved friends, we must worship God in spirit and in truth (John 4:23).

Muslim teachers teach that the Allah of Islam has simple, strict unity that can be easily understood by the human mind, yet they confirm that Allah cannot be personally known.

The amazing truth is the Tri-une God the Bible reveals to us is a knowable God. He can be known and experienced right within the depth of the human heart (as you will fully discover after reading chapters 29 and 30).

God's nature is love

It is significant to notice that because God is a loving God and His nature is unchangeable, His attribute of love must have existed from all eternity. Since love must have an object, the question arises: Before God created any living being, whom did He love? The answer is clear: Within the Divine Unity, there must have existed at least a lover and a beloved. The Bible reveals that there always have been three Persons within God enjoying love—mutually exercised, expressed, and experienced.

According to the Bible, God is love. Love can never be exercised in isolation. God cannot be love and also solitary.

Only the Christian doctrine of the Triune God explains how the attribute of love exists in God's divine nature. The God of the Gospel is not singular and totally alone. He is the all-sufficient God who is able to exist by Himself in love. God wasn't lonely before He created humans. The Father, Son, and Holy Spirit existed in a state of complete, fulfilling fellowship.

It is important here to mention that God created us not because He was all alone and He needed to receive worship or anything from us.

The truth is, God, as described in the Bible, created you and desires to have a relationship with you, so He can give you so many wonderful things which will make you happy now and forever. He wants you and me to enjoy what He has, because He loves us.

Difference in function does not indicate inferiority of nature

We cannot ignore this common sense truth: nature and function are two different things. Three persons in the army share the same type of human nature but they can have different functions.

Long before humans existed, the Father, the Son, and the Holy Spirit chose the roles they would take in the plan for the salvation of the human race.

The one who took the function of the source of creation and of this work of salvation is called the Father; the one who came to earth as our Savior is called the Son; and the one who indwells believers is called the Holy Spirit.

Muslim teachers mistakenly assume that Jesus Christ can't be God because He lived on earth as man. Their wrong assumption is because Jesus' function gave Him an inferior status to the Father's, then he must have been inferior in nature.

To illustrate, a wife's function can be cleaning the house, scrubbing the toilet, changing diapers, etc., that does not make her less human or inferior than her husband, who sits in a nice office spending his day looking at papers and talking on the phone.

Even though Jesus told us that He and the Father have the same nature (John 10:30), He also said to His disciples, ". . . If you loved me, you would be glad that I am going to the Father, for the Father is greater than I" (John 14:28). Jesus is not speaking in this verse about His nature but is rather speaking of His lowly position in the incarnation.

Jesus meant that the Father is greater in office and glory than Jesus was in his humiliated status on earth. The Bible teaches that God the Father is the eternal source of all things to whom both the Son and the Holy Spirit are subject.

The position that the Son assumed while on earth, all the limitations He had as a man and the suffering He went through, does not disprove His deity. All these merely point to a special definition of it while He lived on earth.

God the Father never came into the world as man to be cruelly treated; but Jesus came here on earth and was despised by many people. From this perspective, Jesus meant that God the Father is greater in His position. While on earth, Jesus' function was subordinate and submissive to the Father.

Jesus was telling His disciples to rejoice because He will be returning back to the place He had with the Father before the world was (John 17:5). He would no longer be the subject of attack and ridicule by the religious Jewish leaders. Instead, He would be at the right hand of the Father in heaven itself.

The term "greater" speaks of the position of the Father in heaven over the position of the Son on earth. The Son would soon be leaving this humbled position and returning to His position of glory.

The Bible clearly placed side by side the deity and manhood (human nature) of Jesus Christ. For example, we read in the Gospel that when Jesus and His disciples were in a boat, ". . . a furious storm came up on the lake, so that the waves swept over the boat. But Jesus was sleeping. The disciples went and woke Him, saying, 'Lord save us! We're going to drown!' . . . Then he got up and rebuked the winds and the waves and it was completely calm" (Matthew 8:24–26).

Sometimes a Muslim asks me, "How can you Christians reconcile the Biblical teaching of the true deity of Jesus Christ with the Biblical teaching of the real human nature of Christ?"

As a part of my answer, I usually ask him to remember that in many cases two truths, which seemed completely contradictory to us at one time, are now, after we have gained more knowledge and spiritual light (insight), understood them to be in harmony. Also we need to acknowledge that truth that still seems to us to be contradictory, perfectly harmonize according to God's infinite wisdom, and we will someday understand them.

Capturing glimpses of the Trinity

Noted church historian Philip Schaff summarizes the biblical concept of the Trinity:

> God is one in three persons [that is, three distinct persons of the same nature] . . . The divine persons are in one another and form a perpetual intercommunication and motion within the divine essence. Each person has all the divine attributes which are inherent in the divine essence but each has also a characteristic individuality . . . which is peculiar to the person . . . but the three persons are co-eternal and co-equal.[6]

My dear Muslim reader, by gaining glimpses of the Trinity, now I hope you will begin to appreciate the depth, the power, and the beauty of the Christian faith.

Finally, my dear reader, when you put your faith in Jesus Christ, God Himself will make you realize and even certain that He is the Father who loves you, and He is Jesus Christ who gave Himself for you, and He is the Holy Spirit who indwells you.

If you ask me, "How will I know?" I will share with you a story that I read of a young boy who was outside flying a kite. The kite went so high (up and up) that it was hidden by the clouds. A man asked the young boy, "What are you doing?"

The boy replied, "I am flying a kite."

The man asked, "Are you sure? I can't see anything."

The boy replied, "I know it is up there because every little while I feel a tug."

My Muslim reader, only when you put your faith in Jesus Christ you will experience the Tri-une nature of God.

27

JESUS IS THE ETERNAL SON OF GOD IN A UNIQUE SPIRITUAL SENSE

In the Bible, Jesus is the eternal Son of God in a unique spiritual sense. The expression "Son of God" confirms that Jesus was not the son of any man, but that He came directly from God.

The Qur'an's view of Jesus' Sonship

Based on many passages in the Qur'an, such as Surah 2:116, Surah 6:101, Surah 9:30, Surah 18:4, and Surah 19:35, many Muslims misunderstand the Christian belief in the Fatherhood of God and Sonship of Jesus, incorrectly assuming that God had to have a consort (partner in a sexual relation). They question how, apart from the involvement of a woman, God could beget a son and become a father. In Surah 6:101 the question is asked, "How can He have a son when He hath no consort?"

The Qur'an's argument that it was not possible for God to have a Son because He had no wife reveals that the Qur'an rejects its own misconception of the doctrine of Jesus as the Son of God rather than the true nature of this Biblical doctrine.

It seems that Muhammad only understood the title Son of God in finite and human terms. Another verse in the Qur'an states, "And exalted is the Majesty of our Lord: He has taken neither a wife nor a son" (Surah 72:3).

What the Qur'an rejects as untrue is the carnal idea that God had a son through a physical relationship with a partner. Such an idea is blasphemous also to Christians, who reject such a notion. Therefore, please know that any Islamic rejection of the sonship of Christ is based on a misunderstanding of the Biblical concept of the spiritual sonship of Jesus.

The Bible's view of Jesus' Sonship

When the Gospel states that Christ is the divine Son of God, it does not mean that Christ came by procreation. His Sonship was not the result of a physical relationship between a father and mother. It is of another kind—an eternal, spiritual Sonship (between the Father and the Son), this Father-Son relationship has existed from eternity. We believe that the eternal Son of God is One with the Father from all eternity, is united to Him in One Spirit, became flesh, and dwelt among us. He came to this earth as God's ambassador and was subject to God's authority.

Jesus' Sonship is not a physical (earthly) relationship

When the Gospel teaches that Jesus is "the Son of God," it means God was revealed in His essential nature of love in Christ. Biblical scholar Kenneth Cragg presents an analogy: "When we speak of Beethoven the musician, or Leonardo da Vinci the artist, we mean these men and their full personality in a particular capacity. Capacities which do not preclude their having others, but yet involving them wholly."[1]

In physical birth there is a separation between mother and child. But Jesus came from the Father without leaving Him. Jesus appeared in human form and yet remained in God. Jesus said, "I am in the Father, and the Father is in me" (John 14:10).

God's only begotten Son

When I refer to Jesus as the Son of God, many Muslims recite Surah 112, ". . . He begetteth not, nor begotten . . ." Yes, God was never born because He is eternal. And, yes, it is true that God does not beget according to the Qur'an's use of the word "beget"—in which one becomes a father by sexual means to beget a son—for He is Spirit, not human. In order for God to be called "Father," He does not need to beget in the way we humans do. Mary conceived by the Holy Spirit—not by human flesh—which is the glad tidings of the one-time, holy, pure conception!

Surah 3:46–47 documented Mary's conversation with the angel: ". . . how can I have a child when no man hath touched me?"

The Gospel also documented the conversation in Luke 1:34–35: "'How will this be,' Mary asked the angel, 'since I am a virgin?' The angel answered, 'The Holy Spirit will come upon you, and the power of the Most High will overshadow you. So the holy one to be born will be called the Son of God.'"

Certain English translations of the Gospel state, "For God so loved the world that he gave his one and only Son, that whoever believes in him shall not perish but have eternal life" (John 3:16). Some other Bible translations read that God gave His "only begotten Son." The Greek word, which is translated as "begotten" in the original text is *monogenae*, which means "the one" (mono) and "coming from" (genae) or "the one coming from." In other words, Jesus came from the Father. The expression only begotten or monogenes does not refer to physical begetting but to uniqueness, "one of a kind."

Some translators of the Bible translated this word as "only" while others "only begotten." Both are correct because the meaning is the same—the only divine Son coming from the Father.

The Gospel teaches us that Christ is eternal. He existed before Abraham. Jesus told some Jewish people: "Before Abraham was born, I am!" (John 8:58). He was before the world came into being (John 17:5, 24).

Who else could Jesus' Father be?

Both the Bible and the Qur'an teach as a fact that Jesus was born of a virgin, conceived through God's Spirit. We read in the Qur'an that Jesus is called, "a Spirit from God." According to the Gospel and the Qur'an, Jesus is not related to any human father. Therefore, He is related to God, the heavenly Father. If you object to Jesus being called the "Son of God" in the Bible, can you then explain who else Jesus' Father could be?

To reason that God cannot have a son without a wife, is to assume God has our human limitations. It would be the same as reasoning that God cannot have life without breathing. Although it is true that anything that lives must breathe, God of course does not depend on breathing to live and yet He lives. The Gospel explains that "God is spirit" (John 4:24) and Almighty.

The Arabic word *walad* means "a son born of sexual relations." And certainly Jesus is not a son in this sense. However, there is another Arabic word for son: *ibn*, which can be used without indicating sexual union. For example, because I was born and raised in Egypt, you can call me "the son of the Nile" or "the son of Egypt."

I'd like to ask you a question: Is it permissible for you to forbid anything to God (such as having a Son), which He does not forbid Himself? God is greater than all. No one has the liberty to set limitations on God, because God is able to do anything and sovereign! (Supreme in Authority)

JESUS' RELATIONAL FUNCTION

It is very clear from the Bible that Jesus is the eternal, unique, and divine Son of God. The very title, *Son of God*, immediately suggests Jesus' relational function. Consider that an earthly father and his son share the same human nature, yet the son is subject to his father. Likewise, the expression the "Son of God" indicates relationship between the first two Persons of the Triune God. God the Father and Jesus share the same divine nature, yet Jesus subjected *Himself* to the authority of the Father. Therefore, we see that the expression Son of God indicates likeness or sameness of nature.

The Son took human form almost two thousand years ago and became the man Jesus Christ. Jesus came to earth to do His Father's will and to glorify His Heavenly Father.

The title Son of God is the best language possible to express the close and unique relationship that Jesus Christ has with God the Father. The Bible reveals to us about Jesus: "For in Christ all the fullness of the Deity lives in bodily form" (Colossians 2:9). Jesus is the visible expression of the invisible God (Hebrews 1:3). We rejoice that Jesus came to earth to reveal God to us, and that God did not remain entirely hidden in His glorious majesty far from His creation!

Jesus teaches that He is the Son of God

Jesus referred to Himself as the Son of God in absolute and exclusive terms, we read in the Bible that Jesus said, ". . . No one knows the Son except the Father, and no one knows the Father except the Son . . ." (Matthew 11:27). Jesus said, "If anyone loves me, he will obey my teaching. My Father will love him, and we will come to him and make our home with him" (John 14:23).

If Jesus were nothing more than a human being He would have been committing blasphemy when he said, ". . . that all may honor the Son just as they honor the Father. He who does not honor the Son does not honor the Father, who sent him" (John 5–23).

Jesus also said, "Anyone who has seen me has seen the Father . . . Don't you believe that I am in the Father, and that the Father is in me? . . . Believe me . . . or at least believe on the evidence of the miracles themselves" (John 14:9–11).

Let us look at one example that demonstrates Jesus' claim to be the Son of God who submitted to the will of His Father. In the Gospel, this doctrine is illustrated by "The Parable of the Tenants and the Vineyard." In Luke chapter 20, Jesus teaches a crowd of people about God the Father and Himself:

> A man planted a vineyard, rented it to some farmers, and went away for a long time. At harvest time he sent a servant to the tenants so they would give him some of the fruit of the vineyard. But the tenants beat him and sent him away empty-handed. He sent another servant, but that one also they beat and treated shamefully and sent away empty-handed. He sent still a third, and they wounded him and threw him out. Then the owner of the vineyard said, "What shall I do? I will send my son, whom I love; perhaps they will respect him." But when the tenants saw him, they talked the matter over. "This is the heir," they said. "Let's kill him, and the inheritance will be ours." So they threw him out of the vineyard and killed him. What then will the owner of the vineyard do to them? He will come and kill those tenants and give the vineyard to others. When the people [the religious leaders at the time] heard this, they said, "May this never be!" (Luke 20:9–16) (see also Matthew 21:33–43)

Interpretation of the Biblical parable

The characters in this parable of the tenants and the vineyard are identified as follows:

- The owner of the vineyard is God the Father, who planted the vineyard.

- The landowner's son is Jesus Christ, the Messiah.

- The vineyard is the nation of Israel.

- The tenants are the Jewish religious leaders at that time.

- The landowner's servants are the prophets sent to the nation of Israel.

Jesus' message in this parable

In this parable, Jesus presented Himself as the Son sent from the owner of the vineyard. Those tenant farmers in charge of tending the vineyard killed the owner's Son. The Jewish leaders understood what Jesus was saying—that He was applying this story directly to them and pointing at them as the tenant farmers in His story. We read, "The teachers of the law and the chief priests looked for a way to arrest him immediately, because they knew he had spoken this parable against them. But they were afraid of the people" (Luke 20:19).

Jesus distinguished between the great prophets of the Old Testament, (describing them as the servants of God) and Himself (as the last messenger)—as the beloved Son of God.

Clearly, Jesus' parable teaches that God the Father sent many prophets to the people of Israel to ask them to produce the "good fruits" of righteousness. But the Jewish leadership rejected the prophets and mistreated them. Then God the Father sent His only Beloved Son. However, the Jewish people rejected Him as well and killed Him. Jesus went to the vineyard in submission to His Father's will.

Jesus confronted the Jewish religious leaders

In the Gospel account by the Apostle John, Jesus Himself defends His claim to be the divine Son of God. He declares:

What about the one whom the Father set apart as his very own and sent into the world? Why then do you accuse me of blasphemy because I said, "I am God's Son"?

Do not believe me unless I do what my Father does. But if I do it, even though you do not believe me, believe the miracles, that you may know and understand that the Father is in me, and I in the Father. Again they [the religious leaders at the time] tried to seize him . . . (John 10:36–39)

The Gospel of John recorded that after Jesus healed a sick man on the Sabbath day, the Jews were persecuting Him. Jesus said to them, "'My Father is always at his work to this very day, and I, too, am working.' For this reason the Jews tried all the harder to kill him, not only was he breaking the Sabbath, but he was even calling God his own Father, making himself equal with God" (John 5:17–18).

Jesus did not tell them their interpretation of His words was wrong. Instead He offered more teaching to confirm His identity. (Please read John 5:19–26.)

On another occasion, the high priest asked Jesus, "'Are you the Christ, the Son of the Blessed One?' 'I am,' said Jesus" (Mark 14:61–62). This is an absolute declaration.

Ultimately, Jesus' claim to be the Son of God is what caused the unbelieving Jews to consider Him worthy of death (Matthew 26:63–65; Mark 14:61–63; Luke 22:70).

We read in the Bible, that when Pilate told the Jewish leaders, "I find him not guilty," they replied, "We have a law, and according to that law he must die, because he claimed to be the Son of God" (John 19:7).

Jesus said, "For God so loved the world that he gave his one and only Son, that whoever believes in him shall not perish but have eternal life. For God did not send his Son into the world to condemn the world, but to save the world through him. Whoever believes in him is not condemned, but whoever does not believe stands condemned already because he has not believed in the name of God's one and only Son" (John 3:16–19).

Jesus prayed, "And now, Father, glorify me in your presence with the glory I had with You before the world began" (John 17:5).

Jesus taught that God is His Father and that He is the Son of God. We respond by believing in faith in what God has revealed about Himself. Human reason should not be the final judge.

Man cannot be the final judge on the truth of who God is and who Jesus is. Man should only submit to what God has revealed. You cannot rely on the dim light of human reasoning to judge the infinite, eternal, and most glorious being.

It is significant that not only did Jesus Himself claim to be the Son of God, but John the Baptist and God the Father also testified to this eternal truth. John the Baptist declared, "I have seen and I testify that this is the Son of God" (John 1:34).

We also read in the Bible the testimony of God the Father when John the Baptist was baptizing Jesus: "As soon as Jesus was baptized, he went up out of the water. At that moment heaven was opened, and he saw the Spirit of God descending like a dove and lighting on him. And a voice from heaven said, 'This is my Son, whom I love; with him I am well pleased'" (Matthew 3:16–17).

The Holy Spirit inspired the writing of the Apostle John, who was one of Jesus' disciples and an eyewitness to Jesus' life, death, resurrection, and ascension. We read:

"For there are three that bear witness in heaven: the Father, the Word, and the Holy Spirit; and these three are one" (1 John 5:7 NKJV).

The witness of the Holy Spirit about Jesus was also evident through the testimony of the prophets, including John the Baptist.

God continues to speak to us in the same chapter:

"If we receive the witness of men, the witness of God is greater: for this is the witness of God which He has testified of His Son. He who believes in the Son of God has the witness in himself . . ." (verses 9–10 NKJV).

Those words mean, when you believe in God's testimony about Jesus, God will put the truth in your heart. You will know the truth in your inner being. You will have within you an actual verfication of God's own faithful words.

Verse ten from above continues: ". . . he who does not believe God has made Him a liar, because he has not believed the testimony that God has given of His Son. And this is the testimony: that God has given us eternal life and this life is in His Son. He who has the Son has life; he who does not have the Son of God does not have life" (1 John 5:9–12 NKJV).

Jesus said: "He who believes in Me, believes not in Me, but in Him who sent Me . . . I have not spoken on my own authroity; but the Father who sent Me gave Me a command, what I should say and what I should speak" (John 12:44, 49 NKJV).

The King of Kings sent his Son (the Prince) to all people, and the Son looks like his Father and carries the seal of the Kingdom. If anyone rejects the Son, he automatically rejects the King.

SECTION TEN

WORSHIP, LOVE, AND THE SAVIOR

28

JESUS RECEIVED WORSHIP

It is significant that early Muslim theologians agreed with the teaching of the Gospel that Jesus is worthy to receive worship.

Jesus is worthy to receive worship

Early Islamic Scholar, Ibn Ishaq,[1] quotes a letter sent by Muhammad to the Negus of Abyssinia. In it Muhammad wrote, "I bear witness that Jesus, son of Mary, is the Spirit of God and His Word, which he cast to Mary the virgin."[2]

According to the teaching of early reputable Muslim scholars, Jesus is the only prophet who was believed in while He was still in His mother's womb.

Muslim commentators agree that the prophet Yahya [John the Baptist] was the first person to believe that Jesus was the Word of God.

The following story was reported by Al-Razi, a well-known early Muslim scholar:

"The mother of Jesus met the mother of Yahya, peace be upon them. Both were pregnant, one with Jesus, the other with Yahya. Yahya's mother said to Mary, 'Do you feel I am pregnant?' Mary said, 'I am also pregnant.' The wife of Zekaraiah said, 'I found that he who is inside me bows down to the one inside of you.'" Al-Razi explains, "This is what is meant by John's confirming (or believing in) the Word of God which is Jesus, found in the Qur'an, Surah 3:39. It reads: 'Yahya witnessing the truth of a word from Allah.'"[3]

Yahya bowed down to Jesus according to reliable Islamic records

Abdullah Ibn Abbas (see appendix) who gained the reputation of being the most informed person among the Muslim people as to what God revealed to Muhammad. Ibn Abbas made known that the appropriate response to Jesus as the Word of God is *to bow down to him* and that the prophet Yahya was the first to acknowledge that Jesus is the Word of God. Ibn Abbas says, "His [Yahya] bowing down to Jesus in His mother's womb was his expression of faith in Jesus."[4]

Ibn Abbas further states: "Yahya's bowing down in his mother's womb is his believing that Jesus is the Word of God."[5] Ibn Abbas noted that Yahya was the first to believe and confirm that Jesus is "the Word of God" and "His Spirit."[6]

It is amazing to read of early Muslims believing that *Yahya bowed down to Jesus*, because Yahya was an eminent prophet according to the Qur'an and the Bible.

Bowing down is a clear form of worship

My dear Muslim friend, bowing down is a clear and strong form of worship. Worship is due only to God, who has no partner or equal. The Bible agrees that Jesus is worthy to receive worship because He alone is the eternal, uncreated, divine Word of God. My Muslim friend, God Himself wants us to know that Jesus is His eternal Word and worthy to be worshipped.

Yahya's heart was made alive according to Islamic scholars

In addition, the great Muslim scholar Al-Razi explained why the prophet Yahya was given his name. The name *Yahya* is taken from the verb "to be alive." Al-Razi writes: "Yahya was the first to believe in Jesus, so his heart became alive by that faith."[7]

Only God and His Word can cause a person to be spiritually alive. If you believe and worship Jesus as the divine Word of God, you will be given new life.

Who is worthy to receive worship, Jesus or Adam?

We read in the Qur'an that after God created Adam, He commanded the angels to bow down before Adam. "And behold, we said to the angels, 'bow down to Adam' and they bowed down . . ." (Surah 2:34). (See also 7:11; 15:28-29; 17:61; 18:50; 20:116.)

My dear reader, please allow me to say that the person who deserves to receive prostration is Jesus Christ and not Adam.

The more you read the facts I presented to you in this book and seek God to reveal the truth to you, I am sure that you will discover that, according to all the evidence, only Jesus Christ is worthy to receive this honor.

Every knee shall bow before Jesus

The Gospel, informs us of Jesus' place of honor, ". . . God exalted him [Jesus] to the highest place and gave him the name that is above every name, that at the name of Jesus every knee should bow, in heaven and on earth and under the earth, and every tongue confess that Jesus Christ is Lord, to the glory of God the Father" (Philippians 2:9–11).

My dear friend, the way to know God personally, which I am sharing with you in this book, was never intended by God to be for one special group of people alone. Understanding and personally applying this truth is a common right for all humanity—a right to become spiritually enlightened and alive!

Jesus receives worship

One of my Muslim friends commented that Jesus never said, "I am God. Worship Me."

I answered, "Jesus knew if He made this statement many people would accuse him of blasphemy and his statement will only result in negative impact. The important thing is not whether Jesus made this particular statement or not, but did He talk like he was God? Did He act like He's God? Did He give us enough evidence to conclude that He is God manifested in human flesh? Certainly He did!"

Jesus real identity is established by His actions, miracles, and His words. For example, Jesus promised: "For where two or three come together in my name, there am I with them" (Matthew 18:20).

The Bible documents Jesus receiving worship on many occasions. Here are five instances from the Gospel according to Matthew:

- When wise men followed the star to the Child, they "bowed down and worshiped him" and presented gifts (Matthew 2:8–11).

- Jesus is worshiped by a leper He cleansed (Matthew 8:2).

- When Jesus walked on water and the wind ceased, the disciples "worshiped him saying, 'Truly you are the Son of God'" (Matthew 14:33).

- The mother of Zebedee's sons came to Jesus, "kneeling down to him" (Matthew 20:20).

- Some of the disciples "worshiped him" after His resurrection, on a mountain in Galilee (Matthew 28:16–17).

Three more instances where Jesus received worship in other Gospel accounts are listed below:

- A woman "fell at his feet" and asked Jesus to cast the unclean spirit out of her daughter and He did so (Mark 7:25–30).

- When Jesus ascended into heaven, His disciples "worshiped him" (Luke 24:51–52).

- After Jesus opened the eyes of the man born blind, the man said, "'Lord, I believe!' and he worshiped him" (John 9:32–38).

For additional references to the fact that Jesus received worship see John 20:28; Matthew 9:18; Matthew 28:9; and Luke 5:8.

Note that in all of the instances when Jesus was worshiped, He never refused worship. Not once did Jesus rebuke those who worshiped Him. Although Jesus taught that God was the only one to be worshiped, Jesus permitted people to worship Him.

29

GOD IS LOVE

The glorious revelation in the Bible is that God loves every single person unconditionally. Every person can know God personally and experience His love and salvation! "For God so loved (*ahab*) the world that he gave his one and only Son, that whoever believes in him shall not perish but have eternal life" (John 3:16).

Parable of the lost prodigal son

Whereas the Qur'an states that God does not love prodigals or "wasters" (Surah 6:141; 7:31), a different picture in the Gospel shows God's astonishing love even for prodigals who are recklessly wasteful. In Luke chapter 15, Jesus teaches the parable of the lost prodigal son and his older brother. Jesus first describes the insulting actions of the younger son who decided to leave the family farm and asked his father for his share of the inheritance. It was a selfish and disloyal desire. According to the Middle East culture, it is shameful for a son to ask his father for his share of the inheritance while his father is still alive. A son had the responsibility to stay and help his family until his father died. Then he could receive his inheritance.

Most likely the father had to sell part of his land and/or animals quickly, and probably at a discount, below market price so that he can give his son the money. So the prodigal son took the money, left his father's house, and went far away to squander the wealth in wild living. But when a famine occurred, he ran out of money. The parable then reads:

When he [the prodigal son] came to his senses, he said, "How many of my father's hired men have food to spare, and here I am starving to death! I will set out and go back to my father and say to him: Father, I have sinned against heaven and against you. I am no longer worthy to be called your son; make me like one of your hired men." So he got up and went to his father.

But while he was still a long way off, his father saw him and was filled with compassion for him; he ran to his son, threw his arms around him and kissed him.

The son said to him, "Father, I have sinned against heaven and against you. I am no longer worthy to be called your son."

But the father said to his servants, "Quick! Bring the best robe and put it on him. Put a ring on his finger and sandals on his feet. Bring the fattened calf and kill it. Let's have a feast and celebrate. For this son of mine was dead and is alive again; he was lost and is found." So they began to celebrate.

Meanwhile, the older son was in the field. When he came near the house, he heard music and dancing. So he called one of the servants and asked him what was going on. "Your brother has come," he replied, "and your father has killed the fattened calf because he has him back safe and sound."

The older brother became angry and refused to go in. So his father went out and pleaded with him. But he answered his father, "Look! All these years I've been slaving for you and never disobeyed your orders. Yet you never gave me even a young goat so I could celebrate with my friends. But when this son of yours who has squandered your property with prostitutes comes home, you kill the fattened calf for him!"

"My son," the father said, "you are always with me, and everything I have is yours. But we had to celebrate and be glad, because this brother of yours was dead and is alive again; he was lost and is found." (Luke 15:17–32)

Interpretation of the biblical parable

The older brother symbolizes the "religious" person who never really experienced what it meant to be a son, or appreciate the thoughts and feelings of his loving father. He served his father not out of love, but primarily out of a desire for reward. He did not have genuine love for his brother or his father. He deserved to be punished for being mean and selfish; however, the father displayed grace by lovingly pleading with him to join the feast.

This parable could also be called, "The Parable of the Loving Father." In the Jewish culture of the first century, a respectable old man would not run out to meet his disloyal son who had brought disgrace to his family and village. Yet the father in the parable *did* run out to welcome his son because he loved him passionately and naturally demonstrated his love. It did not matter to him that many of the people in the village would ridicule him, for the father had never ceased to love his son. He still loved him even when the son was squandering his inheritance in wild living. Had the father insisted on judging his younger son according to his good works, this story would have ended with a funeral instead of a celebration!

Even though the prodigal son's sin broke his relationship with his father, the father did not ask him to *earn* his forgiveness. Jesus is teaching us in this parable that God's love for each one of us is never rooted in our worthiness, but rather in His own nature. No amount of good works can make us acceptable to God. We are accepted by grace alone! Certainly Jesus is teaching that God's love is undeserved. God loves sinners and eagerly awaits their return. The heavenly Father patiently waits for the return of even the worst sinners because He loves people regardless of their own unworthiness. God, as described in the Bible, does not love only those who love Him. God demonstrated His inexhaustible love in action—and that demonstration was costly.

God's love in the Qur'an is conditional and arbitrary

The Qur'an, on the contrary, contains no statement that God loves (*uheb*) every living person unconditionally. The commonly used Arabic word for love is uheb. The Qur'an uses this word to reveal God's love only for "those who do good" (Surah 2:195). It states that God does not love (uheb) "those who do wrong" (Surah 3:57). Notice this limited use of the word uheb in the Qur'an. The Qur'an never said that God loves every living person and that God desires to enter into a loving relationship with the people he created.

The God who is described in the Qur'an does not watch over humankind with tenderness and concern. He does not pursue sinful people and seek to save them and to fellowship with them.

The Qur'an shows quite a different picture from what Jesus taught. We read in the Qur'an "Allah loves not transgressors" (Surah 2:190). The Qur'an states: ". . . Allah leads astray those whom He pleases and guides whom he pleases . . ." (Surah 14:4). We also read in the Qur'an: "If We had so willed, We could certainly have brought every soul its true guidance: But the word from me will come true: 'I will fill Hell with Jinns and men all together'" (Surah 32:13).

God, however, as revealed in the Bible, wants to guide every person to Himself and to salvation. "This is good, and pleases God our Savior, who wants all men to be saved and to come to a knowledge of the truth" (1 Timothy 2:3–4).

WHAT IS THE PERFECT FORM OF WORSHIP?

My dear reader, I'm sure you agree that it is important to discover the correct and perfect form of worship that our awesome Creator deserves and asks of us.

Is it the mere performance of religious duties?

Of course God knows that our mere performance of religious duties does not necessarily mean that we love Him, nor does it mean we are submissive to Him. It is possible for someone to perform all the religious duties while his heart and mind are not dedicated completely to God. Our bodies can bow to God while at the same time our hearts and minds are filled with sin. People can try to obey and serve God out of wrong motives such as fear, habit, pride, or prospect of reward. This is not true worship.

The perfect form of worship is loving God with our whole being

A Jewish religious leader asked Jesus, "'Teacher, which is the greatest commandment in the Law?' Jesus replied: 'Love the Lord your God with all your heart, and with all your soul, and with all your mind. This is the first and greatest commandment'" (Matthew 22:35–38).

Jesus taught us that loving God with all our heart, soul, and mind is what God desires of us in worshiping Him. Jesus also taught us that if we truly love God, we will express our love through obedience to Him.

In the Gospel, God is not just asking us to perform religious duties and obey His commandments, but rather He is asking us first to love Him with all our heart, soul, and mind. As a natural result we will want to obey Him. Loving God the way Jesus taught us means surrendering—giving ourselves totally to Him, and desiring to live everyday of our lives to please Him.

Therefore, my dear friend, Jesus' words recorded in the Gospel of Matthew reveal the mind and will of God. There is no higher or better form of worship we could offer to God than to love Him in such a complete way. This love is the perfect form of worship that pleases our Creator because it means giving God all our emotions, thoughts, desires, and our will.

IS IT POSSIBLE TO ENJOY A LOVING RELATIONSHIP WITH GOD?

Let us consider two important questions. First, is it possible for a believer to love God with all his heart, soul, and mind? Second, is the God who desires such love truly worthy to receive this love? (Think about the description of God who rules over this Universe.) My dear friend, to answer these questions, it is helpful for the believer to consider the following three aspects of love:

Is my relationship to God based on *genuine* love?

For your love to become genuine toward God, you must first experience His perfect and eternal forgiveness. Then your heart will be free from fear and guilt and you will be able to love Him. The person who has no assurance of forgiveness from God can not possibly serve God and keep His commandments out of genuine love. Such obedience seeks only the primary objective of trying to earn His forgiveness and reduce His wrath.

Is God's love for me so *full of expression* that it motivates me to love Him in return?

Your motivation to love God depends on how aware you become of His great love toward you. Believers who see and understand God's perfect demonstration of love toward them will respond in a more fervent way in love and thanksgiving toward God.

Can I experience God's love for me *in my own heart*?

Before you are able to feel love toward God, you need first to experience a touch of His divine love in your heart. Then you can have the natural desire from within your soul to love Him in return.

IS IT POSSIBLE FOR THE MUSLIM BELIEVER TO WHOLEHEARTEDLY LOVE GOD?

The answer to this question involves the same three important considerations:

(1) Is the believer's relationship to God based on genuine love?

(2) Is God's love for the believer so full of expression that it motivates him to love God in return?

(3) Can the believer experience God's love in his or her own heart? Let us examine each of these aspects of love.

According to the Qur'an, God is the Master and the believer is merely a slave

Consider all the obligations required of the Muslim who follows the teachings of the Qur'an and Muhammad today in regard to food and clothing regulations, performing the five daily prayers, and all the prescribed details which the Muslim must follow to gain merit from performing the Hajj pilgrimage, etc. We discover that Islam is primarily a religion of outward forms and rituals.

According to the Qur'an, God's love is conditioned upon the Muslim believer's performance. The Muslim believer is treated like a slave. Surah 19:93 states, "Not one of the beings in the heavens and the earth but must come to (Allah) Most Gracious as a *abd* (slave)." Abdullah Yusuf Ali, when translating this verse, incorrectly translated the original Arabic word *abd* as "servant," for abd can only mean "slave." God in the Qur'an is the Master, and the believer is only a slave (abd). A slave (as well as a servant) works to earn a place in his master's house. A slave does not work for the master's sake, but primarily for his own benefits and rewards.

When I was a child, about seven years old, my parents hired a servant to take care of the house. One of her duties was to make sure that I went to bed and was asleep before 9 pm. I remember that she loved watching TV, especially the movies that usually started just before my bedtime. In order for her to be able to watch more TV, she used to scare me by saying, "Samy, you must go to sleep now, or the boogey man and evil spirits will come into your room." She did not want me to go to sleep for my own good or because she loved my parents, but because she was serving her own desires. Looking back, I don't believe that she really loved me.

According to the Qur'an, not only does the Muslim believer's acceptance by God depend on the believer's performance, God the Master still has the right to reject them even if believers were to perform all the religious duties. This relationship is not conducive to heartfelt love. Genuine love cannot come from a servant-slave mentality.

My parents dismissed many servants throughout the years, even when they did a good job. I remember one time when this happened. I cried and complained, telling my parents, "Why did you let this servant go? He helped me in so many ways. This is not fair to me or to my servant." They answered that they were under no obligation to keep him—he was just a servant.

According to the Qur'an, God is an unpredictable judge

According to the Qur'an, God is commonly described as the Judge who never promises complete forgiveness of the believers' sins, nor does He guarantee to believers eternal life in

Paradise. Therefore, it is impossible for the Muslim believer to enjoy real peace in his heart. He cannot be free from fear knowing that God's judgment could be against him. According to Islamic teachers, God may forgive someone for committing serious sin if he wishes, or God may punish and condemn someone for a minor sin.

Surah 5:18 states about God, "... He forgiveth whom He pleaseth and He *uazebo* [tortures] whom He pleaseth ..." Here Ali mistranslated the original Arabic word *uazebo* as "punishes," for uazebo can only mean "tortures." During my work as an attorney in Egypt, I defended hundreds of people accused of violating the Law. I never saw one of them show feelings of love toward the judge. It seemed that the more my client was aware of the law and his offense, the more he was terrified before the judge.

Abu Bakr, one of Muhammad's closest companions whom Muslims believe to be the most exalted person after the prophets, was frightened about his own destiny. In *Teachings of Islam*, in the chapter entitled "Fear of Allah," he was quoted as saying, "I wish I were a blade of grass, whose life ended with the grazing by some beast."[1] He also said, "O, bird! How lucky you are! You eat, you drink, and fly under the shade of the trees and you fear no reckoning of the Day of Judgment! I wish I were just like you."[2]

Consider one of the most popular Islamic records about Umar, a very close companion to Muhammad who was the second leader to the Muslim world and was highly exalted by Muhammad and all Muslim scholars. "When the Muslims were very weak in the beginning [of Islam], the Prophet [Muhammad] prayed to Allah to strengthen the Muslims with Umar's Islam."[3] Yet Umar, also scared of hell, would often hold a straw in his hand and say, "I wish I were a straw like this."

And sometimes he would say, "I wish my mother had not given birth to me."[4]

Love must be genuine

In Surah 23:60, we read: "And those who dispense their charity with their hearts full of fear, because they will return to their Lord." Muhammad himself explained what is meant by that verse. "A'isha said, 'O, apostle of God, is the one who is afraid of God the one who commits adultery, steals, drinks wine, thus he is afraid of punishment?' Muhammad told her, 'No, O daughter of Sedik, he is the one who prays, fasts and gives alms, thus he is afraid that God may not accept these things from him.'"[5]

The fear of God's wrath and eternal punishment in hell makes the Muslims' love self-motivated.

The Muslim believer, therefore, cannot truly love God for God's sake but for his own sake in order to reduce God's wrath and try to gain God's forgiveness and acceptance. However, genuine love must be an exercise of the purest affections of the heart toward God. Naturally, God desires a willing response of love from those who worship Him.

Love must be full of expression

My dear friend, the Qur'an has very little to say about God's expression of love for you and me. The Qur'an does not tell us of any great act of love in the history of God's dealings with mankind. The Qur'an is silent about any deep and strong feelings of love that God has toward us. Throughout the pages of the Qur'an, there is no mention or demonstration of the full measure of God's love toward us.

Every time the word "love" (uheb) is written in the Qur'an it can be translated "approves of" rather than love, without any change of the meaning of the verse. The following verses are an example:

"And spend of your substance in the cause of Allah . . . do good, for Allah loveth those who do good" (Surah 2:195).

"If ye do love Allah, follow me: Allah will love you and forgive your sins . . ." (Surah 3:31). Notice that according to the Qur'an:

God asks people to love Him first and only then in return He will love them back.

God only loves those who love Him.

It is important to note also that the believer's knowledge of God's approval will only be known in the Last Day.

Love must be mutual

It is not possible, according to the Qur'an, for Muslim believers to actually experience God's love in their very own heart. We read in the Qur'an numerous names given to God: "He is Allah . . . to Him belong the Most beautiful names . . ." (Surah 59:24). According to Muslim scholars, there are ninety-nine beautiful names of God in the Qur'an. Note that these beautiful names do not include *AL-Muhebb*, which is the Arabic word for a "loving person." The closest name to indicate kindness in the Qur'an is *AL-Wadu*d (Surah 85:14), which means "The Kind or Amicable One." However this name, AL-Wadud, does not reveal the highest quality of divine love, which is self-sacrifice.

Understanding the love of God in Islam

One of the greatest Muslim theologians in Islamic history, Al-Ghazzali, explains that the expression AL-Wadud means far less than the title would seem to indicate. He wrote a book about the ninety-nine names of God, *AL-Maqsad al-Asna*, in which he states that this title AL-Wadud in the Qur'an is lesser in degree than the title "The Merciful" (*AL-Rahim*). All Muslim scholars agree with his opinion. God is called The Merciful over a hundred times in the Qur'an, and He is called AL-Wadud only twice (Surah 11:90 and Surah 85:14).

It is indisputable that sacrificial love is much stronger, richer, and deeper than mercy. Love is the greatest virtue and characteristic that anyone can have. A person can show mercy to a poor man by giving him a few dollars or something to eat. On the other hand, a father's love toward his child motivates him to sacrifice.

Al-Ghazzali explains God's love as consisting solely of objective acts of kindness and expressions of approval. He denies that the love of God involves any personal feelings. He denies that God feels any love in His own heart toward mankind. Al-Ghazzali states, "God remains above the feeling of love."[6] He confirms this unfortunate teaching in the Qur'an by describing God's love, "Love and Mercy are desired in respect of their objects only for the sake of their fruit and benefit and not because of empathy or feeling."[7] In other words, when God says He loves you, what He means is He will show mercy to you by giving you good things, but you cannot interpret that to mean that He feels anything in His heart for you. The God whom the Muslim scholars describe seems to have no heart.

It is important, my precious Muslim reader, to remember that, according to genuine orthodox Islamic beliefs and teachings about the 99 names of God, they are not part of God's essential being. They are no more than attributes of God. God may or may not express any one of them. Allah can choose to be faithful, forgiving, kind, etc. He can also choose to be unforgiving, harsh, etc.

My Muslim friend, the God whom the Qur'an depicts and introduces to us does not satisfy the thirst and longing of our souls. He cannot give rest or joy to our wandering hearts. Let me illustrate. A certain woman loved a man with all her heart. She wanted to please him and spend the rest of her life with him. Unfortunately, this man only bestowed gifts on her when she pleased him. He refused to let her know whether or not he loved her. And he refused to marry her. He wouldn't even guarantee that he would always be with her. This man wanted her only to be his slave. I ask you, if you were that woman, how would you feel? Would you feel loved? Would your heart be full of love for this man?

Likewise, it is impossible for Muslims to give God the most perfect form of worship, which again is to love God with all their heart, soul, and mind. They are unable to have and to express such love to God through joyful and willing submission to His commandments.

Most Muslim teachers present the Allah of Islam as one to be glorified chiefly in His detachment from His creatures. It appears to them that this is essential to His honor and majesty.

IS IT POSSIBLE FOR THE CHRISTIAN BELIEVER TO WHOLEHEARTEDLY LOVE GOD?

By comparison, the God of the Bible does make it possible for Christian believers to love Him with all their heart, soul, and mind and thus give God "perfect worship."

God in the Gospel is commonly called "the Father"

God allows us to enter into a wonderful relationship with Him as His children. "Yet to all who received him [Jesus], to those who believed in his name, he gave the right to become children of God—children born not of natural descent, nor of human decision or a husband's will, but born of God" (John 1:12–13). The moment you believe in Jesus, a miracle takes place—you are born of God's Spirit and become a child of God!

This new relationship between God and the believer leads to an interactive and personal love. Even though God loves everybody, the moment you are born of His Spirit, God feels the most irresistible attachment to you. I remember seeing a father holding a newborn baby in his hands. To him and his wife, this is the most precious and beautiful baby in the world, regardless of how the baby looks—even if the baby cries, spit up, and smells bad!

God showed me that he loves me much, much more than these parents could ever love their baby. Through the demonstration of love by these parents, I could feel God saying to me "Even though I love every living person, you Samy, are my child. You are more special to me than the people that haven't yet become my children. I know all your mistakes, past failures, present weaknesses, and regardless of anything, you are my most treasured and precious possession. You are born of my Spirit and you are my child! You are a part of Me and I am part of you!" Ever since I have become a child of God, in February 1976, I have been enjoying God's Fatherhood heart.

All that a perfect father wants to be to his children, God is and will do to you when you are born of His Spirit and approach Him in prayer. Because we are His children, there is nothing that can separate us from the love of God (Romans 8:38–39).

In a reverent way I will say this: God feels the most irresistible attraction towards all His children. My precious reader, only through knowing God as your Father can you enjoy the fullness of His deep love for you and be assured of His goodwill and wonderful plans toward you.

Jesus instructed His disciples on how to pray to God. As a model prayer, Jesus said to address God as "our Father" (Matthew 6). Jesus said to His disciples, "The Father himself loves you" (John 16:27).

Some of my Muslim friends told me, "You Christians don't give God the proper respect by making Him your Father; you pull Him down to your level."

I always replied, "The truth is, we have not pulled God down to our level by making Him our Father. Instead, God raised us to the highest level because He has made us His children. We still bow down before Him and approach His throne with awe. And at the same time, we also have peace and confidence because we know that He is our gracious heavenly Father."

We read in the Bible, "How great is the love the Father has lavished on us, that we should be called children of God! And that is what we are!" (1 John 3:1). "Father" is the Christian name for God.

This is one of the most amazing manifestations of the love of God. We were orphans bound as slaves in Satan's kingdom—robbed of dignity, peace, and joy of family. We were filthy, poor, and helpless, judged to spend eternity in Hell because of our sin and miserable condition.

It is truly amazing that the Bible revealed to us God as the most noble and powerful king who fought Satan on our behalf and won the battle through Jesus Christ's death and resurrection.

He broke the chains that were binding us, destroyed the walls that were separating us from Him and from freedom. Now He is personally inviting you; saying, "I want to cleanse you and forgive you. I want you to come to Me. I want you to be part of My kingdom. I want to adopt you into My family. You will bear My name and be My heir."

The Bible clearly assures us, "Now if we are children, then we are heirs . . ." (Romans 8:17). We will always be God's children. While a servant must work to earn his place in his master's house, we as God's children cannot be dismissed. We are not frightened of God as a master whose acceptance we have to strive to obtain.

I love God's word that states, "There is no fear in love but perfect love drives out fear, because fear has to do with punishment. The one who fears is not made perfect in love" (1 John 4:18).

These words mean that those who are not sure that God will forgive their sins will be frightened of God. If fear exists in their hearts that God may punish them eternally, love cannot grow in their hearts toward God.

It is so comforting to know that Jesus said, "'Do not be afraid, little flock, for your Father has been pleased to give you the kingdom'" (Luke 12:32). Heaven will be our home because God has made us His children!

We look to our Father whose kingdom is our home. We can now rejoice that one day we will share and enjoy His glory.

Since true followers of Christ are God's children, He will never condemn them to spend eternity or even one day in hell. However, God does chasten His children here on earth for the purpose of correcting them (Hebrews 12:5–11). But we have the assurance that all His discipline is accompanied by love and forgiveness. Unconditional love and readiness to forgive always characterize His relationship with us as His children (1 John 1:9). My precious friend, God wants you to become a citizen in His Heavenly Kingdom. God is the King and He desires to make you a royal child.

Who is this God that rules the universe?

In the Gospel, the most prevalent characteristic revealed about God is that, "God is Love" (1 John 4:8). God loves us because of who He is, not because of who we are. Because He is a loving God. He offers to care for us.

He is not a God who acts sometimes in a merciful and kind way. He is pure love. His heart is full of emotions of love for you and me. Remember, God asked Abraham to sacrifice his son to prove Abraham's love for God. And God revealed His love for us in this same sacrificial way!

Just as Abraham could not have expressed his love for God in a more fervent way than what he did, God also chose the most radical way to show His love for you and me.

So, my dear Muslim friend, what kind of God do you think rules over this universe? Is He the kind of God who says, "You must obey Me, serve Me, give Me your life," while He is distant in heaven without loving feelings for us? The Gospel does not present such a picture like that of God.

God gave us His Son to prove His passionate and sacrificial love. We read in the Bible, "But God demonstrates his own love for us in this: While we were still sinners, Christ died for us" (Romans 5:8). Again, God did the greatest thing He could possibly do to reveal His deep, strong, and perfect love for you and me. No better proof can be given to mankind than this. God gave us that which is most precious to His heart.

Not only can we see God's awesome love for us in the gift of His Son, but the Bible reveals to us that Jesus' life fully expressed God's own love for us. Jesus revealed God Himself to us. Jesus said, ". . . Anyone who has seen me has seen the Father" (John 14:9).

We can experience God's love through the Holy Spirit

God gives us the Holy Spirit to dwell within us and make us conscious of His love toward us. The Holy Spirit takes up residence in our hearts the moment we place our faith in Christ as our Savior, which enables us to experience God's fatherly love in our hearts and souls. The Bible promises, "And hope does not disappoint us, because God has poured out his love into our hearts by the Holy Spirit, whom he has given us" (Romans 5:5).

We read in the Bible, "Because you are sons, God sent the Spirit of his Son into our hearts, the Spirit who calls out, 'Abba, Father.' So you are no longer a slave, but a son; and since you are a son, God has made you also an heir" (Galatians 4:6–7).

The love of the heavenly Father, made manifest in Jesus Christ, becomes a reality in our hearts and lives through the Holy Spirit whom God placed within our hearts. We read in the Bible, "For you did not receive a spirit that makes you a slave again to fear, but you received the Spirit of sonship. And by him we cry, 'Abba, Father.' The Spirit himself testifies with our spirit that we are God's children" (Romans 8:15–16).

To make this fact a little more clear to you, my precious Muslim reader, imagine a man who adopts a child. After all the forms are filled, the papers are processed, and the adoption becomes legal, the moment comes when this kind man takes the child to his home. The child is shown a room filled with toys. The man gently says to the child, "Do you see this beautiful room? This is your room. Do you see all of these toys? These are your toys. This house is your house, and I am your father who loves you." Then he gives the child a big warm hug. Imagine how valuable and glorious this child will feel in these precious moments. You, too, will have the most awesome experience when the Holy Spirit enters your life.

The wonderful news God gave us through the Gospel is, "And you also were included in Christ when you heard the word of truth, the gospel of your salvation. Having believed you were marked in him with a seal, the promised Holy Spirit, who is a deposit guaranteeing our inheritance until the redemption of those who are God's possession—to the praise of his glory" (Ephesians 1:13–14). The Holy Spirit is the deposit guaranteeing our inheritance until we acquire possession of it. The seal of God is upon us. The Holy Spirit gives us the assurance that our adoption as God's children is forever.

Conclusion after Comparing the Description of God in Islam and Christianity

We can clearly see in this chapter that only the Bible contains the true and complete revelation of God because:

- God, as described in the Bible, created people to give Him the perfect form of worship, which according to Jesus' words is "to love Him with all our heart, soul, and mind." It certainly makes sense that the Creator deserves to receive the perfect form of worship from His creation.

- God as revealed in the Gospel has the most wonderful character. He is absolutely a perfect God. He passionately reveals His magnificent love for us through Jesus Christ's willing sacrifice on the cross. He desires us to become His children and has made it possible for us to experience His fatherly love through the Holy Spirit who dwells within us. It is certainly true that God who rules the world has the most beautiful character.

- God, as described in the Bible, made it possible for us to give Him the perfect form of worship as a natural response to what God has done for us, and in us, and shall do for us forever as believers. Such love and grace! The true Christian can sincerely tell God, "There is no limit to the potential of my love for You. I want to love You, seek You, and serve You everyday of my life."

Important observation about our relationship with God

It is certainly acknowledged that multitudes of sincere Muslims make a genuine effort to please the Creator—the one and living God—who created heaven and earth. The Bible and the Qur'an do contain similarities in their teachings of the attributes of God. Examples are: God is one, He is creator, forgiver, judge, all-powerful, eternal, all-knowing, and merciful.

However, there are serious differences in their meanings of these terms. For example, referring to God as decribed in the Bible, His mercy flows from His *unconditional love* for every person, which is demonstrated by Jesus' voluntary sacrificing of Himself on the cross to pay the penalty for our sins so that we can have eternal life!

The summary of my message to you, my precious Muslim reader, is that we the believers of Jesus Christ have been forgiven by God, have come to enjoy a living relationship with God, have received the Spirit of God in our hearts, and have been adopted by God as His eternal children. He made us heirs of His kingdom. You, too, can have a living relationship with God. You can experience Him as your loving heavenly Father. You can enjoy His forgiveness right now. And you can be assured of His divine presence in your life and can be certain that heaven is your home and destiny.

While Muslims know many facts about God, it is only within the pages of the Gospel that the fullness of God's character and His will are revealed. The reason for writing this book is to help the Muslim person not only reach a true understanding of God, but to pass from death into everlasting life by joining the family of God. This happens when the Holy Spirit comes to dwell within the Muslim person. He or she becomes a new creation in Christ (regenerated) (John 5:24; Titus 3:5).

A word from my heart

Dear reader, I remember clearly the time I put my faith in Jesus. I felt that God was embracing me and giving me a big hug. I can easily say I am in love with God. He is worthy of my life and my affection. I love Him with all my heart. I want to know Him more closely, to serve Him more, and to praise Him. My pleasure and satisfaction are found in giving Him every day of my life. I can say as the apostle Paul did, "For Christ's love compels us . . ." (2 Corinthians 5:14). That is, God's love compels me to forget myself and joyfully submit my life even as a slave in God's hand. I become His slave not out of fear, or obligation, or out of what I could get from Him, but because I love Him.

These remarks are not empty words or theories. They line up with God's truth in the Gospel. My purpose for writing this book is to help you experience in your own heart God's deep and personal love for you. You too, my friend, can experience God in your life as your loving heavenly Father. You can feel His embrace in your heart and enjoy His very presence within you if you go to Him through Jesus Christ. If you step out in faith and go to God telling Him that you don't want to continue living in sin anymore and that you believe that Jesus Christ died for the forgiveness of your sins, then you will experience God's forgiveness. When He enters your life, you will experience His wonderful peace and love immediately, right where you are!

The Fatherly love of God for you, my dear Muslim friend, is unsurpassed. The moment you accept Jesus as your Savior and Lord, you will be spiritually born again and you will experience the heavenly Father's loving arms drawing you to His bosom. Then you will find yourself drawn to Him with the most irresistible attraction. You will fall in love with Him from the depth of your being!

My precious Muslim reader, I beg you, do not strive all your life to try to gain the favor of God. Right now, you can begin enjoying God's favor in the depth of your heart by simply placing yourself in the position to receive it:

1. Admit that you are a sinner.

2. Repent of your sins; decide not to live in sin anymore. (*toba* in Arabic)

3. Put your faith in Jesus Christ as your personal savior

from sin and its penalty.

4. This is your testimony (*shahada* in Arabic) that Jesus is your Savior.

30

JESUS IS UNIQUE BECAUSE HE IS OUR SAVIOR

The Bible teaches that we are all separated from God as sinners in need of the Savior. We all need to be reconciled to God.

Sinners need the Savior

The problem is that sin is an integral part of our human nature. All kinds of iniquity dwell in the human heart, such as lust, envy, greed, pride, hatred, selfishness, and dishonesty. Sin has a vicious control within each person. All human bodies are captive to the power of sin and its ongoing temptations.

Jesus won the battle against Satan and sin

The Gospel tells us that Jesus, the only One who is pure from sin came "in the likeness of sinful man" and "he condemned sin in sinful man [in the flesh]" (Romans 8:3). He lived without committing one single sin. Jesus had complete victory over all of Satan's temptations. Jesus' divine nature guaranteed His victory in the battle against Satan and sin. Jesus won the battle on our behalf. The awesome news of the Gospel is that Jesus came and defeated the power of sin in its own dwelling place inside the human body.

We can be free from the love and power of sin

The wonderful news of the Gospel is that God made it possible for you to be united with Jesus through His Spirit, who will reside within you at the very moment you place your faith in Jesus as your Savior. As a natural consequence of being united with Jesus, you will enjoy the fruits of His victory. You can experience freedom from the bondage to sin for the first time in your life. Jesus said, "I tell you the truth, everyone who sins is a slave to sin," and he also said, "If the Son sets you free, you will be free indeed" (John 8:34, 36). We can only be liberated from the bondage of sin by the power of God within us. We can not be set free by our own willpower.

The Gospel's beautiful message is that the Son of God came as the unique man, Jesus, to save you and set you free from the captivity and love of sin. (Please read Romans 6:4–14.) The Savior Jesus Christ came to do what the law and prophets could not do. "The reason the Son of God appeared was to destroy the devil's work" (1 John 3:8).

Physicians can cure many physical illnesses, but only Jesus can heal sinners and make them righteous.

Jesus warns us, ". . . If you do not believe that I am the one I claim to be, you will indeed die in your sins" (John 8:24 NKJV).

Jesus paid the penalty for our sins

God is just and requires payment for all the offenses (sins) we committed against Him. Jesus made the payment by taking the punishment in our place.

Jesus suffered the most horrible consequence of our sin—death. He endured the cross on our behalf. By suffering the wrath of God toward sin, Jesus paid for the sin of every person.

Because believers in Christ are united with Him, they share in Christ's death and resurrection. "If we have been united with him like this in his death, we will certainly also be united with him in his resurrection" (Romans 6:5).

The Good News of the Bible is that Jesus came to save you and me and set us free from having to pay our own penalty for our sins. The penalty has been paid.

We can feel God's forgiveness in our hearts

The wonderful news of the Gospel is that the moment you believe in Jesus as your Lord and Savior and are united with Him, you can experience for the first time in your life, right within your heart, the forgiveness of God for all your sins. You will enjoy wonderful peace with God. God will look at you as if your old sinful nature had died with Christ. And Christ's righteousness will be counted as yours.

Jesus conquered death

The glorious news of the Gospel is that Jesus came and conquered death itself. When Jesus' bodily rose from the dead and ascended to be with God the Father, He declared victory over death. Jesus reversed the worst consequence of sin, which is eternal separation from God's presence. Christ's resurrection is the first in a long line of resurrections to come of those who believe in Him. True believers in Christ will never die spiritually, but will enjoy eternal life with God forever. We read, "But Christ has indeed been raised from the dead, the firstfruits of those who have fallen asleep" (1 Corinthians 15:20).

Assurance of heaven

You can also be certain within your soul that you are going to heaven. The amazing news of the Gospel is that the moment you believe in Jesus and go to God in repentance, God's Holy Spirit will come to dwell within you, and He will assure you that you are now going to heaven. Paradise will become your home and your destiny. The Gospel declares: "And if the Spirit of him who raised Jesus from the dead is living in you, he who raised Christ from the dead will also give life to your mortal bodies through his Spirit, who lives in you" (Romans 8:11). (See also 1 Peter 1:3–4; Ephesians 2:6.)

The reason that you will know for sure that you are going to heaven is that the same Jesus who lives in heaven will come to live in you now through His eternal Spirit. The living and life-giving Spirit of Christ imparts to you eternal life. Jesus declares to us in the Gospel, "Because I live, you also will live" (John 14:19). It is only through Jesus that you can be united to God!

Jesus bridged the gap between mankind and God

My precious reader, the Son of God came as the unique God-Man Jesus to save us. Jesus fully bridged the gap between heaven (God) and earth (mankind). He made it possible for sinful man to be reconciled with the Holy God.

For this reason, the Gospel declares, "Salvation is found in no one else, for there is no other name under heaven given to men by which we must be saved" (Acts 4:12). Jesus stated clearly, "I am the gate; whoever enters through me will be saved" (John 10:9). Jesus further declared, "I am the way and the truth and the life. No one comes to the Father except through me" (John 14:6).

Jesus satisfies our spiritual thirst

Jesus wants to be your friend. (John 15:14-15) Jesus knows that you need a genuine friend to depend on. Jesus would like to be your perfect friend.

Jesus said, ". . . I have come that they may have life, and have it to the full" (John 10:10). God created us in such a way that we will never be satisfied or enjoy life fully until we have the right relationship with Him through faith in Jesus.

Jesus can satisfy our deepest spiritual longing. He said, "I am the bread of life. He who comes to me will never go hungry, and he who believes in me will never be thirsty" (John 6:35). ". . . Jesus stood and said in a loud voice, 'If anyone is thirsty, let him come to me and drink'" (John 7:37). Your soul is thirsty and seeks to find happiness everywhere but without success. When you go to Jesus, believe in Him and follow His teachings, you will be satisfied forever.

God is inviting you to a life of joy despite any adverse circumstances you may face. Jesus said, "I have told you this so that my joy may be in you and that your joy may be complete" (John 15:11).

WHAT IS YOUR DECISION?

Jesus speaks to all people through the Gospel. He speaks to you, my Muslim friend, because He loves you. Jesus promised, "Come to me, all you who are weary and burdened, and I will give you rest" (Matthew 11:28).

Jesus wants to guide you and help you discover the purpose of your life. "When Jesus spoke again to the people, he said, 'I am the light of the world. Whoever follows me will never walk in darkness, but will have the light of life'" (John 8:12).

Jesus offers eternal life to you and to me. "Most assuredly, I say to you, he who believes in Me has everlasting life" (John 6:47 NKJV).

God's supreme love draws us to Him

My dear friend, I urge you to believe God's Word and take a step by faith. I know from personal experience that the moment you believe in Jesus as your Lord and Savior, you too will actually experience and taste within your heart and soul God's great and wonderful love for you. God wants to make you satisfied. He desires to fill your life with joy, love, hope, and peace. God desires to have fellowship with you, thus fulfilling His eternal purpose. God is speaking to you right now saying,

"I have loved you with an everlasting love; I have drawn you with loving-kindness" (Jeremiah 31:3).

Jesus declares, "For God so loved the world that he gave his one and only Son, that whoever believes in him shall not perish but have eternal life" (John 3:16).

For God	the greatest Lover
so loved	the greatest degree
the world	the greatest company
that he gave	the greatest act
his one and only Son	the greatest gift (Jesus)
that whoever	the greatest opportunity
believes	the greatest simplicity
in him	the greatest attraction
should not perish	the greatest promise
but	the greatest difference
have	the greatest certainty
everlasting life	the greatest possession!

My friend, our loving God yearns for your companionship. He chose *you*—now the choice is *yours*. Romans 10:8–9 tells us how to be saved, "The word is near you; it is in your mouth and in your heart, that is, the word of faith we are proclaiming: That if you confess with your mouth, 'Jesus is Lord,' and believe in your heart that God raised him from the dead, you will be saved."

Your salvation depends on your decision. If you choose to put your faith in Jesus as your Lord and Savior, here is a suggested personal and specific prayer. Pray it if you mean it with all your heart.

God, I want to know You and enjoy Your amazing love. I want to experience Your salvation. I know I am a sinner. I repent of my sins and ask you to forgive me. I do not desire to live in sin any longer. Thank you, Jesus, for taking my place and dying on the cross for my sins. I believe in my heart that God raised You from the dead. Jesus, I ask you to come into my life. Cleanse me of my sin, and be my Savior and my Lord. Help me to walk with God, and submit to His will every day. I pray this from my heart. Amen.

If you prayed this prayer, let me be the first one to welcome you into God's eternal family. I would like to congratulate you on having made the best and most important decision of your life—to receive the miracle of eternal life with God!

Your new life walking with God

My dear brother or sister in Christ, now that you are born again, please pay attention to these important issues:

First, find a church that faithfully teaches God's Word. It is essential to join an *evangelical* church that teaches that one must be born again by the Spirit of God (John 3:3). Please beware of church groups that claim to be "Christians" but do not correctly follow the teachings of the Gospel.

Second, it is important to read the Bible daily. It is the complete, inspired, and reliable Word of God! And remember to spend time in God's presence in prayer so that you will grow spiritually.

Lastly, before I leave you, I want you to know that while we are on this earth, we will all face difficulties. However, God promises that He will be with us, and He will work all things together for our good (Romans 8:28).

My Christian friend, now you are in the beginning of your journey of discovering the fruitful, meaningful, and rich life that God created you to live. By walking with God daily through faith you will experience God's promises for you. And you will be able to enjoy the wonderful blessings and marvelous love that God has for you.

Your servant

Samy Tanagho

Samy Tanagho

APPENDIX

ABDULLAH IBN ABBAS

(Companion to Muhammad)

According to Islamic records, Abdullah Ibn Abbas attached himself to the service of Muhammad. He was attentive and alert to whatever Muhammad did and said. He became one of Muhammad's most learned companions. Muhammad prayed that Abdullah Ibn Abbas be granted not just knowledge and understanding but also wisdom. Muhammad would often pray: "O Lord, make him acquire a deep understanding of the religion of Islam and instruct him in the meaning and interpretation of things." The Khalifah, Umar Ibn Al-Khattab, often sought his advice on important matters of state and described him as "the young man of maturity." (*Companions of the Prophet* #2, published by MELS, 61 Alexandra Road, Hendon, London, NW42RX. Abdul Wahid Hamid 1995, 1998)

AL-BUKHARI

(Recorder of the Hadith, containing Muhammad's words and actions)

Note that we are using the nine-volume translation of the Hadith (by Al-Bukhari) made by Dr. Muhammad Muhsin Khan entitled, *The Translation of the Meanings of Sahih Al-Bukhari*, published by Dar AHYA US-Sunnah Al NABAWIYA. This translation is recommended and approved by all Muslim authorities, including the spiritual leaders of Mecca and Medina. The introduction of Dr. Khan's translation (Volume 1) states that it has been unanimously agreed that Imam Bukhari's work is the most authentic of all the other works in Hadith literature put together. The authenticity of Al-Bukhari's work is such that the religious learned scholars of Islam said concerning him: "The most authentic book after the book of Allah [The Qur'an] is Sahih Al-Bukhari." (page 15 of Vol. 1)

BIBLIOGRAPHY

Note that all Islamic reference books listed below are recognized internationally in the Muslim world. They are re-published annually and distributed in Muslim bookstores worldwide.

Abdul-Haqq, Abdiyah Akbar. *Christ in the New Testament and the Qur'an.* Abdul-Haqq, Evanston, USA (1975)

Abdul-Haqq, Abdiyah Akbar. *Sharing Your Faith With a Muslim.* Bethany Fellowship, Minneapolis, MN (1980)

Abi Hanifah. *Al-Fiqh al-Akbar.* Dar al-Kutub al-Elmeyah, Beirut (1979)

Al-Ahadith Al-Qudsiyyah. *Divine Narratives.* Translated by Dr. Abdul Khaliqkazi and Dr. Alan B. Day, Dar Al-Iman Publishing House, Tripoli-Lebanon (no date)

Al-Baidawi. *Commentary on the Qur'an.* Dar Al-Kotob Al-Ilmiyah, Beirut, (1999)

Al-Ghazzali. *The Ninety-Nine Beautiful Names of God (AL-Maqsad AL-Asna).* Translated by David Burrell and Nazih Daher, The Islamic Texts Society, Cambridge (1992)

Al-Qartaby. *Commentary on the Qur'an.* Dar Al-Kotob Al-Ilmiyah, Beirut, (1996)

Al-Qasemi. *Tafsir (Commentary) of the Holy Qur'an.* Abbreviation to Tafsir Al-Qasemi (Mahasen At.Ta aweel), Beirut, Dar Al-Nafaas (1993)

Al-Razi. *Tafsir-Al Kabir.* Vol. 3, Dar Ehia Al-Tourath Al-Arabi, Beruit (1999)

Al-Razi, Fakhr-ul-Din. *Tafsir-Al Kabir*. Dar Al-Kutub Al-Ilmiyya, Beirut (1990)

Al-Suyuti. *AL-Itqan in Qur'an's Science (AL-Itqan)*. Dar Al-Ketab-Al-Araby, Beirut, (1999)

Alam, Maulana Syed Mohammad Badre. *Descension of Jesus Christ*. Dini Book, Dehli (1974)

Ali, Abdullah Yusuf. *The Meaning of the Holy Qur'an*. Eighth Edition, Amana Publications, Beltsville, MD (1996)

Al-Zamkhashri. *The Kash-Shaf*. Dar Al-Ketob Al-Elmiyah, Beirut (1990)

Anderson, M. *Jesus, the Light and Fragrance of God*. 2 vols., Pioneer Book Company, Caney, KS (1994)

Anderson, M. *The Trinity*. Pioneer Book Company, Caney, KS (1994)

Arberry, A.J. *Revelation and Reason in Islam*. George Allen & Unwin Ltd., London (no date)

Assfy, Z. *Islam and Christianity*. William Sessions Ltd., York, UK (1977)

At Tabari. *The Book of Religion and Empire*. Law Publishing Company, Lahore, Pakistan.

At Tabari. *Commentary on the Qur'an*. (Tafsir). Dar Al-Kotob- Al-Ilmiyah, Beirut, Lebanon (1999)

Bevan, J. *Christianity Explained to Muslims*. YMCA Publishing House, Calcutta (1952)

Bhai, Abdullah. *AL-Masih—the Anointed One*. CMM, Springfield, MO (no date)

Boice, James Montgomery. *Foundations of the Christian Faith*. InterVarsity Press, Downers Grove, IL (1981)

Brown, D. *The Divine Trinity, Christianity and Islam*. Sheldon Press, London (1967)

Broyles, C.C. "The Redeeming King: Psalm 72's Contribution to the Messianic Ideal," in C.A. Evans and P.W. Flint, *Eschatology,*

Messianism and the Dead Sea Scrolls. ed., Williams B. Eerdmans Publishing Company, Grand Rapids, MI (1997)

Bruce, F.F. *The New Testament Documents: Are They Reliable?* Inter Varsity Press, Downers Grove, IL (2000)

Burrows, Millar. *The Dead Sea Scrolls.* The Viking Press, New York, (1955)

Chapman, Colin. *You Go and Do the Same: Studies in Relating to Muslims.* CMS, London (1983)

Cragg, K. *Jesus and the Muslim.* George, Allen and Unwin, London (1985)

Crawford, Craig. *The Prophecies: A Journey to the End of Time.* Prophecy Press (1999)

Durrani, Dr. M.H. *The Qur'anic Facts About Jesus.* International Islamic Publishers, Karachi, Pakistan (1983)

Enns, Paul P. *The Moody Handbook of Theology.* Moody Press, Chicago (1989)

Ersen, Ishak. *Jesus Christ in the Traditions of Islam.* Light of Life, Villach, Austria (1992)

Fadi, Abd Al. *Sin and Atonement in Islam and Christianity.* Markaz-ash-Shabiba, Beirut (no date)

Geisler, Norman and Nix, William. *From God To Us: How We Got Our Bible.* Moody Press, Chicago (1974)

Ghabril, Nicola Yacob. *Themes for the Diligent: The Good Way.* Rikon, Switzerland (no date)

Gilchrist, John. *The Christian Witness to Muslims.* Roodepoort Mission Press, Roodepoort, Republic of South Africa (1988)

Goldsack, W. *Christ in Islam.* The Christian Literature Society, Madras, India (1905)

Guillaume, A. *Life of Muhammad.* A Translation of Ibn Ishaq's Sirat Arasul, London (1955)

The Hadith. CD-ROM. ISL Software Corporation (1996) ALIM.

Hafiz, Sheikh-Ul-Hadith Maualana and Kandhalwi, Muhammad Zakariyya. *Teachings of Islam: Stories of the Sahaabah.* (rev. trans. of the Urdu book *Hikayat-e-Sahaabah*) Translated by Abdul Rashid Arshad, Library of Islam, Des Plaines, Il (pub. date unknown)

Hahn, E. *Jesus in Islam.* (publishing house not available), Vaniyamki, India (1975)

Halverson, Dean C. *The Compact Guide to World Religions.* Bethany House Publishers, Minneapolis, MN (1996)

Hanifah, Imam Abi. *Al-Fiqh al-Akbar.* Dar AL-Kutub al-elmeyah, Beirut (1997)

Harman, Henry, M. *Introduction to the Study of the Holy Scriptures.* Volume I, Hunt and Eaton, New York (1878)

Hughes, Thomas P. *A Dictionary of Islam.* Lahore, Pakistan: The Premier Book House (1986)

Ibn Hisham, Al Sira AL Nabawia. DAR Ibn Hazm publication, Berut, Lebanon.

Imran, Maulana Muhammad. *The Teachings of Jesus in the Light of A-Qur'an.* Malik Sirajudden and Sons, Lahore, Pakistan (1980)

Jadeed, Iskander. *Did God Appear in the Flesh?* The Good Way, Rikon, Switzerland (no date)

Jadeed, Iskander. *How to Share the Gospel with Our Muslim Brothers.* Light of Life, Villach, Austria (no date)

Jadeed, Iskander. *The Cross in the Gospel and Qur'an.* Markaz-ash-Shabiba, Beirut (no date)

Jalalan, AL. *Commentary of AL Jalalan.* (1983)

Josephus, Flavius. *The Complete Works of Josephus.* translated by W. Whitson, Kregel Publications, Grand Rapids, MI (1981)

Kateregga, Badru D. and Shenk, David W. *A Muslim and A Christian in Dialogue.* Herald Press, PA (1997)

Kateregga, Badru D. and Shenk, David W. *Islam and Christianity.* Uzima Press Ltd., Kenya (1980)

Khalid Muhammad Khalid. *The Successor of the Prophet.* Dar
Thabet (1986)

Khaliqkazi, Abdul, and Day, A.B. *Al-Ahadith AL-Qudsiyyah.* Dar Al-
Iman Publishing House, Tripoli-Lebanon (no date)

Khan, Muhammad Muhsin. *The Translation of the Meanings of
Sahih Al-Bukhari.* 9 vols., Dar Ahya Us-Sunnah (1971)

Kramers, J.H. *Shorter Encyclopedia of Islam.* New York (1961)

Larson, Gary N. *The New Unger's Bible Handbook, Revised.* Moody
Press, London (1984)

Lockyer, Herbert. *All the Messianic Prophecies of the Bible.*
Zondervan Publishing House, Grand Rapids, MI (1973)

Maurer, Andreas. *Illustrations, Parables and Stories.* Mercsa,
Mondeor, Republic of South Africa (1994)

McDowell, Josh. *The New Evidence That Demands A Verdict.*
Thomas Nelson Publishers, Nashville, Tennessee (1999)

Morin, Harry. *Responding to Muslims.* CMM, Springfield, MO (1994)

Morris, Henry M. *Science and the Bible.* Moody Press, Chicago (1986)

Nurbakhash, Javad. *Jesus in the Eyes of the Sufis.* Khaniqahi-
Nimatullahi Publications, London (1983)

Obaray, A.H. *Miraculous Conception, Death, Resurrection and
Ascension of Jesus as Taught in the Kuran.* Kimberley, Republic
of South Africa (1962)

Orethke, J.P. *A Christian Approach to Muslims.* William Carey
Library, Pasadena, CA (1979)

Parrinder, G. *Jesus in the Qur'an.* Oxford University Press, New
York (1977)

Payne, J. Barton, *Encyclopedia of Biblical Prophecy.* 5th ed. Baker
Book House, Grand Rapids, MI (1987)

Pfander, C.G. *Balance of Truth.* Light of Life, Villach, Austria (1986)

Pickthall, Mohammad Marmaduke. *The Meaning of the Glorious
Qur'an.* Dar Ahya US-Sunnah Al-Nabawiya (1930)

Qaradawi, al-Yousef, Elewah Mostafa and Ali Gammar. *t-Twahid*. Qatar, (1968)

Register, R.G. *Dialogue and Interfaith Witness with Muslims*. Moody Books, Inc., Chicago, IL (1979)

Robertson, K.G. *Jesus or Isa*. Vantage Press, New York (1983)

Robson, J. *Christ in Islam*. John Murray, London (1929)

Ryrie, Charles C. *Basic Theology*. Moody Press, Wheaton, IL (1981)

Schaff, Philip. *The Creeds of Christendom: with History and Critical Notes*. Edited by David S. Schaff. Vol 1, *The History of the Creeds*. Baker Book House, Grand Rapids, MI (1983)

Shahid, Dr. Samuel. *The Fallen Nature of Man in Islam and Christianity*. AL-Nour, Colorado Springs, CO (1989)

Smith, Chuck. *Answers for Today*. The Word for Today, Costa Mesa, CA (1993)

Smith, John Pye. *The Scripture Testimony to the Messiah*. William Oliphant and Company, Edinburgh, Scotland (1859)

Smith, Wilbur M. *Therefore Stand: Christian Apologetics*. Grand Rapids: Baker Book House (1965)

Tisdail, William St. Clair. *Christian Reply to Muslim Objections*. Light of Life, Villach, Austria (1904)

Walfson, Harry Austryn. *The Philosophy of the Kalam*. Harvard University Press (1976)

Walvoord, John F. *Every Prophecy of the Bible*. Cook Communications, Colorado Springs, CO (1999)

Wismer, D. *The Islamic Jesus*. Gerland Publishing, Inc., New York (1977)

Zwemer, S. *The Moslem Doctrine of God*. Oliphant, Anderson and Ferrier, London (1905)

Zwemer, S. *The Moslem Christ*. Oliphant, Anderson and Ferrier, London (1912)

NOTES

As previously noted, all Islamic reference books listed below are recognized internationally in the Muslim world. They are republished annually and distributed in Muslim bookstores worldwide.

Chapter One:

1. The *Hadith* (Traditions) is the recorded sayings and actions of Muhammad, the prophet of Islam. This record is according to his wives, companions, members of his family, and Muslim leaders. The majority of the Muslim scholars of the world believe that the collections of the Hadith, in Al-Bukhari and Muslim, are regarded as Holy Books in addition to the Qur'an. Therefore, the Hadith is the second source of Islamic religious authority after the Qur'an.
2. Colin Chapman, *You Go and Do the Same: Studies in Relating to Muslims* (London: CMS, 1983), 53.
3. At Tabari, Commentary on the Qur'an (Tafsir), Vol. 4, 649.
4. Ibn Hisham, Alsira Alnabawia, 267.

Chapter Two:

1. Thomas Hughes, *Dictionary of Islam* (Lahore: Priemier Book house, 1986), 62.

Chapter Three:

1. David Shenk and Badru Kateregga, *A Muslim and A Christian in Dialogue* (Scottdale, PA: Herald Press, 1997), 142.
2. See Bibliography (McDowell).
3. Geisler and Nix, *From God to Us: How We Got Our Bible,* 139.
4. See Bibliography (Bruce, Geisler and Nix).
5. McDowell, Josh, *The New Evidence That Demands a Verdict,* 193.

6. (Graham, Franklin. *The Name*, Nashville: Thomas Nelson, 2002), 71–72.
7. See Bibliography (Morris).
8. See Bibliography (Walvoord).
9. Harman, H.M., *Introduction to the Study of the Holy Scriptures*, 488.
10. Ibid, 465.
11. Ibid, 464–465.
12. Ibid, 463–464.
13. Barrows, M., *The Dead Sea Scrolls*, 73–101.
14. Broyles, C.C., *The Redeeming King: Psalm 72's Contribution to the Messianic Ideal*, 23–25.
15. Harman, 52.

Chapter Five:

1. Abdullah Yusaf Ali, in his Footnote 47 explains that the power of will when used aright brings the man nearer to the God-like nature. (Note that the translation of Abdullah Yusuf Ali has become by far the most popular translation of the Qur'an into English in the Muslim world.)
2. Kassis, *A Concordance of the Qur'an*, 483.
3. Pickthall, *The Meaning of the Glorious Qur'an*, 47.
4. Abdullah Yusuf Ali, *The Meaning of the Holy Qur'an*, Note 53.
5. Kassis, *A Concordance of the Qur'an*, 595.
6. Note the *Hadith* is known as the Muslim *Traditions* and is a narration of what Muhammad said or did. It is considered an expression of divine revelation. It is accepted as a chief source of Islamic belief and practice and is second in authority only to the Qur'an.
   • *Sahih Al-Bukhari*, Vol. 8, Hadith No. 611 (according to Khan's Translation and ALIM's Translation).
   • *Sahih Al-Bukhari*, Vol. 9, Hadith No. 423 (ALIM's Translation and Khan's Translation).
   • Ibid, 4:552.

Chapter Six:

1. Smith, Chuck, *Answers for Today*, 128.
2. *Sahih Al-Bukhari*, Vol. 8, Hadith No. 238 (ALIM's Translation and Khan's Translation).
3. Sunan Ibn Majah, Vol 5, 489.

Chapter Eight:

1. AT Tabari, *Commentary on the Qur'an*, Notes 29466–29468.
2. *Shorter Encyclopedia of Islam*, 175.
3. Abdullah Yusuf Ali, *The Holy Qur'an*, 1149, Note 4096.
4. lbn Sa'd, Kitab-al-Tabaqat al-Kabir Vol.1, 41.

Chapter Ten:

1. The word "ransom" means to "buy back." It is the payment demanded for the freedom of a captive.
2. "Redeem" is defined in the dictionary: to free or rescue by paying a price or to free from the consequences of sin.
3. Halverson, D.C., *The Compact Guide to World Religions*.
4. Sahih Al-Bukhari, Vol. 2, Hadith No. 51 (Khan's Translation).
5. Al-Qasemi, *Commentary of the Holy Qur'an* (at Surah 3:45).
6. Farid Esack, "One Being a Muslim" (Oxford: One World, 1999), 5

Chapter Eleven:

1. McDowell, Josh, *The New Evidence That Demands a Verdict*, 201.
2. See Bibliography (Lockyer).
3. Al-Baidawi commenting on Qur'an Surah 2:253.

Chapter Twelve:

1. Al-Razi, commenting on Surah 3:39.
2. Yousef al-Qaradawi and others, *t-Twahid*, 98.
3. Subki, *At-tabaqat al Shafe' eiah al-Kubr*, Vol. 6. 235.
4. Harry Austryn Walfson, *The Philosophy of the Kalam*, Harvard University Press, 1976, p. 251; quoted from Fisal Volume II, 5–6; and Vol. III, 5.
5. Ibid, 240–241 quoted from Al-Tabari, *Annals*, 118, Volume II. 10–11.

Chapter Thirteen:

1. *Al-Ahadith Al-Qudsiyyah, Divine Narratives*, Hadith 112, 156–157.
2. Al-Ahadith Al Qudsiyyah, *Divine Narratives*.
3. Abdullah Yusuf Ali, Note 5365.

Chapter Fourteen:

1. *Sahih Al-Bukhari* 6:71 (ALIM's Translation and Khan's Translation).

Chapter Fifteen:

1. *Sahih Al-Bukhari*, 4:506 (ALIM's Translation and Khans' Translation).
2. *Sahih Al-Bukhari*, Vol. 8, Hadith No. 89 (Khan's Translation).
3. *Sahih Al-Bukhari*, 4:501 (ALIM's Translation and Khan's Translation).
4. *Sahih Al-Bukhari*, 8:319 (ALIM's Translation and Khan's Translation).
5. Ibid, 8:379 (ALIM's Translation and Khan's Translation).
6. Ibid, 5:715: "O Allah! Forgive me, and bestow your mercy on me" (ALIM's Translation and Khan's Translation).
7. *Towards an Islamic Christology II*, The Muslim World, Vol. LXX, No. 2, April 1980, 93.
8. AL-Baidawi, commenting on Qur'an Surah 5:110.

Chapter Sixteen:

1. Shukani, *Fath al- Qadir*.
2. Al-Razi, AL-Tafsir Al-Kabir.

Chapter Seventeen:

1. *Sahih Al-Bukhari*, 4:501 (ALIM's Translation and Khan's Translation).
2. Sunan Ibn-I-Majah Volume 5, No. 4251
3. "Islamic Government Does Not Spend for its Own Grandeur," Kayhan International (September 4, 1985, p.3
4. Ibid
5. *Al-Itqan.*
6. Sahih Al-Bukhari, Vol.5, Tradition No. 266 (Khan's Translation).
7. Refer to *The Successors of the Apostle*, Khalid Muhammad Khalid, 93.
8. Al Jalalan.
9. Sahih Al-Bukhari, Vol. 8, Tradition No. 470 (Khan's Translation).
10. Sahih Al-Bukhari, Vol.7, Tradition No. 577 (Khan's Translation).

Chapter Eighteen:

1. Assfy, *Islam and Christianity,* 6.
2. Halverson, Ibid.
3. Kateregga and Shenk, *Islam and Christianity*, 19.
4. Ibid, 97–98.
5. John Gilchrist, *The Christian Witness to Muslims*, 337.
6. Al-Bukhari, al-Sahih, Vol. 8, Hadith No. 246, 160.

Chapter Twenty:

1. Parrinder, G. *Jesus in the Qur'an*, 121.
2. Abdullah Yusuf Ali, Footnote 2469.
3. Obaray, *Miraculous Conception, Death, Resurrection and Ascension of Jesus as Taught in the Qur'an*, 45.
4. The Azhar University in Egypt has been regarded as the light of Islam for the entire Islamic world.
5. Dr. Mahmud Shaltut, *Quoted in the Muslim World*, xxxiv, 214f.
6. Abdullah Yusuf Ali, Footnote 663.
7. Ibid, Footnote 664.
8. Al-Razi, vol. VI:12, 113.
9. Maududi, *The Meaning of the Qur'an*, 390.
10. Daryabadi, *The Holy Qur'an*, Volume 1, 96–A.

Chapter Twenty-One:

1. Al Akad, Abaas Mahmood, *The Genius of Christ, Dar Al Halal*.
2. Flavius Josephus, *The Complete Works of Josephus*, VI–IX, *Antiquities of the Jews,* Book XVIII, Chapter III, Section 3.
3. Ibid, 379.
4. McDowell, Josh, *The New Evidence that Demands a Verdict*, 216–217.
5. See Bibliography (Smith, W.) 425–426.

Chapter Twenty-Three:

1. Abdullah Yusuf Ali, Footnote 4662.
2. Alam, Nuzul Esa: *Descencion of Jesus Christ*, 37.
3. *Sahih Al-Bukhari*, Vol. 4, Hadith No. 657, also Vol. 3, No. 425 (ALIM's Translation and Khan's Translation).
4. *Sahih Muslim*, English Translation, Hadith No. 7037.
5. *Sahih Al-Bukhari*, English-Arabic, 2:459.
6. Ibid, 9:243 (ALIM's Translation and Khan's Translation).
7. *Sahih Muslim*, Hadith No. 6924 (ALIM).
8. *Sahih Muslim*, Hadith No. 7015 (ALIM).
9. Ibid; Hadith No. 7000.

Chapter Twenty-Five:

1. Al-Qartaby, commenting on Qur'an Surah 4:171.

Chapter Twenty-Six:

1. Halverson, D.C., *The Compact Guide to World Religions*.
2. Al-Ghazzali, *Ihya' Ulumed-Din*, 4:263.
3. Shaarani, *Book of Yawakeet*.
4. Imam Abi Hanifah, *Al-Fiqh al-Akbar*, 33.
5. Parrinder, G., *Jesus in the Qur'an*.
6. Schaff, Philip, *The Creeds of Christendom: with a History and Critical Notes*.

Chapter Twenty-Seven:

1. Cragg, A. Kenneth, *The Call of the Minaret*, 290.

Chapter Twenty-Eight:

1. Ibn Ishaq was an early Islamic Scholar. He left behind two comprehensive works on the life of Muhammad. His work is still considered today an essential source for everyone who wants to learn about Muhammad's life and his companions.
2. A. Guillaume, *Life of Muhammad*, A Translation of Ibn Ishaq's Sirat Arasul, 657.
3. Al-Razi, *AL-Tafsir AL-Kabir*, commenting on Surah 3:39, 211.
4. Ibid.
5. Ibid.
6. Ibid.
7. Al-Razi, *AL-Tafsir AL-Kabir*, commenting on Surah 19:7.

Chapter Twenty-Nine:

1. Hafiz and Kandhalwi, *Teachings of Islam*, ch. II, 41.
2. Ibid.
3. Ibid (ch. VII, 128).
4. Ibid (Umar, ch. II, 42).
5. *The Kash-Shaf* of the AL- Zamkhashri, vol. 3, 187 (see also, Al Jalalan).
6. Al-Ghazzali, *Ninety-Nine Names of God in Islam*, 91.
7. Ibid.

ACKNOWLEDGMENTS

My words cannot express my gratitude to my Living God for guiding and enabling me to serve Him through this book.

Thank you to Volney James, Angela Lewis, John Dunham, and the rest of the group at Authentic for helping get this book into the hands of many readers.

My appreciation goes to Gabriel Straight for providing the technical support for this book.

Special thanks to Bob Baldwin for his generous contribution toward the making of this book a reality.

A WORD FROM MY HEART TO ALL FOLLOWERS OF JESUS

I am inviting all true believers and followers of Jesus Christ to join me by pulling our resources together and uniting in the goal of helping our precious Muslim neighbors experience God's love and salvation.

ABOUT THE AUTHOR

Samy Tanagho was born and raised in Egypt where he studied Islamic law and Islamic religion at Ain Shams University (School of Law) in Cairo, Egypt and later practiced law as an attorney.

Because Samy mastered the Arabic language, he was able to read the words of the companions and followers of Muhammad, which were written only in Arabic. He was able to read the books of the most important Muslim scholars and commentators, who interpreted the words of Muhammad and the Qur'an.

Samy is Chairman of the Board for the Glad News for Muslims non-profit corporation. Samy has been sharing the Gospel with Muslims for over 30 years. His passion is to teach Christians to effectively communicate the Gospel to all people, including Muslims. He speaks on this topic throughout the United States and overseas. His wife, Hala, often joins him to share her story of imprisonment in Egypt for converting from Islam to Christianity.

Samy loves to talk about God's love for all people and encourages believers in Jesus to actively fulfill the Great Commission. Samy's goal is that every Muslim will hear and enjoy God's love and salvation.